A CHILDREN'S HISTORY OF
BRITAIN
— AND —
IRELAND

A CHILDREN'S HISTORY OF
BRITAIN
— AND —
IRELAND

CHRISTOPHER WRIGHT

Kingfisher Books

Kingfisher Books, Grisewood & Dempsey Ltd
Elsley House, 24–30 Great Titchfield Street,
London W1P 7AD

This revised, reformatted and updated edition
published in 1993 by Kingfisher Books

First published in 1986 by Kingfisher Books

2 4 6 8 10 9 7 5 3 1

BRITISH LIBRARY CATALOGUING IN PUBLICATION DATA
A catalogue record for this book is available from the British Library.

ISBN 1 85697 025 6

ILLUSTRATIONS
David Salariya

SENIOR EDITOR
Stuart Cooper

ASSISTANT EDITOR
Janice Lacock

DESIGNER
Kelly Flynn

PICTURE RESEARCH
Jackie Cookson, Elaine Willis

MAPS
Ralph Orme

ADDITIONAL ARTWORK
Shirley Willis, Tony Richards, Nick Harris

Phototypeset by Tradespools Ltd, Frome, Somerset
Printed in Slovenia

CONTENTS

PREFACE

My thanks are due to Margaret Bircumshaw, Carol Wright and Richard Wright, who have read parts of this history in typescript, and to the boys and girls in their classes who have done the same. The schools are Blean Primary School near Canterbury in Kent, Treadworth Junior School and Calton Junior School, both in Gloucester.

I would also like to acknowledge my debt to the authors of the different volumes of Penguin Education's *History of Britain* and the Longman secondary Histories – both model histories for the use of junior readers. I have learned particularly from the imaginative way they present their material. Thoughout the book, I have constantly referred to the one-volume Oxford *Illustrated History of Britain*, and would like to acknowledge my debt to its contributors.

I would like to thank the Children's Librarian of the Children's Book Foundation for her help in the compilation of the Bibliography.

Finally my thanks are owed to Karen Greenstreet for her co-operation and skill in typing my final manuscript.

CHRISTOPHER WRIGHT

PICTURE CREDITS

The publishers wish to thank the following for supplying photographs for this book:

Page 20 M. Holford; 22 British Museum (top), Reading Museum and Art Gallery (bottom); 23 West Country Tourist Board; 30 British Museum; 34 British Museum; 42 National Monuments Record, Air Photographs, Crown Copyright Reserved; 43 Fishbourne Palace; 44 Fishbourne Palace; 49 British Museum; 58 Bodleian Library, MS, Digby 20, fol. 194 (top); 59 British Museum; 60 British Library; 73 ZEFA; 74 Universitetets Oldsaksamling, Oslo; 78 British Library (left); 80 M. Holford; 81 M. Holford; 82 M. Holford; 86 Public Records Office; 88 British Library; 90 Cathedral Gifts, Canterbury; 97 Picturepoint (bottom), M. Holford (top); 99 Copyright Reserved, Reproduced by Gracious Permission of H.M. the Queen; 100 Britain on View (bottom); 102 Master and Fellows of Corpus Christi College, Cambridge; 105 British Library; 114 British Library; 107 Copyright Bibliotheque Royale Albert Ier, Bruxelles. Manuscrit 13076–77 fol. 24 verso; 110 Trinity College, Cambridge; 115 Britain on View; 124 Britain on View (bottom); 125 Scala; 127 National Portrait Gallery; 128 Reproduced by Gracious Permission of H.M. the Queen (top), Royal Armouries, H.M. Tower of London (bottom); 130 National Portrait Gallery; 133 Victoria and Albert Museum; 134–135 Society of Antiquaries; 138 National Portrait Gallery; 147 Fotomas Index; 149 National Portrait Gallery; 155 Reproduced by Gracious Permission of H.M. the Queen; 156 Fotomas Index; 159 Mansell Collection; 164 Mansell Collection; 169 National Portrait Gallery; 173 The Tate Gallery; 178 Mansell Collection; 177 National Trust; 181 Peter Newark Pictures; 182 Peter Newark Pictures; 185 Mansell Collection; 186 Aberdeen Art Gallery; 187 Mansell Collection; 189 Sir John Soane's Museum; 191 Schloss Charlottenburg; 193 Mansell Collection; 195 National Portrait Gallery; 197 Mansell Collection; 198 Mansell Collection; 201 Fotomas Index; 205 Hulton Picture Library; 209 Royal Geographical Society/Fotomas Index; 212 Hulton Picture Library; 215 Trades Union Congress; 216 Mansell Collection; 220 Le Petit Journal; 223 Popperfoto; 225 Popperfoto; 226 Hulton Picture Library; 227 Hulton Picture Library; 228 Hulton Picture Library; 230 Hulton Picture Library; 235 Popperfoto; 236 Popperfoto; 237 Hulton Picture Library; 241 Camera Press; 243 Camera Press; 246 Reflex Picture Agency; 245 A. Ogden & Sons; 248 ZEFA; 249 Frank Spooner Pictures.

2,000,000–75 BC
EARLY PEOPLE

TIME CHART

All early dates are approximate. *denotes events that occurred outside Britain and Ireland.

2,000,000	*First humans emerge, in Africa.		civilizations are developing in China and Indus Valley. *Great Pyramid is built in Egypt.
500,000	*Fire is first used, in China.		
250,000	First humans settle in Britain at Swanscombe, Kent. Old Stone Age begins.	2000	Village developed at Skara Brae, Orkney. Weaving begins in Britain.
200,000	Ice covers northern Europe. Britain is joined to Europe by land-bridge.	1900	Tin is mined in Cornwall.
		1500	Beaker people enter Britain. Bronze Age begins.
40,000	People are living in caves at Creswell Crags, Derbyshire.	1300	Stonehenge is completed.
20,000	*Cave paintings are made at Lascaux, France.	1250	*Jews leave Egypt and settle in Israel.
10,000	Ice retreats north from Britain and Europe. New settlers move into Britain. Middle Stone Age begins. Stone Age factory is in use at Grimes' Graves, Norfolk.	1200	*Iron is first used, in Middle East.
		776	*First Olympic Games are held in Greece.
		753	*Rome is founded.
		600	Celts enter Britain – first iron-using tribes. Heavy ploughs are developed to clear soils.
7500	Settlement made at Starr Carr, Yorkshire.	563	*Buddha is born.
7000	*Farming begins, in Israel and Iraq.	450	Maiden Castle, Dorset, becomes permanent settlement.
6000	Land bridge linking Britain and Europe slowly crumbles. Britain becomes an island.	350	Celts from Germany settle in Ireland.
3500	Village farms begin in Britain. Neolithic (New Stone) Age begins.	310	Greek navigator Pytheas of Massilia sails around Britain.
3000	Settlement made at Windmill Hill, Wiltshire. Silbury Hill, Wiltshire, is built.	200	Celts settle in Taymouth and Moray Firth regions of Scotland.
2700	Stonehenge and Avebury stone circles, Wiltshire, are begun.	100	Lake village flourishes at Glastonbury, Somerset.
2500	Pottery begins in Britain at Windmill Hill. *Advanced	75	Belgae (celts) settle at Colchester, Essex. Extensive trade is carried out between Britain and Europe.

THE FIRST PEOPLE

The story of the human race begins in Africa about two million years ago. The only evidence we have of human beings in prehistoric times is the few remains they have left behind them. These include their bones, the bones of the animals they killed and ate, the remains of the places where they lived, their burial sites, their weapons and their stone tools. With occasional exceptions, their wooden tools have decayed, as have their clothes and buildings. In the case of the earliest people in Africa, tools are the only relics that have survived.

People first settled in Britain in about 250,000 BC. But there are no written records of people living in Britain until Julius Caesar's account of the inhabitants of Kent in 55 BC, about 2000 years ago.

△ *Early people would have spent much of their time making tools by chipping away at large pebbles until they had sharp points and edges. They used the tools for hunting.*

EARLY PEOPLE IN AFRICA

Pebble tools have been discovered in the Olduvai Gorge in Tanzania and in other parts of Africa that must have belonged to the first men and women. They resembled the great apes from which they were descended. They were about one metre tall and had clumsy hands and limbs. Their bodies were probably covered with hair. Their brains were small compared to the brains of modern human beings. However, these first people were different from their neighbours, the apes, because they were able to walk upright, and so their arms and hands were free to perform a number of tasks which gave them an advantage in the struggle for survival.

△ *In earliest times ice covered Britain north of the Thames estuary. Britain was joined to France by a strip of land across the Channel.*

NOMADS AND HUNTERS

Unlike many hunting animals human beings did not have razor-sharp teeth. But they were able to shape stone tools, and used these to attack their prey and cut up its flesh. The early tools were large rough pebbles, which had been chipped away to give them sharp points and edges. Bones have been found which suggest that human beings fought and killed apes and baboons, whose marrow bones they split open with their stone tools, so that they could suck out the juice.

From the beginning people used their intelligence to get ahead of their rivals. Like them they hunted in groups, and travelled about as they hunted. Like modern Australian aborigines they had no permanent homes, but erected wind breaks or shelters of leaves and twigs for the night. They liked to live by lakes or rivers because their prey came there to

▽ One of the most important discoveries made by early people was how to light fires for warmth and cooking. They created fire by rubbing two pieces of flint together near dry grass and twigs until a spark set them alight.

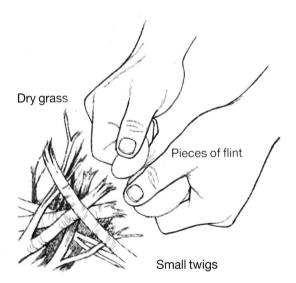

Dry grass

Pieces of flint

Small twigs

drink. As well as larger animals, they lived on frogs, mice, young birds and snakes.

As they travelled, hunting their prey, these early people spread out from Africa into Asia. But they never entered Europe, most of which was covered in ice at the time. They would have died if they had done so, for they wore no clothes and had not discovered fire. In their hotter climate, they had no need of it for warmth, and perhaps they baked their meat in hot ground or fried it on hot stones.

FIRE AND SPEECH

Fire was first used by people in Beijing, China, around 500,000 BC. It was made by rubbing flints together to create a spark that would ignite dry grass and twigs. Fires would probably be kept alight for as long as possible.

At about this time, too, the precious power of speech was developed. Now, for the first time, people were no longer limited to expressing their emotions of love or grief or terror by grunts, or to warning their fellows of danger by a mixture of sounds and signals. They could exchange thoughts, ideas and plans for the next day.

PREHISTORIC BRITAIN

For long periods during the thousands of years when early people were spreading into India, China, Java and Malaysia, most of Britain remained under thick ice.

There were four great ice ages but they were not continuous. In the years between them the climate reached tropical heat. Elephants and hippopotamuses were living north of the river Thames. During those years Britain was attached to the rest of Europe by a strip of marshy land, known as the 'land bridge', across what is now the English Channel.

6000 years ago		**HUMAN DEVELOPMENT** *People now put bone handles on their stone axes, used razor-sharp flints, and made mugs and bowls of pottery.*
10,000 years ago		*People were using bows and arrows to hunt. They painted on the walls of their caves. Stone tools were now very sharp.*
250,000 years ago		*The first Britons used stone hand axes. They hunted, fished and ate berries. They lived in windbreaks and caves.*
500,000 years ago		*People first discovered how to use fire in China. At about the same time they also started to communicate by speaking, not grunting.*
2,000,000 years ago		*The first people lived in Africa, and were like apes, with long arms. They used sharp-edged pebble tools, which they chipped.*

THE FIRST PEOPLE IN BRITAIN

It was during the longest of the warm spells, known as the 'Great Interglacial', that human beings settled in Britain, around 250,000 BC. A section of a fossilized skull, thought to have belonged to a young woman who lived at this time, has been found in Swanscombe in Kent. These are the earliest human remains found in Britain. The settlers were about 1.5 metres tall, and their brains were twice the size of those of the earliest people. Their hands were less clumsy, and with them they made more advanced stone tools. They are called the people of the Palaeolithic period or Old Stone Age.

Like the first people in Africa, these first British people were travelling 'hunter-gatherers', and they continued to be so for over 200,000 years. They hunted animals, but they did not domesticate, or tame them. They killed birds and fished the rivers, ate nuts, berries and roots, gathered limpets from the rocks and shellfish from the streams; but they grew nothing.

TOOLS OF THE OLD STONE AGE

The stone flake tools and hand-axes used by the first people in Britain have been collected in large numbers. The slow improvement in the quality of these tools marks the developing skill of their makers.

At first the tools were flat flakes of stone, knocked off lumps of flint by other stones. They were used to scrape skins and meat, and the pointed ends were for boring holes. Later people learned how to make hand-axes from blocks of stone. Flakes were struck off, but now it was the remaining 'core' which was used and not the flakes. The axes were held in the palm of the hand. They were not fixed to wooden handles until much later. Slowly

△ These Old Stone Age hunter-gatherers are stripping branches for berries. In the background, a hunting party is returning, carrying a carcase slung from a pole.

the tools improved: they became triangular, sharply pointed at one end, and with two cutting edges. They could be used to cut down small trees, to shape wood and scrape skins, and to carve meat.

A NEW ICE AGE

Eventually the Great Interglacial came to an end, and by 200,000 BC the north of Britain was covered in ice. South of the Thames the land was gaunt and treeless, covered only with a thick undergrowth of moss called 'tundra', like modern Lapland.

Most people appear to have left Britain, but it seems that some did settle in ice-bound Britain, alongside the mammoths, reindeer and woolly rhinoceroses.

These settlers used their new, efficient tools to scrape animals' skins and bore holes in them. Then they sewed them into clothes with animal sinew threaded on bone needles. They now lived in caves rather than building windbreaks; they made stone knives, and buried their dead.

NEW PEOPLES FROM THE EAST

During the last part of the fourth and final ice age, about 35,000 years ago, a more developed form of people began living in southern Europe. They had come from the east and they settled in the caves of southern France and northern Spain.

Stone tools had now become very efficient. Their edges and points were razor-sharp. From lumps of stone, craftsmen struck flint blades, blunt at the back so that they could be held in the hand or slotted into bone handles, like a modern penknife. A tool called a 'burin' was used to cut not only stone but bone. Now people hunted with bows and arrows with flint tips, or hurled spears with tips made from antler or ivory. They stitched skin suits with hoods, like duffle coats,

and they made fur boots, like those worn by the Inuit (Eskimos) today. They used antlers to make jagged harpoons, then trailed thongs behind them. The throwers held the thongs tightly so that once harpooned the animals could not escape.

THE CAVE PAINTINGS

The most dramatic achievements of these people are their works of art. Among their creations are a horse carved out of the ivory tusk of a mammoth, the carved head of a woman with an elaborate hair style, and a pebble engraved with the figure of a deer with spreading antlers. Most interesting of all are the cave paintings, which have been found at places such as Altamira in Spain and Lascaux in France. These extraordinary paintings are the first great works of art people have produced.

Some of the paintings are hunting scenes. They show people hunting stags with bows and arrows, or a bison with arrows sticking in its side. At the cave of Les Trois Frères, in France, a man wearing the skin and tail of an animal and a mask topped by great antlers dances on the wall.

Many of the most realistic paintings are deep in the rock, not at the entrance to the caves. The artists worked by the dim light from little lamps made of animal fat.

Nobody is quite sure why these works of art were created between 30,000 and 10,000 years ago. Perhaps the artists saw paintings as a form of magic to bring success in hunting. People may have acted out the hunt in front of the paintings the night before an expedition.

◁ *The cave artists made paint by mixing egg yolks with powdered minerals. They applied the paint to the cave walls with their fingers or with brushes made from animal hair.*

NEW SETTLERS IN BRITAIN

Around 10,000 BC the ice gradually disappeared, until it was only left in high places, such as the Alps, and in the north. With it disappeared most of the animals that prefer cold climates. Trees began to grow over the tundra. As the ice went, some of the cave-dwellers of southern France moved north and west into Britain.

The new settlers brought with them new tools. They had discovered how to fit their sharp axeheads into long wooden handles. Equipped with these new, very efficient axes they began clearing the forest. For the first time, then, men and women were not just living off the earth and its creatures. They were making their own mark.

The new arrivals made boats from the tree trunks they felled. They hollowed them out using fire and stone tools such as the burin, and 'adzes' as well as axes. They also used wood to make paddles.

These people became skilful fishermen. They constructed traps for fish and made nets out of bark, which they floated with bark floats. Instead of living in caves, they now lived in skin-tents, erected on the land they had cleared in the forests or at the sides of rivers or lakes.

The new settlers hunted with flint-tipped spears or bows and flint-tipped arrows. When they succeeded in killing a deer they used the whole carcass. The antlers were used for spear heads, the skins for shoes, or clothes or tents. Some of the meat was eaten immediately; the rest was dried in the sun and stored. The splintered bones were made into needles for stitching clothes or tents and for binding spear heads to the wooden shafts.

▷ *The new settlers brought with them more advanced tools, as well as primitive jewellery.*

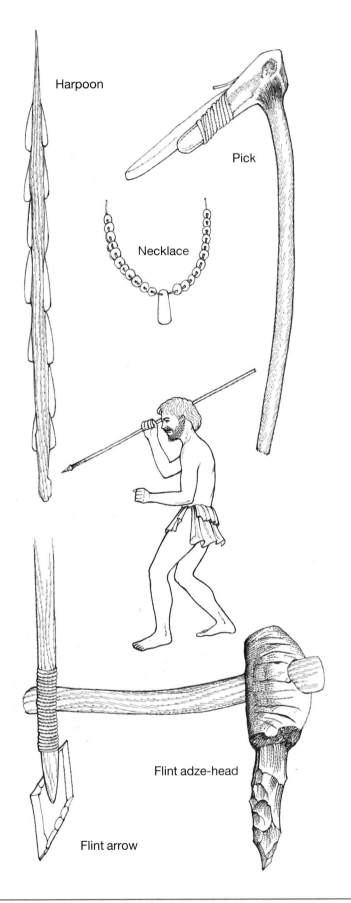

Harpoon

Pick

Necklace

Flint adze-head

Flint arrow

STAR CARR

Evidence of these new settlers has been found at Star Carr in Yorkshire, which was inhabited in about 7500 BC. The settlers cut down trees to make a platform by the lake. They left behind them flint barbs, which would have been mounted in wooden shafts to make arrows; barbed spearheads, made from splinters of red-deer antlers; and a wooden paddle. These people seem to have kept a dog, the first sign of a domesticated animal in Britain.

▽ The people of Starr Carr lived in skin tents on a platform by the lake. Their boats were made from tree trunks and they built traps to catch fish. The hunters wore animal head-dresses.

Like the man drawn in the cave of Les Trois Frères, in southern France, the people of Star Carr wore animal head-dresses when they went hunting. Two head-dresses made from antlers have been found. The hunters also wore deer skins. Their faces would have looked out from deerskin hoods and two antlers would have branched from their foreheads.

About 1500 years later Britain became an island. As the ice thawed, the level of the sea rose, and in about 6000 BC the marshy land bridge which connected Dover and Calais was swept away. The change, far from decreasing contact with Europe, increased it: the age of invaders was about to begin in Britain.

FARMERS AND TRADERS

One of the greatest changes in human life came when people began to stay in one place and farm. They exchanged the life of the hunter and gatherer for the life of the farmer. Instead of caves and windbreaks they lived in huts and villages.

THE FIRST BRITISH FARMERS
The first farmers appeared in Britain about 3500 BC. Farming had begun in the Middle East before 7000 BC.

The earliest British farmers came into England by boat from France. They brought seed-corn, sheep and cattle. They used a wooden plough, and with their wooden-handled axes they cleared the chalky high ground of the south and east.

With farming and settlement in villages came specialization. Some members of the tribe made pottery bowls and spoons. Others became flint-miners. Others herded the cattle or sheared the sheep.

THE WINDMILL HILL PEOPLE
One of the settlements of the first British farmers has been found at Windmill Hill in Wiltshire. The camp seems to have been built more for the cattle than the villagers. The ditches around the site were probably dug to keep the cattle in rather than to keep attackers out. Whereas there are no signs of huts or homes within the ditches, several cattle bones have been unearthed. There would not have been enough food to feed the whole herd through the winter, so many of the cattle would have been slaughtered in the late autumn. The tribe would camp in the enclosure, feast on the meat and sew the hides for their clothes.

INNOVATIONS OF THE NEW STONE AGE
A dozen sites of similar date – 3500–3000 BC – have been found. The remains show that people of the Neolithic period – or new Stone Age – used much more advanced methods than their predecessors. They harvested their crops of wheat and barley with flint sickles. They used red-deer antlers to make picks for breaking up the soil and the shoulder-blades of cattle to make shovels. They kept not only sheep and cattle but pigs, goats and dogs. Some must have been cannibals, for the bones of slaughtered humans have been found. Necklaces of polished stones, shells and bright green jade were being worn. People were carving chalk – a chalk figure, thought to be a goddess, has been found at Grimes Graves in Norfolk.

▽ *Farming of crops and animals started in the Middle East and by 6000 BC had spread over the area coloured pale green on the map below. By 5000 BC it had spread over the dark green area and by 3500 BC the orange area.*

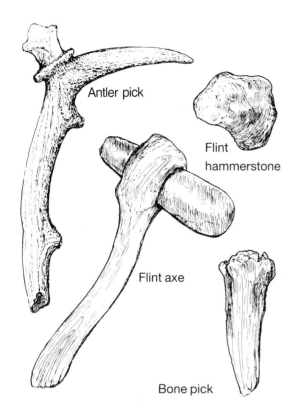

Antler pick

Flint hammerstone

Flint axe

Bone pick

△ Pictured here are some of the mining tools from Grimes Graves in Norfolk.
▷ These miners are extracting flint at Grimes Graves. In the foreground is a chalk goddess and a chalk cup, which was used as a lamp.

FLINT MINING

Of all the new techniques that were now being used the most important were those of flint mining and manufacture. For the stone axes that were in use enabled people to carry on the clearance of the forests which covered the greatest parts of Britain. The flint sickles were sharp enough to harvest the crops of wheat and barley. The flint tips to the arrows proved deadly in hunting, and the harpoons, now too tipped with sharp flints, were used with devastating effect in fishing.

The flint was extracted from mines, such as the one that has been excavated at Grimes Graves in Norfolk. Axeheads have been discovered far away from their place of manufacture, indicating the thriving trade or barter in flints that was carried on all over England, and even abroad to Ireland and the Continent.

DEATH AND BURIAL

These first farmers buried their dead in long burial mounds or 'barrows'. These covered grave 'houses' where a family or perhaps even a whole tribe was buried. At Pimperne in Dorset, turf has grown over the white chalk of which the long barrows were built, so their original dazzling white no longer shines.

SKARA BRAE

At Skara Brae in the Orkney Islands, off the north of Scotland, a whole stone village has been found. It stands by the sea, was built about 2000 BC, and still shows clearly its main features. The one-roomed huts were grouped together and linked by covered passages like a rabbit warren. The roofs of the huts were made of turf and whalebone. Within their stone walls stand recesses, like built-in cupboards. There are stone dressers, two storeys high; beds, with head and foot stones and stone sides; and hearths on the floor for fires made of peat and driftwood.

▽ *At Skara Brae the soil was too poor for crops, so the people kept sheep and cattle. One man returns from hunting, while others cut up deer. Some of the inhabitants collect driftwood.*

The people at Skara Brae buried their dead under the huts, made beads of teeth and bone, and painted their bodies red, yellow and blue. They do not appear to have grown crops. The windswept land would have been unsuitable for proper cultivation. They kept sheep and cattle, clothed themselves in hides, and ate shell fish. In this bleak spot the houses must have made warm comfortable, shelters.

THE BEAKER PEOPLE

The next great step in human development was the use of metals – first copper and then bronze. They were introduced into Britain about 3500 years ago by the 'Beaker People'. They have been called this because of the shape of their pottery mugs, discovered in their round burial mounds, along with the remains of their owners. The Beaker People came originally from

Spain, but traces of their way of life have been found as far east as Poland, as far south as Sicily, as far north as Scotland, and as far west as Ireland. They were skilled sailors, navigating the stormy Bay of Biscay and the North Sea, as well as the shorter English Channel and Irish Sea.

THE BRONZE AGE (1500–600 BC)
Britain had plentiful supplies of tin (in Cornwall) and Ireland had copper and gold. Bronze is a mixture of ninety per cent copper and ten per cent tin. The Beaker People introduced metal-working into Britain and Ireland, and bronze tools began to spread over the two countries. For this reason the years after the migration of the Beaker People about 1500 BC are called the Bronze Age.

△ This is the Long Burial Barrow at West Kennet in Wiltshire. Barrows (mounds) of earth covered the great stones. Inside these chambers the people of the New Stone Age were buried together. Some barrows may have been for one family; others for the whole tribe.

These British bronze smiths must have joined up with brave and enterprising traders. Their bronze goods, like the work of the gold smiths, have been found as far away as eastern Europe. Many have been found in Britain, too, often in burial mounds in southern England.

These smiths were master craftsmen. An exquisite example of their workmanship is the gold cup found at Rillaton in Cornwall and displayed in the British Museum. The gold has been beaten so that it resembles

△ A bronze-smith's workshop of about 700 BC was found in a cave at Heathery Burn in northern England. The smith worked near the entrance, where the light was best. The fire was blown to a very high temperature by bellows. Then a crucible of scrap metal was held in the fire. When the metal melted, the smith removed the crucible with tongs and poured the molten metal into moulds. These were shaped in the form of axeheads, spearheads or cauldrons. When the goods had cooled they were finally hammered into shape.

the waves of the sea, flowing one after the other to the thin delicate brim of the cup.

Bronze tools have also been found all over Britain. The bronze axeheads were hollowed so that wooden handles could be securely fitted into them. Swords were sharp on both sides. Bronze sickles were now used for reaping corn. Bronze harnesses have been found which show that British people must now have been using horses. Wheeled carts seem to have been in use by about 500 BC.

STONEHENGE AND AVEBURY

Perhaps the most impressive things that the Bronze Age people have left behind them are their great stone monuments. The best known are Stonehenge and Avebury, both of which are in Wiltshire.

The builders of Stonehenge had great engineering skills and organizing abilities. The monument consists of a ring of huge upright boulder stones called 'sarsens', joined together across the top by curved cross-stones or 'lintels'. Within the outer circle stood other rings, one of which is made of blue stones transported all the way from south Wales. The outer circle was exactly arranged so that the rays of

△ Beaten gold was used to make this delicate cup, found at Rillaton in Cornwall.

the sun rising on Midsummer Day would strike a particular stone. This may indicate that the stones were used to predict the movements of the Moon or even eclipses of the Sun and Moon.

The prehistoric site at Avebury in Wiltshire, partly New Stone Age, partly Bronze Age, covered 28 acres of land. It was surrounded by a circular bank of chalk. Inside the bank stood over 100 sarsens, which weighed up to 50 tons each and were found locally. Within the outer circle stood two smaller stone circles of about 30 uprights each.

Avebury was probably used as an open air temple. Religious ceremonies would have been held here and the peoples' gods – of fertility, death, harvest, or the seasons – worshipped. The people would sit or stand on the high banks surrounding the circles. They would watch the services being conducted, sometimes with sacrifices, by the chiefs and priests. When

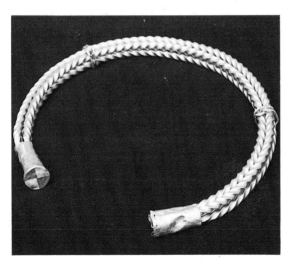

◁ This exquisite gold neck collar – or Torque – was found at Moulsford in Berkshire.

the services were over, they would crowd into the circles, dancing, chanting, clapping their hands and swaying long into the night.

Avebury was linked with a hill temple one mile away by an avenue of upright stones. Windmill Hill is nearby, as is Silbury Hill, built over the same years at Avebury. It is the largest artificial mound in Europe and it has been calculated to have taken about 700 men 10 years to throw up. Also near Avebury is the Long Burial Barrow at West Kennet, where numbers of New Stone Age people were buried together. The whole area must have been one of the most advanced and populated areas in Britain from about 2800 BC to 1500 BC. The Beaker People have left their pottery at Avebury.

CELTIC TRIBES AND THE IRON AGE
Iron is stronger than bronze and so is better for making weapons, nails, and tools such as saws, axes and adzes. Yet, though iron ore was common in Europe and in Britain, it was centuries before people found out how to heat iron to a high enough temperature so that it could be cast in a mould, beaten and shaped. The Hittites in the Middle East were making iron weapons before 1200 BC. But it was not until about 600 BC that iron-using tribes settled in southern England.

These people came once again from Europe. They were Celts, members of an extraordinary collection of peoples who at one time ruled all the land from Turkey to Ireland. We call the Celts who settled in Britain and their descendants Britons. The language they spoke is still used today, for Welsh, Gaelic, Irish and Cornish are direct descendants of Celtic. Many British place names, and the names of rivers and hills, come from Celtic. The Celtic word for river, avon, has given its name to many rivers. Dover, which stands at the mouth of a river, gets its name from a Celtic word similar to the Welsh word *dwfr* and the Cornish *dovr*, meaning water.

▽ *The people of the New Stone Age built great stone monuments, such as this stone circle at Avebury in Wiltshire. It stands where ancient tracks met and was probably a sacred place.*

The Celts could not write in their own language, but Celtic life in Britain has been described by Greek and Roman writers. They stress the Celts' interest in their appearance. The men wore their hair long. They shaved their beards, but grew long moustaches which covered their mouths. Before battle they washed their hair in lime to stiffen it, then brushed it back so it would flow like a horse's mane.

THE BRITONS

The Britons were led by their chiefs and their priests, the Druids. The chiefs were elected, and were sometimes women, like the famous Boadicea or Boudicca. Julius Caesar praised their horsemanship. Their light chariots had iron wheels, and their drivers drove them with reckless courage. They built great hill-forts, which can still be seen, dominating the countryside from the highest points of the downs in Wiltshire, Hampshire and Dorset.

The best known of them all is Maiden Castle in Dorset. This fort, which held great herds of cattle and sheep, was about 1200 metres long, 600 metres wide and defended by earthworks 30 metres high. Some of the forts had shops, workshops, streets and temples. They were the first towns in Britain.

A FARMING PEOPLE

Most Britons were farmers, however. They lived in large thatched huts built of wattle and daub – the same mixture of interlaced twigs and branches (wattle) and mud (daub) which was used to build labourers' cottages until about AD 1600. They kept cattle and sheep. Their farmsteads were protected with a wooden palisade, or fence, and inside they had barns and storage pits for grain. Their most important tool was their heavy plough. This had an iron blade which could turn the earth, and not just furrow it like the light wooden ploughs of earlier farmers. Now the heavy soil of the valleys in the south-east could be farmed, and people began to settle all over England.

WHAT THE BRITISH WERE LIKE

Strabo, a Greek geographer who wrote in the 1st century AD, describes the Celts in Gaul, members of the same people as those in Britain, as

"madly fond of war...so that they are easily handled by those who desire to outwit them for...on whatever pretext you stir them up you will have them ready to face danger even if they have nothing on their side but their own strength and courage. On the other hand...they willingly devote their energies to useful pursuits, and even take to a literary education." [1]

In later years the Irish, Welsh and Gaelic peoples were to prove Strabo right with their poetry and sagas.

The Britons looked after the sick, the wounded and the elderly. They had skilled doctors and seem to have developed remarkably advanced surgery, specializing in operations on the brain. British women had the same right to own property as men, and did not have to hand over their goods when they married. This was a right which British women living only 100 years before today did not have.

The Britons enjoyed drinking – barley ale and mead made from honey for the ordinary people, and wine for the chief and his court. They revelled in great banquets, after which, when the tables had

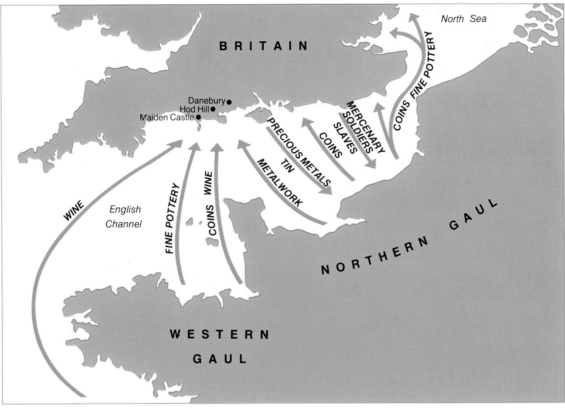

Britain

North Sea

Danebury●
Hod Hill●
Maiden Castle●

PRECIOUS METALS

MERCENARY SOLDIERS

SLAVES

COINS

COINS FINE POTTERY

TIN

METALWORK

WINE

FINE POTTERY

COINS WINE

English Channel

WESTERN GAUL

NORTHERN GAUL

△ *Around 1500 BC trade thrived between Britain and Gaul. The precious metals exported from Britain were copper, bronze, tin and gold. The slaves were probably criminals or prisoners captured in wars between the tribes.*

been cleared, they would listen to their bards and the tellers of the tribal myths and sagas, handed down from generation to generation. In several ways, with their elected chiefs, their regard for women, and the lack of division between rich and poor, they seem more like us than the Romans.

CELTIC TRADE

British boats were made of oak, with sails of leather, pulled up and down by chains not by ropes. The openings between the planks were stuffed with seaweed, which prevented the wood from drying out when the boat was raised from the water.

British traders were in regular contact with Europe, and trade increased as the Roman Empire spread northwards towards the Channel. The Britons imported a lot of wine from Europe. In return they exported woollen cloaks, corn,

tin, hunting dogs – and slaves. Slave chains, found at camps in Kent and Cambridgeshire, are the first evidence we have that slaves were traded from Britain. The slaves were exported for sale in Europe by British traders, either for heavy manual work or for fighting.

Large numbers of Celtic coins have been found, first of silver and then of gold. These are our first examples of British coins. The later ones have the heads of British chiefs stamped on them, with abbreviations of their names in the Roman style. The chiefs, it seems, were copying the ways of the great Roman emperors.

55 BC–AD 407
THE ROMANS IN BRITAIN

TIME CHART

All early dates are approximate. * denotes events that occurred outside Britain and Ireland.

55–54 BC	Julius Caesar makes raids on southern Britain.
7	Cunobelinus is King of Catuvellauni, with capital at Colchester.
5	*Jesus Christ is born
AD 30	*Jesus Christ is crucified.
43	Cunobelinus dies. Romans under Aulus Plautius invade England. Romans occupy Colchester. Romans begin to occupation of England. Roads and towns begin to be built.
48	Romans begin to occupy Wales.
60	First Roman villas are built.
61	Queen Boudicca leads revolt of Iceni. London is burnt. Boudicca dies. New London is started. Romans conquer Anglesey in Wales.
70	*Jerusalem is destroyed. Jews are exiled from Israel.
75	King Cogidubnus builds palace at Fishbourne, Sussex.
77–83	Julius Agricola is governor of Britain.
100	Roman villa is built at Lullingstone, Kent.
119	Caledonian clans in Scotland revolt, wiping out Roman Ninth Legion.
123	Hadrian's Wall is begun.
142	Antonine Wall in Scotland is started.
163	Romans retreat from Scotland to Hadrian's Wall.
196	Romans evacuate Hadrian's Wall. Scottish tribes capture York.
208	Romans occupy Northern Britain and rebuild Hadrian's Wall.
270	*Roman Empire is collapsing. Britain becomes separate nation for nine years.
280	First Saxon raiders attack southern England. Forts of Saxon Shore are built.
287	Albanus (later St Alban) becomes first Christian martyr in Britain.
296	Britain becomes part of Roman Empire again. Emperor Constantius invades Scotland.
306	Constantius dies at York; is succeeded by his son Constantine.
324	*Christianity becomes official religion of Roman Empire.
367	Roman control over Britain is collapsing. Picts and Scots reach London. Roman general Theodosius restores Roman power.
388	Roman troops abandon Hadrian's wall.
396	Picts invade northern Britain.
400	Romans begin to withdraw from Britain.
407	Last Roman troops leave Britain.
410	*Barbarian tribes sack Rome.

THE ROMAN CONQUEST

The Roman Empire was one of the great wonders of the world. At first, its central city, Rome, was only the capital of a small 'city-state' in Italy. During the centuries before the life of Christ, the Romans, with their powerful armies and efficient government, spread their rule throughout Europe and part of Asia. Their language, Latin, became an international language for the educated.

THE ROMAN EMPIRE

By the last century BC, when the last of the Celtic tribes, the Belgae, were moving into southern Britain, the Roman Empire stretched to the English Channel. In France, which was then called Gaul, the Roman legions had reached the river Rhine and were ready to advance east into the Netherlands and Germany. They occupied the Middle East from Turkey to the Red Sea. Spain and Portugal were safely in the Roman net. The British traders who visited Rome must have felt that they stood at the centre of the world.

THE CONQUEST OF BRITAIN

At first, the Romans could not decide whether to extend their empire across the Channel and into Britain, about whose wealth and people they knew only what traders had told them. Some Romans saw little point in further conquest. They said that British tin, iron ore, cloth, corn, gold and slaves could be obtained by trade. But the army chiefs wanted further victories. They imagined leading British captives through Rome to great applause.

△ British traders visited Rome to sell woollen, cloaks in the Roman markets.

◁ The map shows the Roman Empire (orange) just before the invasion of Britain in AD 43. The legions had halted their eastward expansion in Europe at the Rhine for the time being.

CAESAR'S FIRST RAID

One commander who thought like this was Julius Caesar. His soldiers in Gaul were finding it increasingly difficult to quell revolts by the Celtic tribes there who were supported by the Celts in southern Britain. At the very least, it seemed to be worth landing in Kent, a mere 30 kilometres away from Calais, to see whether an invasion might be possible. He described his plans in an account written in 55 BC. He referred to himself, as was his custom, in the third person:

"It was now near the end of the summer, and winter sets in early in those parts... Nevertheless Caesar made active preparations for an expedition to Britain...

Even if there was not time for a campaign that season, he thought it would be of great advantage to him merely to visit the island, to see what its inhabitants were like, and to make himself acquainted with the lie of the land, the harbours and the landing places." [2]

Caesar, as he says, left his sailing late, and did not leave Boulogne until the second half of August, 55 BC. He sailed with 10,000 soldiers, infantry and cavalry, and arrived off the white cliffs of Dover at nine o'clock in the morning. The British had their men lined up along the high cliffs. From there they could easily hurl their javelins right on to the narrow beach if the Romans tried to land. So Caesar

sailed north-east for about 10 kilometres and ran his ships aground on an evenly sloping beach, probably at Deal.

But the Romans still had a desperate fight to get ashore, and their landing very nearly ended in disaster. Their men were given new courage according to Caesar by the standard-bearer of the 10th legion:

"The Romans were faced with very grave difficulties. The size of the ships made it impossible to run them aground except in fairly deep water, and the soldiers, unfamiliar with the territory, with their hands full and weighed down by their

▽ *The first Roman invasion was at Deal on the Kent coast in 55 BC.*

weapons, had to jump down from the ships, get a footing in the waves, and fight the enemy, all at the same time. Their opponents, standing on dry land, fought with all their limbs unencumbered...But as the Romans hesitated, chiefly on account of the depth of the water, the man who carried the eagle of the 10th legion, after praying to the gods that his action might bring good luck to the legion, cried in a loud voice: 'Jump down, comrades, unless you want to surrender our eagle to the enemy; I, at any rate, mean to do my duty to my country and my general.' With these words, he leapt out of the ship and advanced towards the enemy with the eagle in his hands. At this the soldiers, encouraging each other not to submit to such a disgrace, jumped with one accord from the ship, and the men from the next ships, when they saw them, followed them and advanced against the enemy." [2]

After further fierce fighting the British asked for peace. But the expedition soon faced another disaster. Because they were used to sailing in the Mediterranean, which does not have tides, the Romans beached their ships too close to the sea. When the weather worsened, some of the ships were swept away with the tide. The Romans decided to return to Gaul.

CAESAR'S SECOND RAID
Next year, 54 BC, the Romans returned. This time, they set off earlier in the year and in greater numbers, and they landed on 7th July, without meeting any opposition. Once again they lost ships through bad weather and their own inexperience, but they advanced inland and stormed the hill fort at Bigbury, near Canterbury. The British now put all their

forces under one chief, Cassivellaunus, leader of the Catuvellauni tribe, whose headquarters were north of the Thames. The Romans advanced rapidly with their usual efficiency. They were particularly skilled at crossing rivers. The engineers who knew how to cross great European rivers like the Rhine found that the Medway in Kent and then the Thames presented few problems. From the Thames they marched to Cassivellaunus' headquarters at Wheathampstead near modern St Albans in Hertfordshire, and captured it. Cassivellaunus soon surrendered, and with other chiefs of southern Britain, agreed to accept the Romans as overlords. Caesar also made the British agree to pay tribute. However, once he had returned to Gaul, which he did before the autumn storms came, the Romans found it harder and harder to get them to pay it.

Despite the initial success of Caesar's campaign, little else came of his second invasions. Back in Rome, he pursued his

▽ *King Cunobelinus ruled most of south-east England from 7 BC to AD 43. He copied the Roman Emperors and had his shortened name stamped on his coins.*

personal ambitions, and eventually became head of the Roman state. He was then assassinated. The Romans left Britain alone for the next ninety years.

KING CUNOBELINUS

Caesar's enemies, the Catuvellauni, were unaffected by their defeat, and soon controlled most of south-east England. Colchester, in Essex, became their capital, and it was there that a great chief, Cunobelinus (whose name is altered to Cymbeline in Shakespeare's play of that name), ruled for fifty years, living in splendour rather like a Roman ruler. For the Roman Empire on the other side of the Channel held great fascination for the Celtic chiefs. Cunobelinus minted coins stamped with his head in the Roman imperial manner, or showing an ear of corn with the letters CAMV standing for Camulodunum, which was the Latin name for Colchester. During this period trade between Britain and Europe increased: large quantities of red-glazed pottery manufactured in Gaul before the final Roman invasion have been found at sites all over southern England.

THE THIRD INVASION

When Cunobelinus died, in AD 43, one of his sons quarrelled with his brothers and fled to Gaul, where he appealed to the Romans to take over his country. The king of another southern tribe, whose territory covered Hampshire and Sussex, was thrown out by his own people and he, too, went to Gaul with the same request. The new Roman emperor, Claudius, assembled a force of 40,000 men, with Aulus Plautius as their commander, which set sail for Britain. Its landing on the Kent coast in AD 43 was unopposed.

△ Maiden Castle was one of the main British strongholds. The attacking Roman soliders have set fire to the huts outside the castle and are now advancing on the main gate under cover of their famous 'tortoise' of shields.

△ A Roman solider was equipped with a shield, a spear, a short stabbing sword and light armour. The Romans' superior weapons and defences, and their considerable military skills, gave them a great advantage over the British.

The new invaders had learned from Caesar's experiences. They must have had advance knowledge of the British coast, for they first occupied Richborough, at that time an island off the east Kent coast at Thanet. This gave them the sheltered deep-water port that Caesar's army had so badly missed. Here their warships could lie at anchor, and their store ships could unload arms and supplies. The army built granaries and strong rooms for the coins with which the troops were to be paid. Ditches and earthwork defences were quickly built, before they moved on to begin their conquest of Britain.

Forty years later, after they had conquered Britain, the Romans built a towering monument at Richborough. It was faced with marble, and had marble pillars and bronze statues. Standing close to the sea, it served as a reminder to sea farers of Britain's new masters.

THE ROMAN ARMY

The Roman army formed a powerful world of its own. The legions contained experienced infantrymen and smaller groups of cavalry. They had their own skilled craftsmen, and their own engineers. These were the men who built the famous Roman roads, which strode, straight and unwavering, all over Western Europe and the Mediterranean world, and who were

▽ This picture shows an encounter between British farmers and Roman soldiers. One of the Britons is holding a spear. In the background is a British village surrounded by a stockade for defence. Peaceful but suspicious meetings like this one must have been very common in the period following the Roman conquest. (The model hand that is mounted on the end of the Roman standard may have been a good luck charm or a token of loyalty.)

the first to bridge the Thames. They also had their own administrators, who were used to governing conquered peoples. All full-time Roman soldiers had to be able to read and write, at a time when few people anywhere could do either. At this stage the soldiers were mainly Romans or members of other European countries. Later more and more Britons were recruited.

There were good reasons for joining the Roman army. Its soldiers were much admired. They were regularly paid in money, and had excellent chances of promotion. The greatest attraction of all was that after their 25 years of service, soldiers were given small farms (*coloni*). Here they often settled down with British wives and spent the rest of their lives.

THE BATTLE FOR BRITAIN
As a fighting force, no British army, however dashing its cavalry or brave its soldier-farmers, could hope to equal the Roman legions. The Roman catapults and other weapons smashed through the defences of the British hill-forts; and their javelins killed many Britons before they even joined battle. When it came to hand-to-hand fighting, the Romans closed ranks and used their short stabbing swords, which were far more efficient than the long slashing swords of the Britons. And because the Romans had a well-organized system for supplying food and equipment to their army, the soldiers could fight just as long as the weather held; and then start again in the spring as if they had never left off. Most of the British soldiers, however, were farmers who had been called up for battle. When harvest time came, they were eager to stop fighting and return to their small farms to gather the harvest which otherwise would go to waste. Only the

British nobles were professional fighters, like the Romans.

Powerful and confident, the Roman forces defeated the British on two occasions before they reached the river Medway. There they discovered that the Britons had destroyed the bridge. But this did not stop them. They had plenty of experience when fighting in Europe of crossing much wider rivers, such as the Rhine. Some troops, including the cavalry, swam across the river at Rochester, and the rest forded it lower down.

The most important battle took place in the hills on the other side of Rochester, and lasted two days. Finally the Britons gave in and fled. Two weeks later the Romans crossed the Thames and occupied Colchester itself, the capital of the Catuvellauni, where Cunobelinus had ruled with such splendour. The Emperor Claudius led the victory procession, which included elephants, into Colchester. Eleven British kings surrendered, and others soon followed. Other tribes in Britain were no doubt pleased to see the over-mighty Catuvellauni toppled.

Four years later the Romans had reached the river Severn in the west and the river Trent in the north. Here, for the time being, they stopped and consolidated their conquests. In AD 49 Colchester was declared an official 'colony', where retired soldiers could settle, draw their pensions and farm the land. The Romans were in Britain to stay, and their thorough system of colonization now began.

A COLONY OF ROME
Because the Roman Empire was so large, the Romans did not have enough soldiers to keep their power over their conquered peoples by force. So they used other

methods. Local people, particularly the chiefs, shared in governing their own countries. The Romans recruited Britons on a large scale for the army, where they sometimes even became generals. They taught them new crafts and improved their methods of farming. They made them better merchants and sailors. They tried to make allies of the tribes living on both sides of Britain's borders, so they would help in their defence. Many hundreds of years later Britain used similar methods to rule its vast empire in India and Africa.

At the beginning of their occupation of Britain, the Romans ruled a large area of southern and central England. On its eastern border, they made the Iceni tribe in Norfolk their allies. In the north, they signed a treaty with Queen Cartimandua of the Brigantes, who controlled most of northern England. She showed her loyalty by handing over to the Romans the unfortunate King Caractacus of the Catuvellauni, when he fled to her for refuge. He was led through the streets of Rome in chains.

In southern and central England, where the Romans ruled directly, they allowed British chiefs to act as magistrates and serve on local councils of government. No civilian was allowed to carry arms, and the Roman soldiers mostly went off to protect the frontiers or stayed out of sight in their barracks.

Only when it came to collecting taxes did the Romans put all the power in the hands of their own officials. The tax officers were responsible not to the local governor but to the Emperor himself. The Romans controlled trading of all the most important goods. The mines were government run. The lands of captured chiefs became the property of the

△ *These remains of Roman weapons found in Britain date from around the 1st century BC.*

Emperor. Britain was regarded as a rich province and the Romans were determined to squeeze it for all it was worth.

As we have seen, the Romans had declared Colchester a colony. The land which they gave to retired Roman soldiers there was taken from British farmers. Corn was seized as taxes and many local men were forced to join the Army. The Catuvellauni were in a mood to revolt.

THE REVOLT OF THE ICENI
In AD 61 Boudicca, the Queen of the Iceni in Norfolk, whom the Romans had at first chosen as allies, protested because her lands had been seized in the name of the

Emperor. The Romans flogged her and raped her daughters. Such treatment caused a revolt which soon spread from Norfolk over south-east England. Not only Colchester but London and St Albans were destroyed. Captured Romans were killed and tortured. At Colchester 15,000 Romans and their British allies were slaughtered, and a number killed as part of a ritual sacrifice in London. At one

▽ During the revolt of the Iceni led by Queen Boudicca the British burnt London to the ground. Terrible atrocities were committed and the rising lasted two months. At one time the Romans considered leaving Britain altogether, but in the end their military discipline triumphed. "Don't worry about these yelling savages," the Roman general Suetonius said to his troops at Mancetter, "They will break straight away when they recognize Roman courage and weapons." He was proved right.

point the Romans probably considered leaving Britain altogether, but they went on to win a decisive victory, perhaps at Mancetter in Warwickshire.

The Roman writer Tacitus has left us a highly coloured account of the battle.

"Boudicca, with her daughters standing in front of her, was borne about in a war-chariot from tribe to tribe. 'Consider our numbers' she cried 'and the reasons why we are fighting; then you will either conquer or die in this battle. I, a woman, am resolved to do so – you men, if you like, can live to be Roman slaves'."[3]

The legionaries stood their ground. When the Britons were almost upon them they hurled their javelins and advanced in a wedge formation. Boudicca, seeing she was defeated, killed herself. The revolt collapsed. Organized resistance was over.

LIFE IN ROMAN BRITAIN

The land the Romans now took over and ruled as part of their empire was well worth having. Its population seems to have been around two million, double what it was at the time of the Norman Conquests a thousand years later. In the 150 years before the Roman invasion the British had cleared large areas of forest. Farmsteads and villages, generally guarded with a stockade, were surrounded by fields of corn and big expanses of grazing land. The British herded sheep in large numbers and exported corn and cattle.

The Romans introduced farming on a much larger scale – estate farming. They ran big cattle ranches and increased the amount of exports, particularly corn.

One of the main reasons for the Roman invasion had been to obtain valuable minerals – lead, iron ore, gold and tin.

By about AD 47 the Romans were mining silver-bearing lead in the Mendip Hills, in south-west England, and exporting it to Europe. Roman prospectors searched for gold in the Lake District and in North Wales, and they sometimes found it.

As long as they could protect its borders in the south-west and north, and in Scotland and Wales, the Romans believed that their province of Britannia would bring them plenty of profit.

▽ *Large Roman-British estate farms became common in the 1st century AD.*

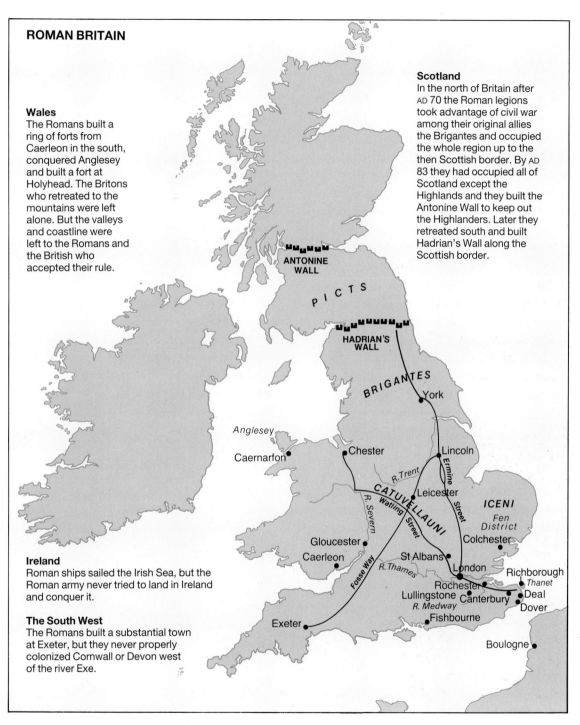

ROMAN BRITAIN

Wales
The Romans built a ring of forts from Caerleon in the south, conquered Anglesey and built a fort at Holyhead. The Britons who retreated to the mountains were left alone. But the valleys and coastline were left to the Romans and the British who accepted their rule.

Scotland
In the north of Britain after AD 70 the Roman legions took advantage of civil war among their original allies the Brigantes and occupied the whole region up to the then Scottish border. By AD 83 they had occupied all of Scotland except the Highlands and they built the Antonine Wall to keep out the Highlanders. Later they retreated south and built Hadrian's Wall along the Scottish border.

Ireland
Roman ships sailed the Irish Sea, but the Roman army never tried to land in Ireland and conquer it.

The South West
The Romans built a substantial town at Exeter, but they never properly colonized Cornwall or Devon west of the river Exe.

The Romans never conquered all of Britain. Their policy was to seal off unconquered territories, to defend the frontiers, and to establish relations with frontier chiefs, whose soldiers would act as a buffer between the British outside the empire and Roman Britain. The Channel and the southerly parts of the North Sea were patrolled by their navy, acting from their base at Dover or elsewhere. The Romans built harbours wherever they could.

ROMAN TOWNS AND THEIR VILLAS

Whenever they conquered a country and settled there, the Romans built towns. In Britain, they built new towns all over England (most of them in the south and south-east), which must have attracted, amazed and impressed the Britons. Often they turned the headquarters of Celtic tribes into Roman towns. In the more distant areas, particularly in the north where there was still danger from enemy tribes, they built forts, which later turned into towns. There were about 100 such forts in Roman Britain. A town or city's modern name often shows that it was once a Roman fort or camp (the Latin word for camp, *castrum*, appears in names such as Manchester, Chichester and Chester).

Roman towns were all built in the same general pattern. The straight streets ran at right angles into each other and there were many open spaces.

The town villas where the well-to-do Celts and Romans lived had plenty of room and their own gardens. They were one-storey houses, built around their own courtyard, and could perhaps be compared to a modern 'ranch-style' bungalow. There would be about a dozen rooms, joined together by a verandah. The most luxurious of the villas had lavatories that flushed, and were heated by underfloor central heating, fuelled by wood or charcoal furnaces called *hypocausts*. The plaster on the walls would be painted in different colours – a deep red was popular, as was a deep pink – and there would be mosaics on the floor. So keen were the Romans on mosaics that Julius Caesar carried his own portable mosaic floor wherever he went, as one might carry a favourite rug about with one today.

Most houses had a wooden framework, and walls of clay, wattle and daub. Workers and shopkeepers lived in low houses, flush with the street. Their floors and roofs were tiled. There were many skilled British craftsmen – blacksmiths and bronze smiths for instance – as well as cobblers, potters, carpenters and other craftsmen. Many of these learned to read and write, as well as to speak Latin. All soldiers in the Roman army had to learn how to read and write. Since more and more of these soldiers were British, literacy

▽ *The streets in Roman Britain bustled with activity. Notice the stone paving, the farmer's daughter selling her vegetables, the baker, the pottery shop, and the people's simple clothes.*

△ The kitchen of a wealthy Roman was very well equipped. The cook, a slave, is at the stove. Around him are large pots – one containing olives – and a milk pail. Some of the pots are made of bronze and some of iron.

now became common for the first time in Britain's history. Schools were formed for both soldiers and civilians.

The population of a Roman-British town was about 5000. Their way of life was truly Roman. Important Britons were made full Roman citizens, and all others who were not farm labourers or slaves were encouraged to wear Roman clothes.

FASHIONS

Both men and women wore the Roman *toga* on formal occasions. This was a semi-circle of white cloth wound round the body. For everyday use, the men wore tunics with short cloaks.

The archaeological excavations at Roman towns such as Richborough and, above all, London, have shown us how fond of jewellery and make-up Roman and Roman-British women were. There is a fine display at Richborough of women's make-up articles: a plated bronze mirror, combs, glass phials for ointment, and ear scoops for extracting wax. There are brooches and finger rings of bronze, silver and gold. In London decorated hairpins of bronze and bone have been discovered, one carved with the head and shoulders of a Roman woman with her hair piled high with a tiara on top of it. (Roman women wore their hair long.) A gold necklace with emeralds, green glass beads, and bronze, iron and gold rings have been found. Pottery bottles have been discovered which would have held ointments and powders. Long spoons were used to scoop out the cosmetics.

▽ *A men's bath house. After he had undressed, the bather first entered the tepidarium (1). Here he gently sweated in the steam and prepared himself for the shocks to come. Then he entered the hot room (2), also full of steam, but this time as hot as a man could bear. But the greatest shock was still to come, when the bather, dizzy with heat made his way into the frigidarium (3) and jumped into the icy pool. After this ordeal he came out into the crowded exercise yard to wrestle or lift weights, or simply to take refreshments or relax by the pool.*

FOOD

The remains of Roman rubbish dumps tell us a great deal about the diet of the inhabitants of London at this time. From seeds left behind we know that figs, grapes and olives must have been imported in large numbers from the Mediterranean region. Many other fruits, including apples, blackberries, plums, cherries, damsons, raspberries, strawberries and mulberries were eaten. A large part of the Roman-British diet was grain and meat – from cattle, sheep and pigs in particular. The animals were brought to the city alive and then slaughtered in special slaughter houses. The skulls of 47 lambs, for instance, have been dug up in Southwark in south London, close to the junction of roads leading from Sussex and Kent. Milk and cheese must also have been important in the diet, but they leave no traces behind them. However, bones of fish such as herring, mackerel, plaice and eel have all been found, as well as thousands of oyster shells (oysters were one of the Romans' favourite foods). Traces of vegetables such as cabbages, carrots, celery and cucumbers have been discovered.

ROMAN BATHS

In the centre of every Roman town stood the public baths. Admission charges were low, and children were allowed in free. They were a social centre, rather than just a place in which to wash. Here townspeople would gather to play dice, to gossip, to do business or merely to kill time, as people in Mediterranean countries still meet in town squares or on waterfronts today. The baths were large and contained a variety of rooms, as in modern Turkish baths. Men and women bathed separately.

WATER SUPPLY

The Romans were the first people to store water in Britain. In some places they built great aqueducts, and channelled water to the towns. The bath houses were supplied in this way, often by lead pipes, and so were the richest town villas.

PUBLIC TOILETS

The Romans were also the first people to build public toilets in their British towns. In Lincoln an underground sewerage system has been excavated, linking the public toilets and the richer villas to the city's cess pits.

THE FORUM AND THE AMPHITHEATRE

In the middle of the Roman town, and dominating it, stood the 'forum' or market place. Here was the city's 'basilica', or town hall, probably with steps leading up to it. Travellers entering London saw the city's basilica standing on top of Ludgate Hill, in the area of modern St Paul's Cathedral, dominating the city and overlooking the Thames. It was more than 150 metres long, longer than any other basilica in northern Europe. Inside, as in a modern town hall, were the council offices, the council chambers and the law courts where the magistrates, most of them local British leaders, would sit. The public buildings were paid for by local rich men and officials, and not by the Roman taxpayers. This encouraged local people to feel pride in their town.

The basilica stood at one end of the forum. On its other three sides there were covered pavements, with columns, where people strolled and admired the shops, as we do in a modern shopping precinct. The owners of the shops lived in rooms behind or above them.

△ *This aerial photograph shows the remains of the Roman theatre at St Albans. The Romans built amphitheatres in several British towns. There they held bull-baiting, cock-fighting, gladiator fights and other events.*

In the middle of the forum stood statues erected in honour of an emperor or governor, or a column commemorating a military victory. Other main buildings were situated in the forum, such as the public baths and the temples. The Romans erected temples both to their own gods and to those of the British.

Outside several of the towns there stood amphitheatres where bull-baiting, cock-fighting and sword-fighting took place. The sword-fighters (gladiators) fought each other to the death, and the crowds placed bets on the results. They watched lions and tigers fighting each other, also, although the shows in general were less lavish than the ones held in the Mediterranean areas of the empire.

THE NEW LONDON

After the destruction of London during Queen Boudicca's revolt, a new city was built that became one of the largest towns in northern Europe. It was the financial centre of Britain and had its own mint. It was the centre of the road network. It was the headquarters of the Roman governor of Britannia and the site of his palace. In two generations since the invasion a city had been built where before stood a straggling collection of huts. It was more technically advanced than anything to be seen in London for the next 1000 years.

The city had a market which must have been popular with local farmers, for agricultural tools have been discovered. They include hoes, sickles, rakes, spades and pruning hooks. The number of bones of oxen that have been found shows that it was they, not horses, that dragged the iron ploughs. Goads used to urge them into action have also been dug up.

The tools found from these years belong to most of the craftsmen you would expect to find in a big and expanding city – builders, carpenters and potters for instance. Blacksmiths have left some of their hammers, anvils and furnace bars, and the remains of iron slag heaps show where the metal was worked. Fragments of the pottery lamps which lit the houses have been found. But no one would have expected the discovery of a collection of surgical instruments similar to a modern surgeon's. Nor would anyone have expected to dig up two wooden yo-yos, or board games of the racing sort, complete with counters and dice, or to find so much evidence of people keeping dogs as pets (they do not seem to have kept as many cats). London had indeed become part of the so-called civilized world.

BUILDING A COLONY

Britons living on the south coast must have been amazed by the construction of the palace at Fishbourne. Its owner was King Cogidubnus. He had been a British leader in south-east England when the Romans invaded and had supported them during Boudicca's revolt. As a reward, the Romans allowed him to go on ruling Sussex and Hampshire, so long as he continued to support them. He was given the title of legate (ambassador) to the emperor and sat in the Roman senate. And he was allowed to live in a magnificent palace at Fishbourne, built in AD 75.

The palace was unlike anything else in Britain. It could be compared in size and splendour only to the palaces of the emperor in Rome. Many foreign craftsmen must have worked there to build it. The stones came from all over the empire.

In the centre of the west wing was a vaulted audience chamber, reached by a flight of steps leading up from the garden. Here the king held court. The main building was entered through a vast hall, at one end of which was a marble-lined pool. More than 60 mosaics covered the floors of the palace.

The rooms had painted ceilings and the walls were covered with large panels of red, yellow and deep blue. The doors and windows were framed with marble mouldings and sometimes friezes of stucco (a kind of plaster) ran around the tops of the walls. One of the friezes showed two

▽ *This model shows what Fishbourne Palace would have looked like. Built in about AD 75 by King Cogidubnus, the palace has been called the largest Roman building north of the Alps.*

birds holding fruit in their beaks and facing each other across vases of fruit. Statues and busts would have decorated some of the rooms.

The gardens were surrounded with wide colonnaded walks, and across their centre and around their edges there were paths lined with box hedges. Fruit trees and flowering shrubs stood in the middle. Fountains played into marble basins.

The splendour of King Cogidubnus' court and the strategic situation of his kingdom illustrates how much the Romans depended on the British for support. After a time the great majority of the soldiers and civil servants were Britons, trained by their Roman masters. It was not a Roman Empire but a Roman-British Empire.

LIFE IN THE COUNTRY

Although some people joined the army, became civil servants, or moved to the new towns, most Britons continued to live and work in the countryside. They usually lived in the same simple timber-framed farmsteads their ancestors had inhabited before the Romans came. They looked after their small farms in the same way, growing just enough to feed themselves and their families. But there were many exceptions. The emperor owned big estates, seized from conquered tribal chiefs. In the south big farmers produced a surplus of corn, which they took to market in the nearest town or exported to northern Europe. Retired soldiers – the *coloni* (colonists) – who were given farms around towns such as York, Gloucester or Colchester often used modern farming methods, learned on military service abroad. In the north and west farmers ran large cattle ranches, and sold their meat

△ *The floors of Fishbourne Palace were covered with mosaics. This section shows a cupid riding a dolphin.*

and hides all over the empire. Britons now inhabited a larger world. They had become members of a national, sometimes an international economy.

ROMAN COUNTRY VILLAS

The villa was the most important Roman introduction to the British countryside. Some of these country houses were small and were really British farmsteads altered after the Romans came. Some were large and luxurious new houses, modelled on villas owned by rich Romans in Italy. They were surrounded by big estates. Some rich men owned several villas and estates, both in Britain and in Gaul. Most of the villas were lived in by Britons, but some were occupied by Romans.

Villa life can be studied in detail at the carefully excavated house which stood at Lullingstone, near Sevenoaks in Kent. It was lived in for 300 years, and was altered and much enlarged. It began as a British farmhouse, of wood and thatch, at the time of the Roman invasion. At the end of the 1st century AD the British owner rebuilt it to look more like a Roman villa.

Towards the end of the 2nd century a wealthy Roman lived in the house and he changed it completely. This Roman may have worked in London and travelled to

work from his country villa like a commuter does today. It would probably have taken him about the same time to reach his office – two hours!

In about 200 the Roman left the area. Nobody lived there again for 100 years. Then a rich British farmer came to live in the villa and farm the lands. After about 360, the villa stopped being lived in, and in about 380 the baths were pulled down and filled in. In the 5th century the buildings were destroyed by fire.

The farm lands attached to Lullingstone covered hundreds of acres of downs and woodlands. Corn was grown on the downs, the woods provided oak for building or for the central heating furnace and acorns for the pigs, while cattle and horses could graze along the river banks. The river runs into the Thames, so that produce could be taken easily by water to London or to the Continent.

▽ *Country villas were a common feature of the landscape in Roman Britain.*

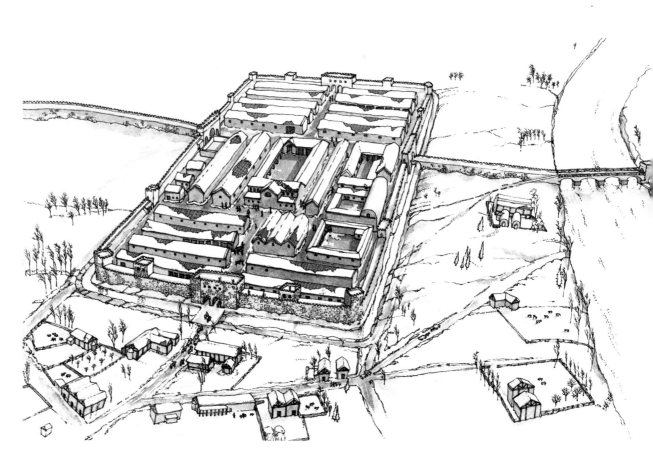

HADRIAN'S WALL

In 122 the Roman Emperor Hadrian visited Britain, the first emperor to do so since the conquering Claudius. During the previous few years, tribes from Scotland had destroyed the Roman forts built to keep them out and had invaded northern England. The Romans had three choices – to move their border south to the river Trent, to conquer all Scotland, or to try to keep the tribes out by a different method. Hadrian ordered that the last be chosen. He built a great wall across England at its narrowest point. It stretched from Barrow-on-Solway in Cumberland to Wallsend-on-Tyne in Northumberland, a distance of about 115 kilometres. It took ten years to complete. Hadrian's Wall remained as a 'frontier of civilization' for 260 years, and much of it still stands today.

△ *Chester's Fort was one of 16 forts built into Hadrian's Wall. The fort housed 500 soldiers in barracks and had granaries, a house for the commandant, a strong room for pay, and – of course – a bath house.*

Hadrian's Wall had four parts: a ditch to the north, measuring 8 metres wide and 2.75 metres deep; the Wall itself; a second ditch to the south; and a military road south of that, which was used to transport troops and supplies. The Wall was a little over 2 metres wide. It was not solid stone, but built of large squarish stones on the outside and packed with broken stones and mortar in the middle. It was 4.5 metres high, with a flat top, sometimes turfed, so that patrolling sentries could walk along it. On the north side of the sentry walk there were an extra 2 metres of narrow parapet to protect the sentries from enemy attacks. Every 500 metres a turret was built for the soldiers who patrolled the Wall, and every Roman mile (about 1400 metres) a 'milecastle' was built on the south side of the Wall. The milecastle housed around 40 men. It contained a gateway through the Wall so that soldiers could march out, when necessary, for battle.

Every 8 kilometres there was a large fort, making a total of 16 in all. Each of the forts housed about 500 soldiers, and contained supplies and services. There were granaries with raised floors so that the corn would not become damp and rot. There were barracks for the soldiers, a house for the commandant, workshops for the blacksmiths and carpenters, a hospital, and bath houses. The forts had protective walls and turrets.

The ditch to the south of the Wall was built for two purposes. If the Brigantes tribesmen of northern England turned against the Romans and attacked the Wall from the south, the ditch would serve as a defence against them. If armies from Scotland succeeded in breaking through the Wall from the north, it would serve as an extra barrier.

The Wall gave the Romans new confidence. By 140 they had advanced deep into Scotland. In 142 they built a wall of turf, 60 kilometres long, connecting what is now Glasgow on the river Clyde with Edinburgh on the Firth of Forth. It was called the Antonine Wall, after the emperor who ruled at the time. Only about 6000 soldiers were needed to patrol it. But twenty years later the Roman army retreated from Scotland to Hadrian's Wall, and never returned to occupy Scotland.

Within 35 years the Romans abandoned Hadrian's Wall. In 196–197 the troops were withdrawn. The governor of Britain, who was trying to become emperor, wanted their help in his battles in Gaul. The Scottish tribes saw their opportunity, and advanced deep into northern England, capturing York. Whole stretches of the Wall seemed to have been demolished. The vital importance of the Wall to the security of the empire in Britain was obvious for all to see.

▽ *This soldier is on sentry duty on Hadrian's Wall. For hundreds of years the Wall marked the northern limit of an empire which stretched from Northumberland to Iran.*

When the governor's ambitions had been defeated the Roman garrisons returned to the Wall. About the year 208 it was rebuilt. From then on, though badly damaged, it withstood all attacks from the north. But in the south, Roman power in Britain was coming under increasing attack from pirates, raiders and colonists from overseas, while Rome itself was nearly overwhelmed. In 388 the troops abandoned the Wall, and the great construction was left to crumble.

ROMAN ROADS

The most lasting memorial the Romans left behind them in Britain was their famous road system. The road engineers began building soon after they arrived, and by the time they left had built about 5000 Roman miles of magnificent straight, wide roads. These were still being used 1300 years later, although the people who came after the Romans had no idea how to repair them and many became no more than tracks. Traces of the Roman paving stones, running straight across the countryside, can still be seen today. I myself came across such stones in a wood near Dover recently and followed the straight track for a mile until it was lost in a farmer's field.

Although the Romans built their roads originally in order to move troops quickly across the country, soldiers were not the only users. Farmers taking their produce to market, traders from all over the western world, Roman and British officials going about their duties all travelled by road. The road system was a great communications network, bringing British people into closer touch with each other and with the rest of the empire.

▽ *The Roman road engineers laid their roads straight. They were built to last and many can still be seen all over Britain.*

The Romans laid their roads as straight as the land allowed. They lasted so well because they were thoroughly drained. The first job of the Roman road engineers was always to dig deep trenches in the soil, into which layers of cobblestones, crushed rubble and concrete would be piled. On top of these deep foundations would be laid a surface of large paving stones, carefully fitted together. The surface would be curved at the edges (cambered), so that water ran off into drainage ditches at the road sides. Milestones stood every Roman mile.

TROUBLES IN BRITAIN

We think of the years of the Roman-British Empire as a block of peaceful time. In fact periods of peace were interspersed with wars and rebellions. Much of the 3rd century was a time of chaos throughout the empire. There were civil wars, and at one point Britain joined a separate empire – 'the Empire of the Gallic provinces' – which contained France, Spain, and parts of Germany. Many Roman Emperors were assassinated. There was high inflation. By 270 the whole empire seemed about to collapse. Rich villa owners in Gaul emigrated to Britain to escape attacks by tribes from across the Rhine. For nine years Britain was a separate nation under a rebellious Roman officer. By 296 Britain was back under the control of the Emperor Constantius. He saved London from destruction and led an invasion of Scotland in 306. He died at York, and it was there that the army proclaimed his son Constantine the new Emperor. He became known as Constantine the Great, and regarded Britain as his favourite province. Britain was peaceful and prosperous again for a while.

△ The Chi-Ro mosaic at Lullingstone provides evidence of Christian worship in Roman Britain.

CHRISTIANITY IN ROMAN BRITAIN

For the first 300 years after Jesus' death there were few Christians in Britain and those there were suffered terribly. Most of them were soldiers in the Roman army like Albanus, executed for his faith at the city we now call St Albans. The situation changed when the emperor Constantine was converted to Christianity. This became the official religion of the empire, and Britons who worshipped their nature gods were persecuted. At Lullingstone the remains of a Christian chapel has been found. It was built about AD 365 above a room in which the old British or Roman worship seems to have continued. On the walls of the chapel were painted figures of men at prayer and the Christian sign. This was the two Greek letters Chi and Rho – CHR – which stands for 'Christos' – Christ in Greek. But after the Romans left people went back to their old gods and before long there were hardly any signs that Christianity had ever come to Britain.

DECLINE AND FALL

Britain was peaceful during the reign of Emperor Constantine, but for years the empire had been in trouble. Civil wars were fought, emperors were assassinated, and politicians and generals fought each other for control. Tribes were attacking the borders of the empire in Europe from the 3rd century onwards. They had come from the Russian steppes and moved into central and eastern Europe. They saw the wealth of the empire, and believed the Romans were too weak to defend it.

The Roman army was not as efficient as it had been in the early days. Many soldiers were foreigners, and later some officers and even generals were foreigners too. The foreign soldiers were not always as loyal to the emperor as the Romans themselves were. Sometimes they changed sides during a war with an invading tribe. Without strong armies, and with troubles at home, the Romans could no longer defend and control their vast empire. That they had done so for so many centuries is one of the wonders of history.

SAXON INVASIONS

By 300, the Romans were very worried about the tribes from Germany who were attacking British shores. These were the Saxons though the Romans tended to call all tribes by the same name, 'barbarians' (because their strange languages sounded to them like animal noises – 'bar, bar'). The Saxons advanced deep inland looking for wealthy towns and villas to loot. The governors of Britannia had always been reluctant to allow a town to build a circuit of walls, for it could make the town

△ This coin, discovered at Richborough, is dated 410 – about the year the Romans left. One side (above) shows a Briton cowering before a Roman on horseback. The Roman galley and gatehouse are vividly portrayed.

difficult to control. Now town governors began to build walls round their towns, particularly those near the coast, to keep out invaders. A chain of forts was built from the Wash to the Solent, and placed under the command of a man who was known as the Count of the Saxon Shore.

The forts had massive walls, from which stone-throwing machines threw balls of stone more than 30 centimetres in diameter. Unlike the forts the Romans built when they invaded, these were to defend the British people; not barracks from which the troops would attack them.

The monument at Richborough that the Romans had originally built to celebrate their great victory over the British now had a new use as a look-out post. The sentries peered anxiously out across the English Channel, searching for the dreaded Saxon pirate ships. From a magnificent monument with shining bronze statues dominating the Channel, Richborough had become a place from which repeated dangers could be spotted.

THE FLIGHT OF THE LEGIONS

In 350 a Roman general in Germany tried to turn the western part of the Roman Empire, including Britain, into a separate empire. This rebellion was defeated, but the British were savagely punished for supporting it. Then in 367 Picts from Scotland and tribes from Ireland invaded the north of England and reached as far south as the Thames. At the same time, the Saxons and the Franks attacked southern England and northern Gaul.

The army was not prepared for attacks from several different directions at once. Like the rest of the Roman army, the army in Britain had become undisciplined and weak. Instead of defending Britain against the invaders, many soldiers deserted. They joined the enemy who roamed the country in small bands; or they roamed about on their own, robbing towns and farms. A strong task force under a commander called Theodosius was sent from Rome to re-establish order. He recaptured London and defeated the Saxons at sea. Bands of barbarian soldiers were rounded up. Deserters were pardoned, and the army reorganized. Forts were rebuilt; towns and cities repaired. Villas were still inhabited and farmed. A new system of signal stations was set up on one section of Hadrian's Wall. Everything seemed to have gone back to normal. But again the peace proved short-lived.

At the beginning of the 5th century, the real ruler of the Western Empire was a Vandal who took the Roman name of Flavius Stilicho. He withdrew part of the Roman army out of Britain to fight for him in Europe, for he hoped to take over the whole empire. Soon the rest of the Roman army left Britain as well. The British were left to fight the Saxon invaders alone. In 440 a group of British leaders asked for help from Rome, but their request was ignored. The Romans were overwhelmed by troubles of their own, and seemed to have lost interest in Britain. It was no longer part of the Roman Empire.

▽ *The Saxon Shore Forts were built to defend the whole south-east coast of Britain.*

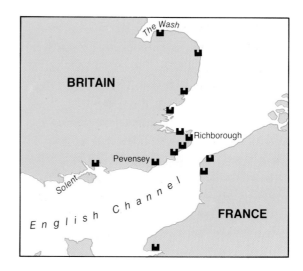

THE BREAKDOWN OF ROMAN CIVILIZATION

Once the Roman troops and civil servants had departed, the local chiefs and big landowners were left in charge of the country. Most of the signs of Roman wealth and organization vanished with extraordinary speed. By 430 coins were no longer regularly used.

People still went on living in towns for a while. But soon nobody repaired the roads or kept up the town walls. The forts and Hadrian's Wall were neglected; the villas slowly deserted. People went back to living on their own small farms, and growing just enough food for themselves and their families.

It seems extraordinary that a way of life which had existed for nearly 400 years should vanish, leaving so few traces behind. The Romans had attempted to get the British to share in their way of life – to help govern the country, to join the army, and to follow Roman methods of trade, industry and farming. In the towns the potters, the jewellers and the blacksmiths were British. Roman engineers may have planned and supervised the building of the great roads, but British workers built and repaired them. The forts and walls were constructed according to Roman designs used all over the empire, but the work was done by the British.

▷ *After the Romans left, their villas were abandoned, although most of them had been lived in by British owners. Their maintenance was beyond the capacities of the British and the villa way of life was soon forgotten. Local farmers took away their wood, tiles and stones. In the towns the houses crumbled away, while the walls were used as quarries by local people for hundreds of years to come.*

In the light of all this, how was it that British landowners, accustomed to living the leisurely and comfortable life of the villas, deserted them, leaving thieves to take the bricks and tiles? How could Christian men and women go back to the gods of their ancestors? How could town-dwellers lose interest in the towns in which they had once taken such a pride, let their forum, basilica, theatre or bath house fall to pieces, and move to the country again? When you know how to build a road, why let it go to ruin and return to using a rough track? Why give up such seemingly important skills as reading and writing? It is all very strange.

400–1042

INVADERS AND SETTLERS

TIME CHART

* denotes events that occurred outside Britain and Ireland.

By 400	Anglo-Saxon mercenaries had begun to settle in Europe.	757	Offa becomes King of Mercia.
400–450	Saxons start permanent settlements in England.	774	Offa becomes *Bretwalda*. (supreme ruler) of all England.
432	St Patrick starts mission to Ireland.	780 on	Norwegian tribes settle in Orkneys, Shetlands and Isle of Man.
450	Vortigern, the Welsh king, invites Saxons to settle in Thanet, Kent. Jutes accept.	787	First Viking raid on England.
		By 800	Wales is divided into four main kingdoms.
457	Jutes defeat Britons at Crayford, Kent, and conquer all of Kent.	800	*Charlemagne is crowned Emperor of Western Europe.
476	*Goths conquer Rome. End of Western Roman Empire.	835	Norwegians capture Dublin.
		865	Danish Grand Army lands in eastern England.
About 500	King Arthur leads Britons to victory over Saxons at Mount Badon, Dorset. Saxons settle most of southern England.	866	York becomes the centre of a Norwegian empire.
		871	Alfred is King of Wessex.
527	*Justinian Emperor of Eastern Roman Emprie (Byzantine).	878	Alfred defeats Danes near Chippenham. Treaty of Wedmore divides England between Saxons and 'Danelaw'.
563	St Columba founds Iona community.		
570	*Muhammad is born.	899	King Alred dies.
588	Aethelric creates kingdom of Northumbria.	911	*Viking settlement is formed in Normandy.
597	St Augustine starts mission to England.	924–975	King Athelstan and Edgar of Wessex unite most of England in peace.
600	England divided into seven Saxon kingdoms.	959	St Dunstan is Archbishop of Canterbury.
About 620	Sutton Hoo burial mound built.		
632	*Muhammad dies.	980	Danes renew raids on England.
635	Lindisfarne monastery is established.	976–1016	Ethelred is King of Wessex.
About 650	*Beowulf* is written.	1016	Danish King Cnut is elected 'King of all England'.
664	Synod of Whitby formed.		
732	*Muslim invasion of Europe halted at Battle of Tours.	1035	Cnut dies. Seven years of fighting for succession follows.

ANGLES, SAXONS AND JUTES

After the Romans left, the Saxons, Angles and other tribes from North Germany, the Netherlands and Scandinavia took over England. They settled in the same areas as those once occupied by the Romans. Many Britons retreated into Wales and western England. Many more remained behind to become aliens or slaves in their own country.

Some Saxon tribespeople were living in England even before the Romans departed from the country. They were probably employed by the Roman authorities to guard London from attack. From about 450 they were joined in large numbers by Angle and Saxon tribespeople sailing from the northern coast of Europe.

EVIDENCE OF THE INVADERS
Unlike the Roman colonists these new invaders could neither read nor write and have left no records behind them. Once again we have to rely for evidence on the archaeologists. Three hundred years after the invasions, however, a monk known as the Venerable Bede wrote an account of his ancestors' origins. Here is part of it:

"They came from three very powerful Germanic tribes, the Saxons, Angles and

▽ When the Saxons' fighting men reported that it was safe to come to England, whole families arrived to colonize their new lands, bringing all their possessions with them.

These Saxons merchants are carrying wool to sell in a town. Although Britain grew more isolated after the Romans left, the Saxons traded from the time of their earliest settlements, both inland and overseas.

Jutes. The people of Kent, and the inhabitants of the Isle of Wight are of Jutish origin. From the Saxon country came the East Saxons, the South Saxons and the West Saxons. From the country of the Angles ... which is called Angulus, came the East Angles, the Middle Angles, the Mercians and all the Northumbrian race (that is all the people who dwell north of the river Humber)." [4]

The names of counties such as Essex and Sussex, and of regions such as East Anglia, Wessex and Mercia, are derived from those of the peoples Bede describes.

We can never be sure why these tribes left their homelands to settle in an unknown country. Perhaps their country was overcrowded and there was a food shortage. The first raiders, as Bede says later, reported that the new land was fertile. In their own countries they were being pressed by fierce tribes, the Huns and the Goths, arriving from the east.

Perhaps, like many migrating peoples, the tribes were just looking for adventure. The Anglo-Saxon poem *Beowulf*, written about 700, describes one Saxon voyage:

"Time passed on; the ship was on the waves, the boat beneath the cliff. The warriors eagerly embarked...Men bore bright ornaments, splendid war trappings, to the bosom of the ship. The men, the heroes on their willing venture, shoved out the well-timbered ship. The foamy-necked floater like a bird went over the wave-filled sea, sped by the wind, till after due time on the next day the boat with twisted prow had gone so far that the voyagers saw land...Then the sea was traversed, the journey at an end. The men mounted quickly to the land; they made fast the ship...They thanked God that the sea voyage had been easy for them." [5]

VORTIGERN AND HENGIST

By 450 full scale invasions had started. In that year a Welsh king, Vortigern, ruled much of England including Kent. His people lived along the old border between England and Wales. They had been allies of the Romans, and had adopted many Roman ways. When Saxon raiders kept landing along the Kentish coast Vortigern decided to invite some of them to help him defend his shores, offering them land in east Kent as a reward. Here is Bede's account of what happened:

"the race of the Angles or Saxons, invited by Vortigern, came to Britain in three warships and by his command were granted a place of settlement in the easternmost part of the island. They pretended they were going to fight on behalf of the country, but their real intention was to conquer it...A report of the fertility of the island and the slackness of the Britons, reached their homes, and at once a much larger fleet was sent over, with a stronger band of warriors." [4]

The warriors, according to the *Anglo-Saxon Chronicle*, a history of the Saxon peoples written some time after 800, were

led by two brothers, Hengist and Horsa. The names mean 'Horse' and 'Mare' respectively and, like the brothers themselves, may well be fictitious.

THE DEFEAT OF THE BRITONS

The new settlers soon attacked their British hosts and won a number of victories. By 600 they controlled most of England. The British were forced into northwest England, Devon and Cornwall and Wales. Some sailed to Brittany, as the name shows, and settled there. The Saxons did not have things all their own way. About the year 500 the Britons won a victory at a place called Mount Badon. They were said to have been led by the great British King Arthur, about whom many legends later developed. The little that is known about Arthur suggests that he was a military commander, not a king.

THE KINGDOM OF ENGLAND

From about 600 the country which came to be called England – the Angles gave their name to the whole area – was roughly divided into seven kingdoms that were run on tribal lines. Some of their boundaries were determined by natural features. Kent was divided from Sussex by Romney Marsh and the great forest of the Kentish Weald. East Anglia was bordered by the river Stour and the Fens. Further north there were no such limits. Two powerful northern kingdoms, Mercia and Northumbria, swallowed up the lands of weaker neighbours. King Offa of Mercia built a great ditch, known as a 'dyke', to separate his land from the Welsh. Much of the dyke still exists, bearing his name. In the west Wessex stretched to British Cornwall. It was destined to become the greatest English kingdom.

Those Britons who did not flee west worked as free labourers or slaves of the Saxon farmers. The Britons formed by far the greatest proportion of the population. During the 6th century, there were only about 100,000 Anglo-Saxons in Britain, one tenth of the population. Slowly the races merged together.

Life in Anglo-Saxon Britain was very different from that of Roman times. The towns and villas, money and writing, organized armies and law courts had disappeared. The Anglo-Saxons replaced them with their own way of life, which was more like life had been in Britain before Roman times.

◁ *The Anglo-Saxons did more than any previous settlers to clear and plough lands which no one yet had farmed. In this scene an overseer is supervising farm workers who are cutting and carrying corn.*

△ *Much of our knowledge of early Anglo-Saxon life and Christianity comes from Bede's works. This decoration from a manuscript of Bede's life of St Cuthbert shows Bede writing.*

LOYALTY TO FAMILY AND TRIBE

The Anglo-Saxon tribes were farming people. They lived in the countryside in groups of about 50, each made up of the family and relations of one man. The laws were based on loyalty to your family and lord. If you were killed, your family would kill the murderer or one of his family. If someone else in your family was killed, it was up to you to punish the killer. If you did not, you would never be forgiven. Above the family were the lords and the chiefs. Loyalty to them was as vital as loyalty to the family. You would never be forgiven if you broke your oath of loyalty.

▷ *This map shows the areas settled by the Anglo-Saxons. Cornwall remained British, and Wales and most of Scotland stayed independent.*

SAXON PLACE NAMES

Most English place names are of Saxon origin. Common Saxon names are *bury* (fort), *chester* (Roman camp), *ham* (home), *hurst* (wood), *ing* (tribe or family), *minster* (monastery), *strat* or *stret* (Roman road) and *ton* (farm or village). In place names the words are combined with the name of a chief or a description of the place. For instance, Canterbury means the fort of the Cantii tribe, Hastings is where chief Haesta's family lives, Stratford-on-Avon marks the ford over the river Avon on the Roman road.

SAXON RELIGIONS

The Saxons were a superstitious people. They believed in magic, charms and incantations. Most people believed in witches and their male equivalent,

warlocks, who were supposed to be in league with the Devil, and to do fearsome things. These beliefs survived after the Saxons became Christians and became mixed up with Christian beliefs, although the Church tried to stop it.

ANGLO-SAXON GODS

The Saxons worshipped many gods. They believed they would protect them in battle or during storms, that they would cure their children of illness or make their crops grow. They also worshipped trees, springs, stones and rocks. Their holy places were outside, in sacred groves in the woods or forest clearings.

The names of some of the Saxon gods are remembered today in our days of the week. Tuesday is named after Tiw, Wednesday after Woden. Both were gods of war. Thursday was called after Thor, god of thunder, and Friday after the goddess Frigg, Woden's wife.

SUTTON HOO

One of the most remarkable archaeological discoveries ever made in England was that at Sutton Hoo, near Woodbridge in Suffolk, overlooking the estuary of the river Deben. Here a great burial mound, dated at around 620, has been excavated. It is probably the tomb of an East Anglian king. In the barrow was found the remains of a rowed ship, 24 metres long, with iron rivets in its side, to fasten the overlapping timbers. In the middle of the ship lay a stupendous treasure. Fortunately the grave had not been rifled by thieves.

The treasure discovered at Sutton Hoo was amazingly lavish. There was the lid of a purse made of ivory, decorated with garnets and gold. There was a belt-buckle,

△ *This helmet was reconstructed from hundreds of iron fragments found in the burial ship at Sutton Hoo. The nose and mouth were made of bronze, as were the eyebrows and moustache. Many of the treasures discovered at Sutton-Hoo are in the British Museum.*

which is the heaviest solid gold object ever found in England. There were shoulder clasps which glittered with garnets, the red jewels which the Anglo-Saxons particularly loved. There were gold coins from France, silver spoons and bowls from Egypt and the lands of the eastern Mediterranean, and a helmet, shield and sword from Sweden. There was a lyre with a wooden body, six wooden pegs and strings made of gut or horsehair.

ANGLO-SAXON LIFE

One of our distant ancestors described human life as 'nasty, poor, brutish and short.' Though this gloomy view of life did not apply to all Anglo-Saxon people, especially to the tiny minority of the wealthy, it summed up much of Anglo-Saxon life all too accurately.

DANGERS AND DEATH

Many children died at birth or before their first birthday. Mothers often miscarried and rarely had more than two surviving children. People were surrounded by natural and artificial dangers.

A poem that was written at the time called *The Fates of Men* lists the various ways in which people would be likely to die. They might be killed by wolves, starve to death, die in a storm, fall from a tree,

▽ *The farming methods of the Anglo-Saxons are shown in their calendars. This one, for January, shows oxen ploughing the heavy soil. In Anglo-Saxon times more land was farmed than ever before. Not for nothing have they been called the people who colonized England.*

or be burned alive (either at home in a thatched house or at work in a thatched barn). They might be murdered during a feud (a fight between families), or die in battle. They might be hanged for breaking the law or killed in a drunken brawl. Strangely enough, the writer of the list has left out death from cold and, most common of all, from plague.

TRAVEL PROBLEMS

A journey during Anglo-Saxon times could be frightening. Most of Britain was still forest, much of it thick, dark and impenetrable. In the heart of the forest lived outlaws – people who had been forced to flee from ordinary society, perhaps for committing a crime or because they had made enemies of powerful people. If anyone was unlucky enough to stumble across one of their forest settlements they were likely to be killed on sight. The same thing might happen to any stranger arriving at a settlement if he did not immediately show that he was there on peaceful business.

△ *Many Anglo-Saxon towns were built within the remains of old Roman walls, such as this one from about AD 700.*

◁ *In this Anglo-Saxon settlement a woman is grinding corn with a quern.*

In many parts of the country bogs or marshes made travel almost impossible. The most difficult of these areas were the Fens in East Anglia.

After the Romans departed from Britain, people soon stopped repairing the roads they had built, and movement from one part of the country to another became almost as difficult as it had been during early British times. The untended Roman roads grew to resemble the old long-distance footpaths of earlier days. Travel by river or by sea became the quickest way to move around the country.

Forests, marshes, moors, crumbling roads – they all helped to make the people living in Anglo-Saxon Britain isolated from each other.

Many Anglo-Saxon settlers began clearing the forests, a job which was to be continued by successive generations for over a thousand years. Using fire and axes, and often relying on pigs to clear the undergrowth, the Anglo-Saxon settlers slowly and laboriously colonized England.

FARMING

Once they had cleared an area of land, the free Anglo-Saxon peasants and their British labourers and slaves began to farm it with their heavy ploughs, which were drawn along by oxen. Each peasant was given a share of the farmed land. Often the good and the inferior land was fairly divided by giving each peasant several strips of land of varying quality in the two or three large village fields. This arrangement is known as the 'open-field' system and it operated in much of England for the next thousand years.

The main crops grown on the farms were corn – barley, rye and wheat. The basic foodstuff – bread – was made from these and baked at home. Beer was made from barley. Peas, beans and flax (used for cloth making) were other popular crops. There was no sugar, and bees were kept for their honey and for mead, the popular alcoholic drink made from it. The villagers kept pigs, cattle, goats and sheep. Eggs would not only be taken from chickens, but from geese, ducks and all sorts of wild birds, including seagulls.

▽ *In addition to working the land, Anglo-Saxon peasant farmers had to be adept at handicrafts. Here a woman weaves cloth, using a loom, while her husband makes a wicker basket. Their house is made of logs and thatch. They are slightly better off than the serfs, who lived with their families in huts that were so small it was not possible to stand upright.*

ANGLO-SAXON SETTLEMENTS

At the very top of Anglo-Saxon society stood the king, and his thanes (lords). The kings had their own large estates, as did their thanes, which were managed by their bailiffs. For the king and his court were always moving. They would descend on a thane, stay as long as they chose, and eat him out of house and home. Below this very small number of powerful men came the peasants. Many were *ceorls* (churls), free men who owned strips of 90–100 acres in the fields. Others rented their homes and smaller quantities of land, strips of 20 acres or less. They paid rent in money and goods (eggs, barley, a sheep) to their thane. They would also have to work for him two days a week. They, like the *ceorls*, employed serfs (forced labourers) and thralls (slaves). Something very like a feudal system was developing in Anglo-Saxon England long before the years of the Norman Conquest.

HOUSING

Saxon houses varied according to a man's position in society. Because the Saxons built in wood, thatch and wattle, which do not last, we have to rely on archaeologists to tell us how the kings' halls or farmers' huts of Anglo-Saxon times would have looked. We can also read descriptions of Anglo-Saxon buildings in writings of the time. In *Beowulf*, for example, a magnificent king's hall is described. Its roof is tall; its walls made of long planks held together with iron. You enter through double doors. Inside, the wooden walls are covered with magnificent tapestries which shine with gold. The floor is of stone. The king's thanes sleep here on beds and mattresses with their weapons beside them in case they were attacked.

Some of the houses and huts which ordinary people lived in have been excavated too. The richer farmers lived in thatched wooden longhouses, built in the shape of a rectangle about 20 metres long and 5 metres wide. Most people's huts, however, were probably more like one, belonging to a farmer of the 6th century which has been excavated at Dorchester on Thames. It was roughly circular and about 5 metres across. The roof and walls were of thatch, laid on stakes set into the ground. The floor of the hut was about three quarters of a metre lower than the outside ground. It was of earth or gravel. The smoke from the open fireplace found its way out through a special hole in the roof or through the entrance. There was no door. The whole family would have lived in the one room.

Apart from the various houses and huts, other buildings in the Saxon settlement included a chapel and a weaver's shed, and a corn mill with a grain store and bakery attached. A small building with a pit was the public toilet.

THE LAW

Anglo-Saxon law was very severe. Runaway slaves were killed, as well as certain kinds of thieves, people thought to be witches and those who helped outlaws. The death penalty was inflicted in a number of ways – by hanging, beheading, stoning, burning and drowning. For less serious crimes people could be branded with a hot iron, scalped, scourged (whipped) or blinded. Their ears could be cut off or their tongue wrenched out. As the author of *The Fates of Men* describes, it was common for a traveller to see the dead bodies of criminals hanging on 'gibbets' or gallows outside city gates.

Law was based on the idea of a man's *wergeld*, which means 'life-price'. If he was killed his relatives were entitled to compensation from the murderer. If he was wronged or injured, compensation should be paid to him by those who wronged him on a scale fixed according to the gravity of the crime. Compensation was paid in money or goods and varied according to the wronged person's position in society. According to the laws of early Wessex a thane's *wergeld* was six times that of a churl. Thralls could be killed without *wergeld*. If the price was not paid, then vengeance ('the blood-feud') could be exacted.

One of the features of Saxon tribal life was the *moot* or meeting of the people. This is where cases were tried and the accused had to swear their innocence. They could do this by producing 'oath-helpers', men who would swear that their oath was true. The higher the oath-helper's rank in society the more weight his testimony would carry. Or the trial would go to 'ordeal'.

One of these 'ordeals' was by water. The accused would be roped to a man on the bank and thrown into a pond or river. If he sank the accused would be hauled to land and declared innocent. It was believed that the water had received him with open arms and shown the *moot* the truth. If he floated he was guilty, for the water had rejected his body.

Other 'ordeals' were those by fire. The accused had to carry a red hot bar of iron. If the blisters disappeared in three days he was declared innocent.

Only a few crimes were punished by death. One was witchcraft and another disloyalty to your thane. Outlaws, if discovered, were killed.

ANGLO-SAXON TRADE

Most Anglo-Saxons hardly ever left their own farms or settlements. But there were always pedlars, who visited even the most isolated farms with their medicinal ointments and glass beads, their herbal remedies and their newly sharpened knives. There were merchants who carried wool or cloth to the nearest market town, and then there were the bravest traders of all – those who risked the dangers of attack by robbers on land or by pirates at sea to buy and sell goods in Europe or even further afield.

Foreign trade was for the wealthy. Anglo-Saxon merchants traded regularly with Scandinavia (Norway, Sweden and Denmark) and with Frisia (Holland). French merchants carried wine to London, which Bede described as "an emporium of many peoples coming by land and sea."

In return the English exported wool and cloth to France, and their merchants were to be found even at the mouth of the Vistula on the Baltic coast. From about 600 the Saxon kings were minting their own coins, and King Offa of Mercia minted beautiful silver pennies which were used all over England.

English ports and inland centres of trade began to grow within the old Roman walls (York, Canterbury, London), around a royal palace (Southampton) or close to a large monastery (Winchester). Money rather than barter was increasingly used.

▷ *The Saxons loved to feast, particularly after battle and during the long winter months.* Beowulf *describes one such 'lofty' hall with long trestle tables and benches. They would be pushed back after the feast. Then the minstrels would play their lyres and the bards would recite the sagas of their tribes.*

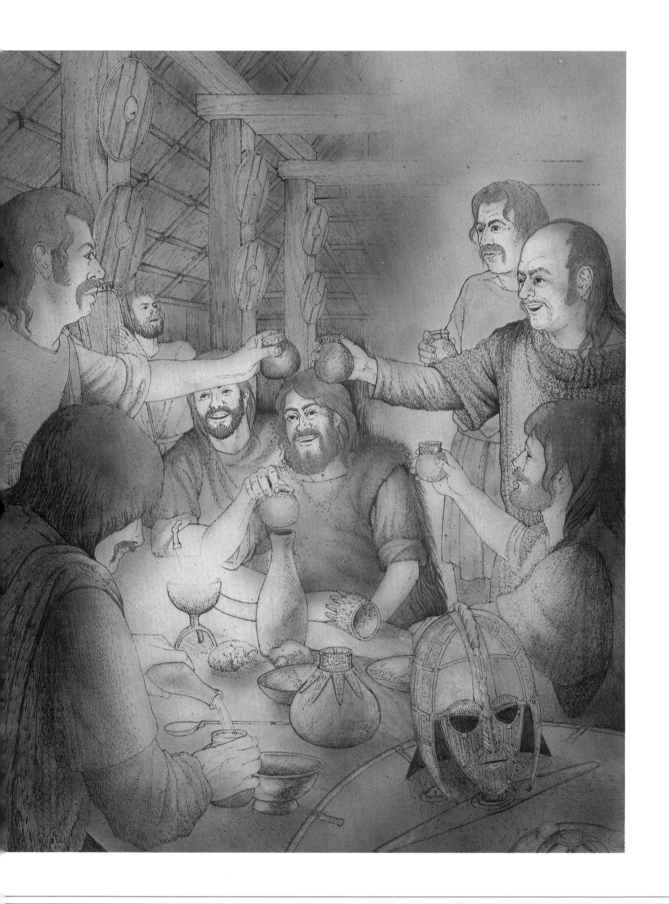

PICTS AND CELTS

When the Anglo-Saxon tribes first conquered and settled in England, many British people who had lived there fled to Wales. There, for a while, they were left alone by the Saxons.

WALES

At this time, Wales was split into separate kingdoms, many of them tiny. After about 600 Welsh armies started raiding parts of England to steal cattle, goods and slaves.

By 800 there were only four main Welsh kingdoms – Gwynedd in the north, Powys in the centre, Dyfed in the south-west and Gwent in the south-east. The rulers of these kingdoms tried to conquer the rest of Wales, such as Hywel Dda, who died in 950. His code of laws formed the basis of Welsh laws for centuries. During his reign, literature was written in Welsh for the first time. Welsh traders travelled all over France and the Mediterranean region.

Most of the Welsh were farmers, raising sheep and cattle. They were independent men who recognized no authority other than their own king's. So too were the skilled craftsmen – jewellers, blacksmiths and goldsmiths. But the serfs and slaves, who worked the big estates, were not regarded as true Welshmen by law.

SCOTLAND

The people living in the Highlands were isolated from other parts of the country by mountains. They knew only their own chiefs and families, and did not regard themselves as part of a Scottish nation. In the 7th century, Scotland was inhabited by four different peoples.

In the north and north-east lived the Picts, one of whose languages was Celtic. Their rulers were descended from the female in the family and they had their court at Scone near Perth. By the eighth century the Picts were claiming to be the rulers of all Scotland.

▽ *The people who farmed Welsh settlements of about AD 900 lived in beehive-shaped huts with thatched roofs and low walls.*

△ Many of the islands off northern Scotland were colonized by Norwegian tribes. In this settlement in the Shetland Islands (about AD 800) the buildings are of local stone, thatched with reeds tied down with weighted ropes.

The tribes on the west coast were the Scots, who had migrated from Ireland and who gave their name to Scotland. They spoke Celtic or Gaelic.

In the Lowlands to the south were the British tribes who had lived there since Roman times. Although they conquered lands and built up large kingdoms for a while they were too often fighting amongst themselves to protect these kingdoms from the Picts, or from the fourth people, the Angles.

The Angles had advanced into northern England from Yorkshire to form the kingdom of Northumbria. At one time they advanced as far as the Firth of Forth at Edinburgh, but they were forced back by armies of Scots and Picts. In 1018 the king of the Scots and Picts reached the modern English frontier.

Scotland was greatly influenced by settlers from Norway. Between 780 and 850 many Norwegian peasants arrived in the islands of Shetland and Orkney, and in the north of Scotland. They fished and farmed and hunted the seals. Other Norwegians settled in the Hebridean islands and Galloway.

It was in the Orkneys that the Norwegians became most powerful. The islands became the centre of a Norwegian empire of the North Sea, which traded with Iceland, Greenland and even perhaps North America. In time, these Norwegians became part of the Scottish peoples.

Attacks by the Norwegians and English helped to create the feeling among the different peoples that they belonged to one nation – Scotland. Malcolm II (1005–1034) claimed to be king of all Scotland, apart from the Norwegian lands in the north. His son inherited a country which seemed to be united.

IRELAND

The Anglo-Saxons did not go to Ireland. Most people in Ireland at this time were descended from the Celtic settlers who first came in 300 BC. The Irish composed great sagas (stories) about their past, which were a mixture of fact and fiction.

By Roman times Ireland consisted of five kingdoms, known as the Five Fifths of Ireland – Ulster, Meath, Leinster, Munster and Connaught. But it was not until the 10th century that the descendants of Ulster's Niall of the Nine Hostages, whose court was at Tara in Meath, claimed to be kings of all Ireland. In the next century Brian Boru of Munster claimed to be the High King of Ireland.

Most people were farmers. The Irish also grew flax which they wove into fine linen. Their sheep produced good wool from which woollen cloaks (brats) were made. People kept pigs for their meat and fished and hunted. The Irish could travel

△ The Irish produced extremely good clothing. The father here is wearing a woollen cloak or 'brat', fastened with a brooch. This indicates that he may have been a chief.

long distances in stormy seas in their currachs. These were round boats made of wicker frames and covered with animal hides. Irish houses, of wattle and mud, were built within defended circles.

In 835 Norwegians seized Dublin and advanced inland. In 914 they took Waterford, and in 920 they captured Limerick. It seemed as if they might turn Ireland into a Norwegian kingdom. But in 1014 they were defeated in battle by the soldiers of Brian Boru. They accepted the authority of Irish kings. A century later their descendants had become Irish people.

THE BEGINNINGS OF CHRISTIANITY

After the Romans left, Christian belief began to decline in England and by 500 it had almost died out completely. In Wales and Ireland, however, the situation was quite different.

CHRISTIANITY IN WALES

In much of Wales the Church still lived an organized life, complete with bishops and local parish clergy. During the fifth and sixth centuries devout Christians set up monasteries (called *Llans* in Welsh, as in Llandudno). Here groups of Christians lived lives of prayer, Bible study, farm work, and service to the poor or sick. The monks were in touch with their brothers in Ireland, Cornwall and Brittany.

IRELAND AND ST PATRICK

The conversion of Ireland to Christianity was carried out by St Patrick, the greatest Christian personality of these early years of whom we have knowledge. He lived on the west coast of England. His father was British but was a Roman official. His grandfather had been a Christian priest.

At the age of 16 Patrick was captured by pirates and taken to Ireland, perhaps to Antrim, where he lived as a herdsman. One night he believed he heard a voice in his sleep which told him to leave for the

▽ *St Patrick, like most of the early missionaries, went everywhere on foot. Here he is seen (on the right) talking to a fellow traveller.*

coast. He did as he was directed and found a boat waiting for him which took him to France. Here he trained as a priest before he returned to England. In 432 Patrick returned to Ireland as Bishop to the Irish, who greeted him with suspicion. They thought Patrick was bringing a "strange and troublesome doctrine...from far away...that would overthrow kingdoms and destroy their gods".

Patrick expected to be killed or injured. Yet in spite of opposition he succeeded in converting Ireland to Christianity. He set up an organized system of bishops and

◁ *The monastery at Kells, County Meath, is shown as it would have been about 1100. The monks lived in the beehive-shaped huts. In the middle of the enclosure is the stone chapel. When the monastery was attacked, by Vikings or thieves, the monks retreated into the tower.*

priests, and encouraged the building of monasteries. After his death in about 461 other Christians went out from these monasteries and completed his work. A hundred years after his death, most of Ireland was Christian when England had forgotten Christianity.

IONA AND LINDISFARNE

In about 563 an Irishman, Columba, travelled with 12 companions to the tiny island of Iona, off the southwest corner of Mull in western Scotland. Here, in this wild and lonely spot, he built a monastery and from it travelled widely in Scotland, preaching to the northern Picts, and converting many to Christianity. (The southern Picts were already Christian.)

Later, another monastery was built at Lindisfarne, an island off the coast of Northumberland in the north-east of England. It was built in about 635 by Aidan, a monk from the Iona community. From Lindisfarne, Aidan and his monks travelled among the Northumbrian people, working their way south. By the middle of the 7th century many people in northern England were Christians.

Aidan and Columba both thought of Ireland as the centre of their church. Now Wales, Ireland, Scotland and the north of England all belonged to the Celtic branch of the Christian Church. It was separate from the main branch of the Church, whose head was the pope in Rome. The separation was to cause great problems.

THE MISSIONARIES FROM ROME

Forty years before Aidan began building his monastery at Lindisfarne, the conversion of southern England to Christianity had begun. This was also carried out in the first place by monks. But the monks owed obedience to the Roman Catholic Church and its head, Pope Gregory. Gregory now decided to try and convert England. He described the people as "placed in the corner of the world...worshipping sticks and stones". In 597 Augustine, head of a monastery in Rome and a friend of Gregory's, landed in Thanet, Kent, with 40 monks.

The king of Kent, Ethelbert had a Christian wife Bertha, daughter of the king of the Franks in Paris. So he already knew something about Christian beliefs.

▽ *The area coloured green on the map shows where Celtic Christianity was first practised.*

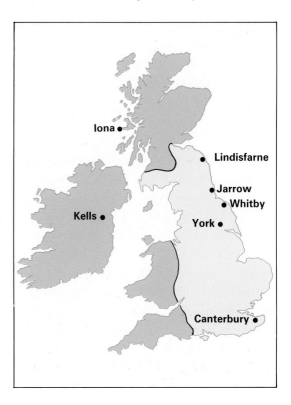

He decided to meet the visitors and hear what they had to say. Although their message did not convince Ethelbert straight away, he said he would offer them hospitality and would not forbid them from trying to convert people to their faith. After a while, Ethelbert himself became a Christian. Augustine built Canterbury Cathedral on the site of an old Roman church, and a monastery which was named after him.

THE NORTH OF ENGLAND

From Canterbury Augustine and his missionaries began to move north. Ethelbert was a useful ally. He claimed to be overlord of the East Saxons and made it possible for a church of St Paul in London to be built, since London was in East Saxon territory. By about 620 they ventured into northern England.

Once again the Christians were helped by a Christian queen, Ethelburgh, who came from Kent. When King Edwin of Northumberland married her, he promised to allow her to continue worshipping as a Christian and to consider becoming one himself. Soon the king ordered a council of his advisers to discuss the beliefs of the new religion and the old. The missionaries won the argument. King Edwin was baptized at York, where another Christian minster (monastery) was built.

However, after King Edwin died in battle in 632 people stopped taking any notice of the Roman Church. Edwin's successor, King Oswald, asked for missionaries from the Celtic Church to join him, and, as we have seen, Aidan was sent from Iona to build a monastery at Lindisfarne. For the next 30 years, Christians in Northumberland followed the Celtic Church.

THE CHURCH UNITES

Slowly, with many changes of mind and returns to the old worship of 'sticks and stones', the rest of England became Christian. Sussex and the Isle of Wight were two of the last areas to do so. But because Britain was divided into two Christian faiths – with Ireland, Wales, Cornwall, Scotland and the north of England being members of the Celtic Church, and the rest of the Roman Church – there were continual problems. Finally a great 'synod', or conference, of Christian leaders from the Celtic and Roman Churches was held at Whitby in Yorkshire in 664. There the Celtic Christians agreed to join the Roman Church and accept the pope as their head. From then on, for the next 900 years, there was only one Christian Church in Britain – the Roman Catholic.

THE MONASTERIES

As they went about, gradually converting the whole of Britain to Christianity, the missionaries set up monasteries, or 'minsters', wherever they could. These were simple collections of buildings within an enclosure, and sometimes linked with a farm. The Christians tried to build them in stone, for they regarded wood as 'heathen' (or non-Christian).

The buildings were designed for only a few monks to live in. They would consist of a church, a dormitory, individual huts for the monks, a guest house and a dining hall (called a refectory). Some of them were double communities – of both monks and nuns.

The minster formed the local Christian centre. Here babies were baptized, the sick were nursed and the dead were buried. Children would be taught to read and

△ *These are the remains of the monastery at Tintagel in Cornwall. It was built by Celtic Christian monks about AD 470 and is the earliest known monastery in Britain.*

write, and a few clever boys would gain a knowledge of Latin and the Bible. Monks would go into the countryside, preaching the Christian message. In time they set up small churches in the nearby settlements. Later these became the parish churches to be found in every English village.

KEEPING OLD TRADITIONS

Saxon gods and British gods continued to be worshipped secretly for many years. Wherever possible, the missionaries built their churches in places where the old gods were worshipped, and held their services at the same time of year as the Saxons had held theirs. By doing so, they hoped to make it easier for people to change over to the new religion.

The Christian festival of Easter was held at the same time as the heathen or 'pagan' services dedicated to 'Eostre', the goddess of spring. Christmas was celebrated at the same time as the heathen festival of Yule.

Many of the Christian carvings must have resembled the old heathen idols. Just as the early Saxons thought that holy wells, magic circles, incantations and magic charms would protect them against evil, so the later English Christians believed that holy water, the chanting of a prayer, the relics of a saint or the carved figure of Christ on the cross would protect them in the same way.

PEOPLE FROM THE NORTH

At the end of the 8th century several murderous raids were made on the north of England. The Saxons called these raiders 'the men from the north'. They came from Norway and from Denmark.

VIKINGS FROM NORWAY

Norway was short of land. Its population was rising, and the land could not feed everyone. There was only enough land for each family's eldest son. The rest had to find another way of getting their living. Because they lived in the 'fjords' (*viks* in Norse) the Saxons called them Vikings.

By the 8th century Norwegian sailors were sailing far out into the North Sea looking for new lands to attack and loot. The raids they carried out on northern England were a few among many others.

Many Danes too sought new lands. It was they who invaded eastern England. And for every one Dane or Norwegian

▽ *This is a reconstruction of a Viking ship found at Oseberg in Norway. The keel was made from a single oak trunk, with oak ribs, cross-beams and planks. Tarred animal hair stuffed between the planks made the ship waterproof.*

who landed in England looking for plunder, there were three more who followed after them intent on colonizing the conquered land.

The longboats the Northmen travelled in were shallow – easy to beach and sail away again. They could be rowed far up the river estuaries which penetrate eastern England. Their targets were often monasteries because the monks could not defend themselves and they contained so many riches. In 865 the Danish Grand Army landed on the east coast of England. By 870 the army was poised to invade Wessex, the major English kingdom.

ALFRED AND DANELAW
The king of Wessex, Alfred, decided to try and buy peace. He paid the Danes money to stay away from his kingdom. The payment was called 'Danegeld' and for five years the Danes kept the agreement. During that time they conquered Mercia and began to colonize it. In 878 the Grand Army split. One group divided Yorkshire up into Danish colonies. Another, led by King Guthrum, attacked Wessex. Alfred took refuge in Athelney marshes and recruited more men.

Alfred did not stay long in the marshes. He marched towards Chippenham where Guthrum had his headquarters. After a fierce battle, Alfred's men were victorious. The Danes eventually asked for peace. Guthrum, with 30 of his chiefs, agreed to be baptized into the Christian Church.

A frontier line between Wessex and the Danish territory was agreed following the line of Watling Street, the old Roman road that ran from London to Chester. By the treaty of Wedmore, signed in 878, Alfred recognized the land that lay to the east of Watling Street as Danish, the territory of

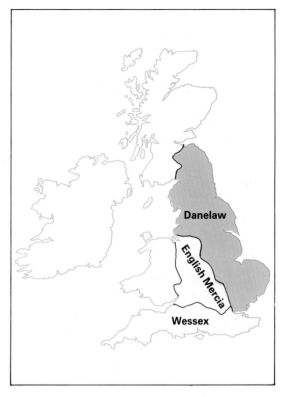

△ By the Treaty of Wedmore (878) King Alfred allowed the Danes to colonize eastern England, which then became known as the Danelaw.

King Guthrum. It had taken the Danes just 13 years to conquer one third of England, a territory from which they were never to be removed, and which was now known as the 'Danelaw'.

ALFRED THE GREAT (871–899)
After the treaty of Wedmore Alfred was accepted as overlord of all England apart from the Danelaw. His strong rule, wise policies and encouragement of religion and learning earned him the title 'the Great'. He treated the Danes well. Both sides seem to have wanted to keep peace.

But Alfred knew that he must ensure England was strongly defended in case of more attacks by the Danes. He was the first English king to build a fleet of fighting ships. Alfred had no professional army. Instead he organized the *fyrd*, in which all free men had to serve. It was made up largely of farmers. Half the men were on active service. The other half were at home on their farms, ready to be called up at short notice. After a few months the two would change over.

Alfred built fortified towns – burhs or boroughs – from which people could defend the country. They became the thriving towns of the next century.

THE ENGLISH LANGUAGE

One of the most important of Alfred's achievements was his summary of laws which had to be obeyed all over his kingdom, which now comprised two-thirds of England. The new system of law was written down in the language of the ordinary people, called *Englisc* or English. Before then, English had not been written down. In fact very few people could read or write in English. The priests and monks were the only educated people, but their books were in Latin.

Alfred set out to encourage English books, often translations from the Latin. The best known was *The Anglo Saxon Chronicle*, which was written under Alfred's supervision. By putting together in one history book the accounts of the Saxons in England, and by writing them in English, Alfred helped to make all his people see themselves as members of one English nation – just as his system of laws had done. He called his country 'Angelcynn, the land of the English folk'.

Alfred was a deeply religious man. He wanted the English Church to be rich and strong. After his reign, England had many monasteries full of hard-working monks. Parish churches grew up all over the land.

THE DANELAW AND VIKING YORK

The Danes settled peacefully into the Danelaw. They did not expel or enslave the English. They were friendly with the people of Wessex, preferring them to the Norwegians who had settled in Lancashire and Cumberland. But it was those same Norwegians, this time from Dublin, who conquered York in 866 and made it the centre of a Norwegian kingdom.

York became a thriving town, described by *The Anglo-Saxon Chronicle* as "wealthy beyond words...because of the riches of merchants who gathered there." It was a town of merchants and small craftsmen, living in thatched wooden or wattle and daub houses.

ENGLAND AND THE DANES

Under the Wessex Kings Athelstan (924–939) and Edgar (959–975) most of England became united, peaceful and prosperous. Many new monasteries were founded. These became famous as centres of prayer and learning and help to the poor and sick. Towns grew up around the *burhs*, and the population of London grew to around 10,000.

Then, in the 980s, men from Denmark came to raid England again. The Danish King Swein ruled Denmark and Norway. He had a strong army of paid soldiers. Ethelred, who was king of Wessex from 979 to 1016, and was known as 'the Unraed' ('the ill-advised'), knew that he could not defeat such an army. So he collected 'Danegeld' from his people – large sums of money which he paid to the Danish soldiers to persuade them to leave.

▷ *This Viking smith in his forge is hammering rods of wrought iron to make the blade of a sword. His helper pumps the bellows.*

After the death of Ethelred the Wessex Grand Council of noblemen, known as the Witan, whose job it was to elect a new king, chose King Swein's younger son, Cnut, to be king of all England. They thought it would be preferable to have a Danish king than to go on paying the Danish armies Danegeld to stay away or having to fight them.

△ *The map shows the extent of the territories over which Cnut reigned.*

KING CNUT

Cnut was crowned king in 1016. He promised to preserve English laws, and he married Ethelred's widow in an attempt to demonstrate his Englishness. He helped to build new churches, and encouraged people to construct them out of stone so that they would last.

In 1019 Cnut's father died and he became king of Denmark and Norway as well as England. So that there would be strong rulers to look after the country while he was away, he divided England into four separate earldoms – Northumbria and East Anglia, ruled by Danish earls, and Mercia and Wessex, ruled by English earls. Unfortunately there was great rivalry between the different earls, and Cnut's death led to seven years of fighting over a new king.

△ *This drawing is from the* Liber Vitae*, a medieval manuscript. It shows Cnut, now a Christian king, and his wife placing a cross on the altar of the new minster at Winchester.*

1042–1189
THE
NORMANS

TIME CHART

* denotes events that occurred outside Britain and Ireland.

1042	Edward ('the Confessor') is King of England.
1051	Godwin's Rebellion.
1054	*Roman Catholic and Eastern Orthodox Churches split.
1058–1093	Malcolm III Canmore is King of Scotland.
1066	January: Edward dies. Witan elects Harold II King. September: Harold II of England defeats Harold Hardrada of Norway at Stamford Bridge, Yorkshire. October: William of Normandy defeats Harold II at Battle, Sussex. Christmas Day: William is crowned William I, King of England, in Westminster Abbey, recently built by Edward the Confessor.
1067	Rochester Castle is started.
1069	'The harrying of the North'.
1072	Rebellion in the Fens by Hereward the Wake is suppressed.
1072	William I invades Scotland and forces Malcolm III to pay him homage.
1076	*Turks capture Jerusalem.
1078	Tower of London is begun.
1079	Scots invade northern England but are forced to retreat.
1081	William I leads expedition to St David's, South Wales. Normans colonize South Wales and the Marches.
1084–1086	Domesday Book survey.
1087	William I dies. William II ('Rufus') becomes king.
1088	*Urban II becomes pope.
1090	Ely and Norwich cathedrals are started.
1096	Durham cathedral is started. *First Crusade.
1099	*Crusaders capture Jerusalem.
1100	William II dies. Henry I becomes king.
1120	Prince William, heir to throne, drowns in *White Ship*.
1135	Henry I dies.
1138	Civil war starts between Stephen and Matilda, and continues for 13 years.
1142	*Frederick Barbarossa becomes Holy Roman Emperor.
1154	Henry II becomes king and starts Plantagenet line. Henry develops 'common' law.
1162	Thomas Becket becomes Archbishop of Canterbury.
1170	Thomas Becket is murdered.
1171	Henry II lands in Dublin and receives submission of some Irish princes.
1173	Thomas Becket is canonized.
1174	First pilgrimage to Canterbury.
1187	*Turks recapture Jerusalem. Third Crusade starts, to win it back.
1189	Henry II dies. Richard I becomes king.

THE NORMAN CONQUEST

The disputes about who should follow Cnut as King of England were settled when the Witan chose Ethelred's son Edward in 1042. He was Alfred's great great-great-grandson. His reputation as a devout Christian earned him the name 'the Confessor', meaning 'strong believer in the faith'. He was later made a saint.

KING EDWARD THE CONFESSOR

During Edward's reign England became the strongest kingdom in Europe. Its towns developed in size and wealth, and villages grew up in the countryside. There was a recognized system of raising an army, and the kings could call upon ships to defend the Channel ports. The tax system was famous for its efficiency.

RIVALRY AT COURT

Yet the country's ruling groups were deeply divided. Edward's mother, Emma, was a Norman. He himself had been brought up in Normandy and was as Norman as he was English. He preferred Norman advisers at his court to English, to the fury of his English earls. Rivalry between the two groups reached flash point in 1051 when, after quarrels between Normans and English in Dover,

▽ This section from the Bayeux Tapestry shows Harold swearing loyalty to William, one hand upon the altar, the other on a chest of holy relics. Harold later maintained that William had forced him to take the oath, and that therefore he was entitled to break it.

◁ *Harold's coronation by Archbishop Stigand is shown in this part of the Tapestry. Harold holds the sceptre and the orb, symbols of monarchy.*

Edward ordered Earl Godwin of Wessex to burn the town. Godwin refused and an open rebellion, in the south-east, followed. After Godwin's death his son Harold Godwinson became the champion of the English against Edward's Norman friends and the strongest subject in the country.

FOUR MEN CLAIM THE THRONE
Edward died on 5 January 1066, leaving no heir to succeed him. There were four men who claimed the right to the title 'king of all the English'. One of them was William, Duke of Normandy. Edward the Confessor had lived in Normandy during the reign of King Cnut, and William swore that Edward at one time promised him that he would be King of England when he

▽ *Another section of the Tapestry tells the story, like a strip cartoon, of William's Conquest of England. This part shows provisions being carried for the invasion.*

△ Here the Tapestry depicts Harold's death at the Battle of Hastings. He is shot in the eye with an arrow, then cut down by a mounted knight.

died, which may well have been true. He also swore that Harold had promised him his loyalty when Edward died. But if Harold ever swore such an oath he had been forced to, when he had been wrecked on the Norman coast a few years before.

The second contender for the throne was Harold Hardrada, from Norway, who hoped to unite England with Norway again. The other contenders were two brothers, Harold of Wessex and Tostig, Earl of Northumbria.

THE NEW KING
Harold of Wessex had been named king by Edward on his deathbed. The Witan elected him immediately, and he was crowned king. But the other three men would not accept this. The people of Northumbria revolted against Tostig, so he fled across the North Sea to give his support to Harold Hardrada. Now King

Harold faced the prospect of two invasions – one from across the North Sea by Harold Hardrada, Tostig and their supporters, and one from across the Channel by William and his army.

It was William whom King Harold feared the most. Throughout the summer he stationed his army along the south coast and his navy off the Isle of Wight. Duke William had an invasion army ready in northern France, but strong winds from the north forced the army to stay in port. By early September, Harold could keep his troops together no longer. They were eager to return home for the harvest. He let them go, and sent his fleet back to London. Many of the ships were lost on their way in storms.

VICTORY IN BATTLE

No sooner had Harold let his men and ships go than dreadful news arrived. The winds that had kept William in port helped Harold Hardrada and Tostig to sail swiftly south from their base in the Orkneys, where the Norwegian army and fleet were gathered. They sailed up the Humber with 200 warships, landed, and won a battle near York. But Harold acted quickly. He marched north, gathering an army on the way, and defeated Harold Hardrada and Tostig at Stamford Bridge, near York, on 25th September 1066. Both his rivals were killed.

THE BATTLE OF HASTINGS (1066)

Then Harold received the news that William had landed at Pevensey Bay on the Sussex coast near Hastings on 28th September. His army rapidly marched south. The two forces met at Senlac Hill, near Hastings, and on 14th October 1066, at 9.30 a.m., they joined battle. The place they fought at became known as Battle, a name the village there still has today.

Harold seems to have had about 6000 men under his command – more than William's army. But most were on foot, and all of them were tired. His men were drawn up on the top of Senlac Hill. The fighting lasted eight hours and more and was ferocious. William's men, led by trained knights on horseback, advanced repeatedly up the hill. But the English formed a wall of shields and kept tightly together, so the knights had to retreat.

If the English had stayed put, they might have won the day. But in late afternoon their discipline broke. A group of English, sensing victory, charged downhill after a retreating group of Norman soldiers. The Normans rallied their forces, turned, and put them to flight. Seeing their success the Normans feigned further retreats. At the crucial point they rounded on the pursuing English, cut them off from their comrades, and slaughtered them.

Towards nightfall the Normans charged once more up the hill. This time they broke through the English shield wall, which now surrounded a much smaller force. In the half-light Harold was killed and his men overwhelmed. William's victory was complete.

THE SUBDUING OF ENGLAND

William now made for London. There was no time to lose if he was to occupy the capital before winter. The quickest way of getting to London was to march along the coast to Dover and from there to follow the old Roman Road to London.

At Canterbury William received the first surrender. The men of Kent gave him hostages and swore an oath of loyalty. Men from Winchester, the old Saxon capital, submitted to him.

It was not until he reached London Bridge, the only bridge over the Thames at that time, that he met serious resistance. He decided not to attempt the capture of the bridge but to cross the Thames at Wallingford and encircle London.

William now began to burn and destroy the countryside, a policy of terror he was to repeat in other parts of the country. In his march round London he had reached Little Berkhamsted south of Hertford before the English cracked. There a group of English earls offered William their loyalty. The road to London was open.

William was determined to complete his victory as soon as he could. He was crowned king in Westminster Abbey on Christmas Day 1066.

BRITAIN UNDER THE NORMANS

Although William was now king, only southern England had been conquered, and the Kentish revolt of 1067 showed that the conquest was skin-deep. Worst of all the English were supported by William's enemies overseas. The men of Kent were helped by Eustace of Boulogne. English armies stationed in Devon and Herefordshire were supported by troops in Ireland, led by Harold's illegitimate sons. All these risings were put down but William's most dangerous enemies were still to strike.

'THE HARRYING OF THE NORTH'
In 1069 there was a general rising led by Edgar 'the Aetheling', one of the old Wessex royal family. The rising covered much of the country north of the Humber, and was supported by a Danish fleet. (King Swein of Denmark, whose country was no longer united with Norway, had become one more claimant for the English throne.) Edgar's army took York and began to move south.

His success encouraged further English resistance. Once again there was a revolt in Herefordshire. Now it spread as far north as Chester and Stafford. There were more risings in the south-west, again supported by Harold's sons from Ireland.

William immediately marched north, sending armies to the south-west and west to deal with the lesser challenges. The Danes retreated to their ships in the Humber estuary. William took and burned York, marched north as far as the river Tees, and crossed the Pennines to capture Chester and Stafford. Wherever his armies went in the north they put into practice the policy of terror they had used around London in 1066. Their cruelty became known as the 'harrying of the north'.

The soldiers were ordered to destroy every town, village and house between York and Durham. They were to burn every barn and haystack and kill every human being and animal they found. As it was winter, thousands died of cold and hunger if they survived the soldiers' swords. The terrible lesson was learned: it did not pay to revolt.

HEREWARD THE WAKE
English resistance, however, was still not finally defeated. In the Isle of Ely a Lincolnshire *thegn*, Hereward, known as 'the Wake' or 'Watchful One', led a last-ditch stand. Hereward made Ely his headquarters. It stood above the rivers and marshes of the Fens, which were then undrained. His position appeared impregnable, for only local people knew where the paths through the swamps lay. William's men tried to make a path across the water, but it sank. Later the Normans captured the island. Hereward escaped but in a few years surrendered. The English gave no more trouble.

SCOTLAND VERSUS THE NORMANS
Led by King Malcolm III 'Canmore' (meaning 'Bighead') the Scots crossed the English border and raided northern England. When William had defeated Hereward he marched north in 1072. He struck deep into Scotland and carried out a combined campaign by land and sea

▽ *The first Norman castles were motte and bailey castles like this one. A wooden fort was built on the motte (mound) and the garrison lived in the bailey (enclosure). They could be built very quickly – in eight days at York.*

to the north of Edinburgh. Malcolm was forced to swear homage to William and make peace. Seven years later the Scots again crossed the border and invaded England. They were thrown back, the Normans invaded Scotland, and homage was renewed.

▽ *The first permanent castles the Normans built were keeps (towers) made of stone. The Tower of London dominated the river Thames where it approached London.*

THE NORMANS IN WALES

For the first 100 years after the Conquest the Normans could only settle in the lowland areas of south Wales (Pembroke, Gower, Glamorgan and Gwent) and the areas along the Welsh borders, called the Marches. The powerful Norman baronial families could exercise little power over the rest of Wales, where the mountains proved formidable barriers, and the Welsh lived independent lives.

CASTLE BUILDING

William knew that he would have to rule with force, so everywhere the Normans went they built castles. They were used as barracks for the occupying troops. The stone 'keep' (tower) of a Norman castle looks like a clenched fist. It served to remind the local people of the price they would have to pay for rebellion.

At first, the army built 'motte and bailey' castles. The mottes were mounds of earth on which a wooden keep was built. Connected to them by wooden bridges were the baileys, enclosures where the garrison would live in normal times, ready to retreat to the motte in time of war.

After a few years the Normans began building castles which would last. They now had stone keeps, with walls five metres thick. The biggest and strongest Norman castles were built in north Wales. They were built at the end of the 13th century and were strong enough to withstand any direct attack.

Within 20 years castles were built along the south coast and the Welsh borders. London and other centres were brooded over by their Norman fists. But the castles were to pose problems in the future, when they became the centres not of the king's power but that of his rebellious barons.

THE DOMESDAY BOOK

William I wanted to know who owned the land in his new kingdom and how much it was worth. In about 1084, when the Danes were again threatening invasion, he organized a survey which would tell his officials how much tax each landowner could pay towards the cost of raising a new army. The survey took two years to complete and became known as the *Domesday* (or Judgement) *Book*. Most of it has survived and is kept in the Public Record Office in London. It does not cover northern England and the sections on some important towns have been lost. But the book gives us an accurate picture of England 20 years after the Conquest.

The difference between rich and poor at that time was staggering. The English population was about a million. Three-quarters of the country's wealth – land, oxen, cattle and pigs – was owned by the king and around 300 landowners. Two hundred were nobles, of whom only two were English. One hundred were leading churchmen, archbishops, bishops and heads of great monasteries.

△ *The* Domesday Book *was used until 1900 to settle land disputes. Copies can still be seen in the British Museum and Salisbury Cathedral.*

According to the *Domesday Book*, the rest of the land was farmed by small farmers. Some of them were free men who owned their own land. But most had to work for part of each week on the local lord's farm. They also had to do extra work for him during harvest time. One tenth of the people were still serfs so they owned no land. About 90 per cent of the population worked on the land.

THE INFLUENCE OF THE CONQUEST

Following the Norman Conquest, England and northern France became one nation, with one king and one small group of barons, who owned huge estates on either side of the English Channel, in control. England became involved in French quarrels, since the Duke of Normandy owed loyalty to the king of France. For centuries Englishmen died fighting on French battlefields. The English law courts carried out their business in Norman-French. Romantic Norman stories about the love affairs of lords and ladies became very popular.

NORMAN KINGS AND THE FIRST PLANTAGENET

It was not for nothing that William I, Duke of Normandy, became known as William the Conqueror. But although the rule of William I and his sons, William II (1087–1100) and Henry I (1100–1135), was harsh it brought some advantages to England. Trade greatly increased, because of closer links with Europe. As a result towns grew larger and wealthier. Life grew more peaceful and orderly, since no-one dared to challenge the king's power.

William II maintained the Crown's strong authority, despite quarrels with the church and the barons and despite wars in Normandy. So too did his younger brother Henry I, when he quickly succeeded William after his death in a hunting accident in the New Forest. But he too was deeply involved in Normandy, which led to heavy taxation on his English subjects. England's future would depend to a large extent on whether he could leave an undisputed succession to his heir. In 1120 his son William was drowned in 'The White Ship', when he was crossing the Channel. His daughter Matilda was next in line. But powerful men at the English Court were determined to see that she should not succeed her father, even though the English barons had twice sworn to be loyal to her.

CIVIL WAR 1135–1154

Matilda was married to Geoffrey, Count of Anjou, the most powerful state in northern France. But the marriage had antagonized the English barons, who had tried to insist that she should not marry any man who was not English without their consent. The very fact that she was a woman made many of them fear that she would be unable to hold the country together. So they turned to Henry I's nephew, Stephen, who was in Boulogne when the old king died. Stephen crossed the Channel, received the help of important Londoners and the support of Winchester, where his brother was bishop and where the royal treasury was based. His supporters argued that their oaths of loyalty to Matilda were not binding, because they had been forced to give them. Within three weeks of Henry's death Stephen was crowned King of England at Westminster Abbey.

For two and a half years Stephen ruled peacefully. But in the summer of 1138 the powerful Robert of Gloucester declared his support for his half-sister Matilda. The next year Matilda landed in Sussex, which was in Stephen's control. Instead of imprisoning her, Stephen let her join Robert in Bristol. From that time on there were two opposing courts, and England slid into 13 years of civil war.

During this time the barons, who were always jealous of royal power, and keen to increase their own, took advantage of royal weakness. They built new castles for themselves without permission and avoided paying the taxes they owed the Crown. They often refused to provide either Stephen or Matilda with fighting men for their armies.

Those who suffered most in this situation were the ordinary people. Merchants received no naval protection from pirates. Towns were looted by robbers from the country. Small farmers suffered when armies fought battles over their crops and stole their livestock.

By 1153 everyone in England, except perhaps those barons who were taking advantage of the wars to seize more power for themselves, longed for peace. In this year Stephen's son and heir, Eustace, died, so there was no-one to follow him on the throne. Two years earlier, Geoffrey of Anjou had died, and his and Matilda's eldest son, Henry, had become lord of their lands in Normandy. Now Stephen and Henry made an agreement that Stephen would rule England for the rest of his life, but that on his death it would be ruled by Henry.

HENRY II – THE FIRST PLANTAGENET
Stephen died a year later, and was succeeded by the 21-year-old Henry II. By adding England to his possessions he became the strongest king in Europe. His empire stretched from the Spanish border to Scotland. By marrying Eleanor of Aquitaine, who was 12 years older than Henry, he had doubled its size. Later he added Brittany to his lands. He was called Henry Plantagenet, from the Latin names for the yellow broom flower which was his father's emblem. He started a new line of English kings called the Plantagenets.

Henry had red hair. He was broad-shouldered, stocky and rather bandy-legged. He was a madly energetic man and loved to travel quickly from one part of his empire to another at short notice. Under Henry government came from the travelling court, not from the capital.

△ These are the four Norman kings. William I and William II are on the top row, Henry I and Stephen below. The first three established Norman rule, but it fell apart under Stephen.

Henry II was determined to show the people of England that the king was in charge once more. The barons had been doing as they liked during the civil wars. Henry ordered that any castle which had not been built under royal licence should be destroyed. Three hundred were burned or pulled down. The barons had private armies which were under the command of their knights. These armies were meant to be ready to fight for the king whenever he wanted them to do so. All over England these gangs of armed young men were roaming the country, causing trouble. Henry encouraged the barons to pay him a special tax called 'scutage' (shield money) instead of providing him with troops. With the money, the king paid his own troops and so developed a professional army. More knights now settled down to live in their castles and farm their lands.

REFORM OF THE LAW

Henry II is chiefly remembered for founding our modern system of law. Alfred's system of trials and punishments had been forgotten. In the time of Stephen and Matilda most of the courts that tried offenders or settled disputes were under the control of the local lords. The lord decided what the law was and often pocketed the fines instead of handing them over to the king. Henry developed the system of 'common law' – law common (the same) throughout the whole country – that we use today.

Royal judges, appointed by the king and not by the barons, travelled all over England. They held trials, which were known as 'assizes', in royal courts called 'assize courts'. The royal judges used common law to judge people who were accused of serious crimes. If the people were found guilty, the judges passed sentences of punishment on them, rather than making them pay compensation to their victims, which was the old system. But the royal courts only tried the richer people. Everyone else was still tried in the lords' courts.

THOMAS BECKET

The most bitter dispute in which Henry II was involved was with the Archbishop of Canterbury, Thomas Becket. For hundreds of years churchmen had been allowed to be tried in their own church courts. In fact, anyone who could read or write could claim to be a clergyman and so be tried in a church court. Punishment in these courts was much less harsh than it was in the king's courts.

Henry wanted to change the system so he made his best friend, Thomas Becket, Archbishop of Canterbury. Becket had previously supported Henry in his long quarrel with the Church. But when he became Archbishop, Becket supported the church courts loyally.

In 1170 while Henry was in Normandy, he received news that he was once again being defied by his troublesome Archbishop. He flew into a furious rage, and shouted out: "Will no-one rid me of this turbulent priest?"

Four knights took the king at his word and set off for Canterbury Cathedral. When they arrived, the Archbishop was standing at the High Altar, conducting the evening service. There he would have been safe. Even the knights in their rage would

△ In Norman England, stories of courtly love were the romantic fiction of the day. They were narrated in illustrated manuscripts and became extremely popular.

not have murdered him in such a holy place. They were in another part of the cathedral, calling out to him to come down and talk to them. Becket did so, pushing aside his priests who tried to stop him. A fierce argument followed and the knights killed him.

Almost immediately miracles were being reported. People who prayed to Becket to help them claimed that they were healed. The pope made him a saint. Hundreds of thousands of pilgrims came from all over Europe to pray at Becket's shrine in Canterbury Cathedral.

Henry announced his bitter shame at his part in Becket's murder. He walked barefoot through Canterbury while the monks lashed his bare back. As for the quarrel about the church courts, no king dared to raise the matter for centuries.

△ This stained glass window in Canterbury Cathedral shows Henry II and Thomas Becket as friends – before their bitter quarrel which ended with Becket being murdered.

IRELAND AND WALES

The Irish were ruled by kings of their different clans. In 1166 the king of Leinster fled to Henry II to ask for help against his enemies. He raised a Norman force under Richard, Earl of Pembroke, called 'Strongbow'. The army conquered land around Dublin, and when the king of Leinster died in 1171, Pembroke, who had married his daughter, succeeded him. He offered his lands to Henry II as overlord, who landed in Ireland and received the submission of Pembroke and some Irish chiefs. Henry was supported by a Papal Bull (order) that permitted his conquest of Ireland. So started the long English involvement in Ireland.

In Wales Henry was twice defeated by Owain, king of Gwynedd in north Wales. A Welsh challenge to Henry's position ended with Owain's death, but the independence of north Wales continued.

SCOTLAND

In the north the Scots were forced to restore Cumberland, Westmorland and Northumbria to England. During the last 15 years of Henry II's reign, King William of Scotland paid him homage.

HENRY II'S SONS

Henry had four sons – Henry, Richard, Geoffrey and John. John was made Lord of Ireland. Henry announced, long before his death, that when he died his lands were to be partitioned among the eldest three. They had, however, no real power during his lifetime. This led to repeated revolts, in which the sons were backed by their mother Eleanor and by the king of France. Henry and Geoffrey died before their father. When Henry II died he was at war with Richard.

THE FEUDAL SYSTEM

Long before William conquered England and introduced the system known as the feudal system, or feudalism, the English had developed a way of life which resembled it in many respects. It arose out of people's needs for protection against criminals, or foreign raiders, or the armies of neighbouring lords, at a time when there were no police or national armies to defend them.

NORMAN ENGLAND

The Normans organized this protection system more systematically and in a military manner, suited to the needs of kings who were always at war.

At the top stood the king who, in theory, owned all England. He kept much of it for himself, particularly the forests, which covered one-third of the country. Much of the rest was let out to his barons – dukes, earls and bishops, the church leaders. They in turn let out lands to their professional fighters, the knights, who fulfilled the barons duties of fighting for the king. Beneath them came the largest group, known as the 'villeins', who leased a little land from their lords in exchange for two or three days' work a week. Finally there were the serfs, who made up about one tenth of the population and were no better than slaves.

▷ *The Norman kings loved to hunt deer and wild boar in forests which were specially preserved for royal use. An example is the New Forest in Hampshire. Any man who was caught poaching a deer in a royal forest was punished by having his eyes put out.*

The small landowners (yeomen) and townspeople were outside the system. Feudalism did not apply to most of the west or east of England but was normal everywhere else. About the year 1500 it died out – officially.

THE FARMING YEAR

The villein's working year was determined by the hours of daylight and the weather. In January hours were short and work on the frozen land often impossible.

This is a reconstruction of the manor of Raleigh in Essex, as it is described in the Domesday Book in 1086. The castle (1) is separate from the lord's house (2) within the bailey.

Inside the bailey the lord and his sons are returning from riding, hens are being fed, the vegetable garden dug, and there is a pig stye.

A moat, with ducks on it, surrounds the manor house and would have protected it from attack. The castle contained the vital well. The manor house has two storeys.

The villein's houses (10) are built round the church (11). This has a square tower and low roof in the Norman manner.

The village fields are divided into strips, belonging to the villeins and the lord. One bears wheat (7), another barley (8).

The third field (9) is being rested, and cattle are grazing on it. Neither the lord's house (2), the bailiff's house (4) nor the blacksmith's forge (5) have chimneys. Smoke escapes through a vent.

The farm buildings (3), like all the other buildings on the estate, are thatched. The lord has a large deer park (12).

In the orchard (6) apples are being picked. There is a vine-yard (13). The cultivation of grapes, for wine-making, was common in medieval England.

Ploughing by oxen (bullocks) would be under way by March. Sowing of the seeds would start in April.

Haymaking started in June. All the men who had rights in the hay meadow would cut the field. When the grass was dry it would be raked and built into a haystack.

In August the corn was harvested. Then the wheat or barley was cut and bound into sheaves. When dry the sheaves were carried to the corn stacks. The corn was spread on the barn floor and beaten with flails to separate the grain from the husks (threshing). The grain was taken to the miller's and ground into flour for bread.

A great Christmas feast marked the year's end. People could not feed animals through winter so they were slaughtered. The meat was eaten or preserved in salt.

Women and children worked in the fields all year. The women also had to work for the lord. Life was hard for the villagers. Few people lived past 50.

△ *Villeins' houses were made of wattle and daub walls supported by wooden beams. The floors were earthen, the roof thatched, and there were no windows.*
▽ *The water mill, on which the village depended, was always owned by the lord. Here sacks of grain are being brought to the water mill for grinding, and sacks of flour are being carried away.*

1189–1485
THE MIDDLE AGES

TIME CHART

*denotes events that occurred outside Britain and Ireland.

1189	Richard I becomes king. Massacre of Jews at his coronation.	1349	Black Death reaches England.
1190	Richard joins Third Crusade.	1366	Duke of Clarence passes Statutes of Kilkenny
1192	Richard and Saladin sign treaty to end Third Crusade.	1377	Poll Tax introduced. Edward III dies. Richard II becomes king, aged 10.
1199	Richard killed fighting in France. John becomes king.	1380	John Wyclif becomes first English Protestant.
1215	Magna Carta is signed.	1381	Peasants' Revolt.
1216	King John dies. Henry III becomes king, aged nine.	1399	Richard II dies in prison. Henry IV becomes king – first Lancastrian king.
1264	Battle of Lewes.		
1265	De Montfort's Parliament sits (first English parliament).	1400	Welsh rising under Owain Glyndŵr.
1272	Henry III dies. Edward I becomes king.	1409	Glyndŵr's rising is defeated.
		1413	Henry IV dies. Henry V becomes king.
1277	Edward I invades North Wales.		
1284	Wales is conquered. Statute of Wales.	1415	Battle of Agincourt.
		1422	Henry V dies. Baby King Henry VI succeeds.
1290	Jews expelled from England.		
1291	*Crusades effectively end.	1429–31	*Joan of Arc leads national French wars against English.
1296	Edward I invades Scotland. Wallace's rebellion.	1453	*Turks capture Constantinople.
1298	Battle of Falkirk. Wallace is executed.	1453	England withdraws from France except Calais.
1306	Robert Bruce becomes king of Scotland. French support Scots.	1455	Wars of Roses begin.
		1471	Henry VI dies. Edward IV becomes king.
1307	Edward I dies. Edward II becomes king.	1476	Caxton starts up his first printing press, at Westminster. (Printing first invented by Chinese.)
1314	Scots defeat English at Bannockburn.		
1327	Edward II is murdered. Edward III becomes king.	1483	Edward IV dies. Richard III becomes king.
1337	Hundred Years' War starts.	1485	Battle of Bosworth. Richard III killed. Henry VII becomes first Tudor king.
1347	*Black Death (bubonic plague) reaches Europe.		

CRUSADERS AND REBELS

The phrase 'the Middle Ages', like its adjective medieval, describes the centuries that fell 'in the middle' of ancient and modern times. It is a convenient term, but can be misleading. Life does not change overnight when one 'age' gives way to another.

THE CRUSADES

Henry II was succeeded by Richard I, who spent the greatest part of his reign on crusade. The crusades – or 'wars of the cross' – had been occurring ever since the Turks had captured Jerusalem at the end of the 11th century. The Turks were followers of the Islamic religion and of the great religious teacher Muhammad. Unlike the previous Arab rulers of Jerusalem, the Turks refused to allow Christian pilgrims to visit their holy places, such as Bethlehem, where Jesus was born, or Jerusalem, where he was crucified. The indignant Pope Urban II declared a Holy War against the Turks and in 1099 the crusaders captured Jerusalem.

RICHARD I AND THE THIRD CRUSADE

In 1187 the Turks recaptured Jerusalem. The Third Crusade was announced, to win it back. In 1190 Richard I joined Emperor Frederick I of Germany and King Philip II of France in an unsuccessful campaign. Frederick drowned at sea, while Richard and Philip quarrelled. Philip returned to France and plotted with Richard's brother John to seize Richard's lands. In 1192 Richard heard news of a rebellion in England, so he made peace with the Turks and started for home. But he was captured in Italy and handed over to the new German emperor, Henry VI.

For 13 months Richard was imprisoned, while his officials tried to raise a ransom of 150,000 silver marks. When Richard was released, in 1194, he returned to

▽ Many crusaders started from France or Italy. They aimed to capture Jerusalem or Bethlehem from the Turks so that Christian pilgrimages could start again. Venice was their main port; Cyprus and Malta were military bases.

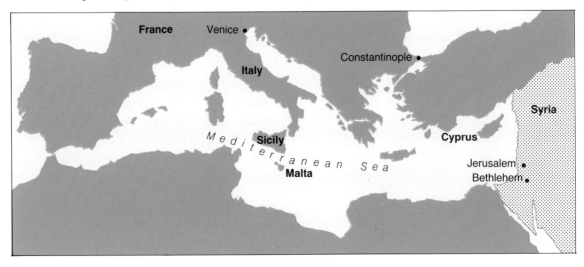

△ *This manuscript painting shows Richard I's imprisonment in a German castle. He rests his cheek on his hand in sadness. He was held captive by the emperor of Germany, Henry VI, who is standing outside the jail.*

△ *The effigy of Sir John Holcombe is at Dorchester Abbey in Oxfordshire. Sir John was killed in Israel during the Second Crusade and knighted on the battlefield. His legs are crossed in the Crusader fashion.*

England to punish those who had plotted against him. He was killed fighting in France five years later. He is remembered as a great warrior king – Richard, Coeur de Lion, Richard the Lion Heart.

KING JOHN (1199–1216)
Richard was succeeded by his brother John. He spent most of his reign in England but was not popular. Both barons and people were indignant about the heavy taxes they were being forced to pay. They were also furious when John tightened the royal forest laws which prevented his subjects entering them.

When John objected to the appointment of Stephen Langton as Archbishop of Canterbury, the pope placed an interdict on Britain and excommunicated John.

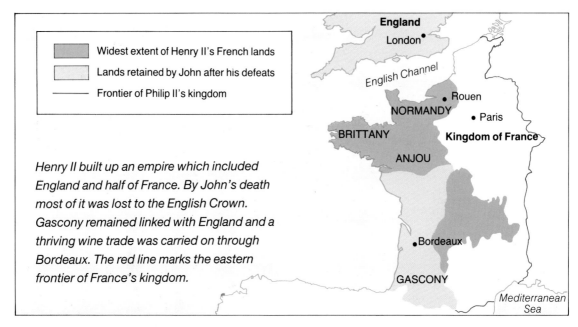

Widest extent of Henry II's French lands

Lands retained by John after his defeats

Frontier of Philip II's kingdom

Henry II built up an empire which included England and half of France. By John's death most of it was lost to the English Crown. Gascony remained linked with England and a thriving wine trade was carried on through Bordeaux. The red line marks the eastern frontier of France's kingdom.

This meant that all churches were locked and the only services allowed were baptisms, and confessions for the dying. The interdict lasted for six years.

MAGNA CARTA

In 1214 King John was in France, fighting to regain his lost lands. The English barons revolted and forced a number of conditions on the king. These were listed in the Magna Carta – the great charter. For many centuries it was seen as the basis of English liberties. At the time, however, it was not thought of in such a way.

The Magna Carta applied only to the minority of the people – the rich and powerful. When the Charter said that no 'free man' could be punished without a proper trial it meant only a man who was free of duties to his lord – and there were not very many of them. When the Charter said that taxes could not be raised "except by the common consent of our realm" the barons meant their own consent. Many years later the rights that the Charter guaranteed were extended to everyone.

THE FIRST PARLIAMENT

Magna Carta did not bring peace. In 1216 John was succeeded by his nine-year-old son, Henry III. England was ruled by a council of barons until 1264. The barons' leader, Simon de Montfort, led an army of nobles and defeated Henry at Lewes, taking him prisoner. Simon called a Great Council, or *Parleyment*, to discuss what to do. It contained two representatives of each county and each main town. These were the knights (county squires) and the burgesses (wealthy townsmen).

So the English Parliament was born. In time the Great Council divided into two houses at the Palace of Westminster. In the House of Lords sat barons and bishops. Knights and squires sat in the House of Commons. It was 650 years before the people were represented in the Commons.

▷ *In the Council of Edward I, the king sat with Alexander, king of Scotland, on his right and Llywelyn, prince of Wales, on his left. Beneath are the bishops, with their mitres, a lord, with his coronet, and commoners.*

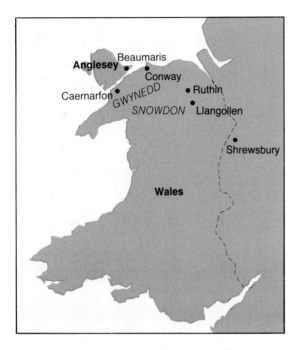

△ This map shows the English bases in North Wales. The Welsh farmers were moved out and their lands were given to English settlers.

REBELLION IN WALES

The Normans had settled in many parts of Wales, but had left the most mountainous parts of North Wales alone. Here the princes of Gwynedd grew strong and hoped to rule the whole country. So powerful was the last of their line, Llywelyn ap Gruffydd (Llywelyn the Last), that he was recognized by Henry III as Prince of Wales. In return he recognized Henry as his overlord.

Neither side, however, could trust the other. When Henry III died in 1272, Llywelyn failed to attend Edward I's coronation. Five years later Edward launched a campaign on sea and land against Gwynedd.

▽ Harlech Castle is one of 14 English castles built by Edward I in Wales. Castles were sited at key points to overawe the Welsh.

Always before, the Welsh had retreated to their mountain refuges around Snowdon, certain that no invader could enter such country for long. This time they met their match.

Edward's soldiers advanced along the coast of north Wales, supported by his fighting ships. They built great castles at key points such as Conway, Caernarfon and Beaumaris. From these bases they destroyed the corn crops in the surrounding areas and killed cattle and sheep. The Welsh in the mountains were starved out. Finally Llywelyn was killed. By the Statute of Wales (1284) Gwynedd was absorbed into England.

Edward I built 14 English castles with walled towns around them. They became the area headquarters of the English. Welsh farmers were evicted in favour of English colonists. In 1301 the completion of the conquest was marked when Edward I's son was crowned Prince of Wales at Caernarfon Castle.

AN INDEPENDENT SCOTLAND

In the 13th century English Kings claimed to be 'overlords' of Scottish kings. The Scots had their own coinage and customs officers. In Europe Scotland was seen as a separate nation.

When in 1290, however, there was a disputed succession to the Scottish throne Edward I claimed his right as overlord to choose the next king. He chose John Balliol, with the support of the Scots. But Balliol showed signs of independence and Edward I marched into Scotland and removed him from the throne. When he returned to England he brought with him the coronation stone from the abbey of Scone. His intention was to show that he was the true king of Scotland now.

But Sir William Wallace led a national Scottish rebellion. Edward again marched his forces north and defeated the Scots at Falkirk (1298). Wallace was dragged to England for trial and his head was impaled on London Bridge.

The Scots' new leader was Robert Bruce. He was crowned king at Scone in 1306, and secured the support of the French. This 'auld alliance', as the Scots called it, between the two countries was to continue for centuries.

After repeated Scottish defeats, Robert Bruce's luck changed. Edward I died and his successor, Edward II, led the English at Bannockburn in 1314. Although they had more soldiers than the Scots, the English were defeated. Fourteen years later, Edward III recognized Robert Bruce as the rightful King of Scotland.

DOMINANCE OVER IRELAND

It was Henry II who first began the English attempt to conquer Ireland. His army captured Dublin and the area around it, which was known as the Pale. But English power stopped there and the real rulers of the country were the great barons, such as the Earls of Ormond and Kildare. Robert Bruce's brother Edward landed in Ireland in 1315. He received support from Irish chiefs and was crowned king of Ireland, only to be defeated and killed three years later.

When the Duke of Clarence was sent to govern Ireland in 1361 he found that many Englishmen in Ireland were friends with their Irish neighbours. This prompted him to pass the Statutes of Kilkenny, which forbade the English to marry the Irish. The statutes also banned the Irish language in English-held territories, along with Irish laws and customs.

KINGS, BARONS AND PEASANTS

The feudal system only worked when the king held it together. If he failed to do so, the country split into warring groups led by powerful barons. Troops trampled the crops in the fields, killed animals for meals round their camp-fires, and looted shops in the towns. Traders were afraid to take their goods to market, and merchants trading across the Channel found their ships hijacked and their precious cargoes robbed. Instead of uniting around the king in his troubles, his advisers looked round the court to see who was likely to become the new king.

DEPOSING THE KING

There was always the threat of trouble when a king was believed to be weak, when he was under age, or spent too much time abroad, when he surrounded himself with unpopular favourites, or when he taxed his people heavily. If things got out of hand, the king might well be deposed and murdered.

The first king to be deposed was Edward II (1307–1327). The courage he showed at Bannockburn was generally admitted, but many people never forgave Edward for losing the battle. After two years of bitter civil war, the king put the leader of the barons, Thomas, Earl of Lancaster, on trial for treachery. He was found guilty, and executed as if he was a common criminal. In the end, Edward's wife, Queen Isabelle, took their son Prince Edward and joined forces with the king's enemies. Edward II was taken to Berkeley Castle in Gloucestershire and murdered.

THE HUNDRED YEARS' WAR

Edward III (1327–1377) became the next king. When the old French ruling family died out in 1337, he claimed to be king of France. This claim, repeated by his successors, started a series of wars called the Hundred Years' War. He and his son Edward, called the Black Prince (who died in 1376 before he could become King) won a number of battles in France, such as Crécy (1346) and Poitiers (1356).

▷ *The decisive battle in the Scottish struggle for independence was the one fought at Bannockburn in 1314. Many English nobles were captured and they were only released on payment of huge ransoms.*

△ *The effigy of the Black Prince lies on top of his tomb at Canterbury Cathedral.*

But the success of the English did not last. By 1370 only Calais and Gascony remained under English control. The barons were no longer prepared to provide the king with soldiers for his army, and the tax collectors were unable to raise sufficient taxes to pay for horses, armour and weapons. The English could not afford to protect their own south coast ports. The ports of Rye and Winchelsea were burnt and looted. The authorities levied those most unpopular of taxes, poll taxes, which demanded the same amount from rich and poor.

POLL TAX RIOTS

When Richard II (1377–1399), Edward's ten-year-old grandson, became king, poll tax riots were raging, and it was obvious that many people were determined not to pay the hated tax. On 1st June 1381 the king's Chief Justice was sent to Brentwood in Essex to deal with trouble that had arisen over the tax. He was met by an enraged crowd shouting that they would kill all the "lawyers, jurors, and royal servants" they could find.

Ever since the Black Death, which had reached England in 1349, the country had been seething with anger. The Death killed about one person in three. This meant that the surviving labourers could ask for higher wages – and receive them – because their lords had no alternative. Villeins insisted on paying rent instead of working the old labour services. At first the lords were forced to give them what they asked for. But when the population began to rise again, the lords lowered their wages and insisted on the old services. The government supported the lords. Many villeins ran away. Others joined together to force the lords to give in.

THE PEASANTS' REVOLT

In Kent a lord threw one of his villeins, who had been captured fleeing from his estate, into Rochester Castle. A crowd of peasants released him and marched on Maidstone, where they freed John Ball, a priest who had been at odds with the Church for years. Then the peasants stormed Canterbury, led by Wat Tyler, a blacksmith, hoping to capture the despised archbishop, whom they held responsible for the poll tax. When they found him gone, they made for London.

BLACKHEATH CAMP

They received strong support wherever they went and on 12th June thousands of Kentish men and women camped outside London on Blackheath. People from Essex reached Mile End at the same time. The Mayor of London William Walworth, ordered the city gates to be shut.

Accounts of the rebel camp at Blackheath tell us how well-disciplined the people were. The rebel leaders, concerned for the safety of their country, gave orders that none of their supporters should leave

△ *The peasants camped at Blackheath. Here they rested and listened to John Ball, before moving in to occupy London.*

the coast, in case the French took advantage of the revolt to invade. The thousands of people who had risked their lives to march on London listened in rapt silence to the speeches of John Ball, who challenged the very idea of feudalism and the division of human beings into social classes. He called for an end to the great divisions between rich and poor, asking passionately: "When Adam dalf (dug) and Eve span, who was then a gentleman?" As a later chronicler wrote scornfully of the rebels: "According to their foolish minds there would be no lords thereafter but only kings and commons".

REBELS CAPTURE LONDON

On the next day, 13th June, London fell to the rebels. The gates were opened to the men and women of Kent and those from Essex, and the crowds surged through them. But now the leaders lost control.

The palace of the archbishop at Lambeth was ransacked, along with the Savoy Palace of the king's uncle, John of Gaunt. The grand houses of foreign merchants were set on fire and angry mobs rampaged through the streets. Soon the peasants ringed the Tower of London, where the king, the archbishop, the treasurer and the mayor had taken refuge.

RICHARD MEETS THE REBELS

Early the next morning the boy King Richard II rode out of the Tower to meet the rebels at Mile End. He promised Wat Tyler that labour services would end, that land would be rented at fourpence an acre, and that no man would be compelled to serve another. While Richard and Tyler were talking, men broke into the Tower, seized the archbishop and the treasurer and beheaded them.

△ *This picture from Froissart's* Chronicles *shows Richard II meeting the rebels at Smithfield during the Peasants' Revolt. Wat Tyler is about to be killed by the Mayor of London.*

The next day many of the rebels started for home, convinced that their case was won. Tyler and the king met again, this time at Smithfield. Tyler is said to have been insolent to Richard. A scuffle broke out and Mayor Walworth killed Tyler.

But the king saved the situation. When they heard Tyler was dead, the rebels raised their bows. Richard rode out alone in front of them. "Sirs, will you shoot your king? I will be your captain," he cried. He rode to some nearby fields and

the peasants followed him. The mayor took advantage of the lull and sent for support. Soon the peasants were encircled in the fields. They were allowed to return home. Now that Wat Tyler was dead, there was nothing to stop the lords and the king's ministers from restoring control.

The peasants had won support in other counties but everywhere their supporters were rounded up and cruelly treated. If the king had ever meant to keep his Mile End promises his advisers must have over-ruled him. On 2nd July the promises were withdrawn. Ball and Jack Straw, another peasant leader, were executed along with hundreds of others, many without trial. The government forgot about the poll tax.

THE REIGN OF RICHARD II

During Richard's minority England was governed by his uncle, John of Gaunt. Richard's advisers continued to dominate him when he was grown up. There was a brief civil war when he tried to break free of them, but at the end he had to accept the execution of his supporters as traitors.

In 1394 Richard led an expedition to Ireland which proved costly and had to be financed by more taxes. Again he clashed with his barons, and sent the Earls of Warwick and Nottingham into exile. He arranged the murder of his uncle the Duke of Gloucester. In 1399 he was captured by his cousin Henry Bolingbroke and taken to Pontefract Castle in Yorkshire. Here he died a year later, probably murdered.

THE BLACK DEATH

Diseases of all sorts were an unavoidable part of normal life for medieval people. Because of them few people lived past 40.

The conditions of daily life promoted disease. There were no drains. In the towns open sewers ran down the middle of the streets. The houses huddled closely together, their upper stories overhanging the street. Housewives threw the contents of their chamber pots straight into the middle of the street from their upstairs windows. The droppings left by the horses, pigs, cows and sheep as they walked the town's roads, rotted where they lay. The slaughter houses, like the markets for live animals, did their business in the middle of the towns. People rarely washed their bodies or their clothes. In any case there was no public supply of clean water. (People were puzzled when almost all the monks in Christ Church Priory at Canterbury survived the Black Death, while the monks at nearby Rochester did not. It was discovered that the Canterbury monks had recently installed a supply of fresh water, piped from a spring three kilometres away.)

The worst outbreak of plague in medieval England was that which erupted in 1349 and became known as the Black Death. Afterwards the fear of plague overhung England until the Great Plague three hundred years later. Doctors today would say that the plague was probably a combination of illnesses, all of which were fatal. The most common version was spread by fleas carried by black rats. The plague's symptoms were large swellings on the neck, underneath the arms, and between the legs. Sufferers developed black spots and a high fever. Three-quarters of people who caught the plague died, usually within about five days.

The plague swept across Europe with devastating results. Something between one third and one half of Europe's

△ Rattus rattus, *the black rat, was responsible for spreading the most common of the plague illnesses. The disease was transmitted by the fleas that lived in the rats' fur. Infected rats were brought to Britain in merchant's cargoes.*

population was killed by it. We do not know for certain where it started – but it was probably in China and India. It reached Sicily in 1347, England in 1349, and Scandinavia in 1353. Painters portrayed the plague as a corpse riding a horse, killing everyone he met. There was no cure for the plague.

The Death was carried into England by rats which flourished in the holds of ships trading with Europe. Within a year about one third of English people died. The Plague struck Scotland, Ireland and Wales later, but less severely.

Within 12 years the Death was back. In some villages the whole population died or fled. Such a village was Tusmore in Oxfordshire where the village fields were turned into parkland. 'Plague villages' can be found all over England, though in fact their abandonment was not always caused by the Black Death.

▽ *This illustration from a medieval manuscript shows a burial scene during the Black Death. Only the wealthy were buried in a coffin. Most plague corpses were thrown into open pits after dark and burned with lime.*

THE POWER OF THE CHURCH

In medieval Britain every village had its own church. They were built of stone, not of wood. Men and women were married there, children were baptized there, and the dead were buried there. The churches were also used for all sorts of social occasions which the whole village would attend. Nearly everyone went to church on Sunday, and the festivals of Christmas and Easter, and the birthdays of popular saints, were declared rest days. (They were the holy days, and we still refer to them as holidays today.)

In the churchyard stood the village stocks, where those who had committed minor offences sat. Their ankles and their wrists were clamped in front of them, while passers-by insulted them and threw rotten eggs or mud at them.

THE VILLAGE PRIEST

Each village had its own priest. Before 1200 priests could marry. After that time they could not. The priest, who had a small farm beside the church called the 'glebe' land, was a farmer like everyone in his congregation. This meant he had a great deal in common with them, and this helped him in his work of telling them about the teachings of Jesus.

Everyone in the village had to give one-tenth (a 'tithe') of their animals and crops each year – the best tenth – to the priest as his wages. The crops were taken to the tithe barn on the glebe land at harvest time. Villagers hated paying tithes, and their collection caused ill-feeling between priests and their congregations which lasted for centuries.

The village priest could often barely read or write, and spent much of his life working on his land. Sometimes he did not understand the Latin services he spoke, or the words of the Bible he read out. But though he may have seemed ignorant to learned men, he was more educated than anyone else in the village. Sunday after Sunday he conversed with the people about the meaning of life and death, and held the Holy Communion service (the Mass). During this service the people felt joined in spirit with Jesus and with those who had lived before them, particularly their own ancestors.

◁ *This monk is tending the sheep in the hills above Fountains Abbey in Yorkshire. The monks at the abbey used the most modern agricultural methods of their time.*

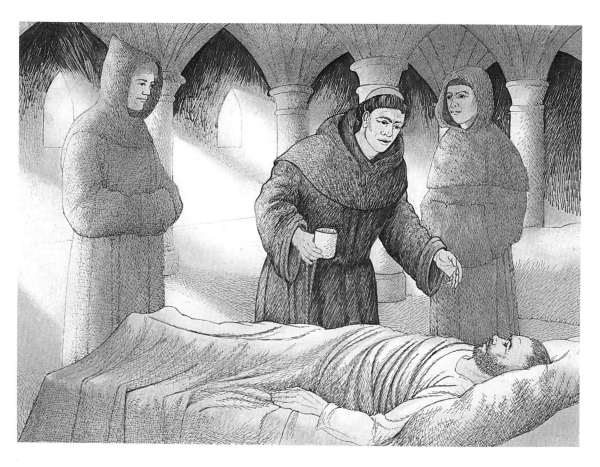

△ *Medieval monks cared for the sick in hospices, from which our hospitals developed.*

CATHEDRALS

All over England the finest monuments of the Middle Ages still stand – the cathedrals. They dominate their cities, still dwarfing the surrounding houses. Their spires or towers can be seen from miles around. Within their walls are fine examples of craftsmanship – stone altar screens, wooden choirstalls, marble tombs and stained glass windows.

RELIGIOUS HOUSES

In every part of medieval Britain there were monasteries and nunneries. These communities owned much of the land, and monks, such as the Cistercian sheep-farming monks in Yorkshire, used the most modern farming methods. They built hospitals for the sick, and gave travellers who came to their doors food and a bed for the night. Their schools were the only places where clever children could be educated, and there were fine libraries.

Not only did the monks collect and study books; they made them. Before printing was introduced into England in the 15th century, books were written and illustrated by hand on parchment (sheep-skin) or vellum (calf-skin).

Though the monks, nuns and village priests devoted much time to farming or to helping the poor and sick, the heart of their life lay in prayer. Without such regular contact with God they believed their life would lose its real point.

January a time of rest

February digging and planting

March pruning vines

April carrying a
flowering branch

May hawking

June mowing hay

July cutting corn

August threshing corn

September picking apples

October sowing winter corn

November gathering acorns
for the pigs

December killing a pig

MAKING A PILGRIMAGE

Among the travellers who knocked on the doors of monasteries and nunneries to ask for hospitality were the pilgrims. These were people who set out on foot or on horseback to visit a holy shrine. They might go to St Albans Cathedral, built where the first English Christian martyr was killed in the 3rd century; to the tomb of King Edmund in Bury St Edmunds; or to the most popular place of pilgrimage – the shrine of Archbishop Thomas Becket at Canterbury. At one time one million pilgrims came to Canterbury from all over Europe, each year.

Many people went on pilgrimages because they were holidays, and it was fun to travel all over Britain and beyond. Others went to be cured of their illnesses, believing that if they prayed at a saint's shrine or touched his or her relics, they or the people for whom they prayed would be cured. Other pilgrims went to give thanks or to ask forgiveness.

In time some monks and nuns failed to live up to their founders' ideals. When they entered the monastery they had vowed to have no possessions or money, to avoid the other sex, and to obey their superiors. Now some of them were lazy, ate and drank too much and mixed freely with the outside world.

THE FRIARS

In Italy St Francis of Assisi had created a new order of dedicated Christians – the friars. They lived and worked in the ordinary world, though they vowed to give up all possessions and to remain unmarried. They helped the over-worked parish priests and gave food and clothing to the poor. The friars became well known as preachers and teachers, and were highly respected. From the 1230s onwards they were familiar sights in the roads and streets of Britain.

EDUCATION

The Church provided the only education there was, and it did so partly to train priests. The great majority of the population could neither read nor write. But the Church was always on the look-out for clever boys whose parents could not afford to pay the fees which the grammar schools charged – where they existed. These 'poor scholars' would be taught at the Church's expense and in return they would become priests when they grew up.

From the earliest times the Church had provided the civil servants who administered the nation's business. They required education beyond that provided by the grammar schools which were attached to cathedrals or convents or monasteries. During the 12th and 13th centuries the universities of Oxford and Cambridge developed for the clergy and civil servants. They were controlled by the Church and taught mainly theology, mathematics, Latin (the international language) and law.

The Church controlled all knowledge and all art. The sciences were regarded as means of illustrating God's wisdom in creating the world. All men and women had to accept the Church's teaching or face a cruel death. Jews were massacred and tortured. In 1290 the Jews were expelled and were not allowed to live in Britain for another 350 years.

◁ This 14th century calendar of the farming year shows some of the different activities which occurred during 12 months.

THE BATTLES FOR THE KINGDOMS

Henry Bolingbroke, now Henry IV and founder of the Lancastrian line of kings, spent much time rushing around his kingdom trying to suppress rebellions. When the Earl of Northumberland led a northern rising with Scottish support, Henry was faced with the possible loss of all England north of the Humber. This was avoided when the Scots were defeated at the Battle of Bramham Moor in 1408 and Northumberland was killed.

OWAIN GLYNDŴR'S WELSH REBELLION

The most serious challenge to Henry came in Wales. Here Owain Glyndŵr, who claimed to be descended from an old Welsh royal family, raised a rebellion in the north-east of the country.

By 1406 it seemed possible that Glyndŵr might be crowned Prince of Wales. He was allied to the English barons who were trying to overthrow Henry IV, and had allies in Scotland and in France. He drew up an agreement with the pope for a Welsh Church. However, the Scots, the French and the English barons made their peace with Henry IV. Then in 1408 Glyndŵr's armies were decisively defeated. The war was over by 1410.

From that time Wales and England were united. The Welsh kings – the Tudors – who ruled England in the 16th century strengthened the union. Welsh law gave way to English law. The official language was English, in which public affairs had to be conducted, but Welsh continued to be the spoken language in most of Wales.

HENRY V AND FRANCE

Henry IV died in 1413 and was succeeded by his son Henry V, who is regarded as the last great warrior king. The 26-year-old king led fighting in northern France, where the English won battle after battle. Henry's victory at Agincourt in 1415 meant that most of France was now under the control of the English. In 1420 Henry made a treaty with Charles VI, the sick king of France, which marked the height of English power in France. The treaty decreed that Henry was to marry Charles' daughter Catherine and was to be regent of France during the king's illness. After Charles' death Henry was to become king of France.

△ In 1400 Owain Glyndŵr led a national Welsh rebellion against the English monarch and he was almost successful.

△ *Joan of Arc was burnt at the stake by the English. She led the French war of liberation.*

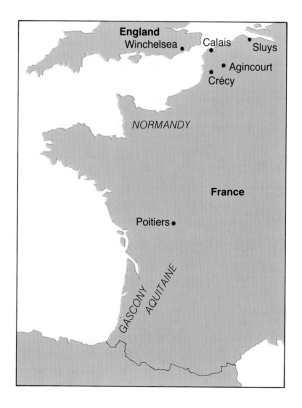

THE LOSS OF FRANCE

The international situation was transformed by Henry V's death from dysentery in 1422, when he was campaigning in France. His son Henry was only a baby. During the following years of Henry VI's minority, the English in France were on the retreat.

A young woman, Joan of Arc, who was later made a saint by the Catholic Church, led a national war against the English invaders. By 1450 the English were driven out of Normandy. Three years later they lost all of Gascony, and with it the flourishing wine and cloth trade. Only Calais remained in English hands. The Hundred Years' War was over. From now on the English and French were separate and competing neighbours.

HENRY VI'S WEAK RULE

Henry VI collapsed after the loss of Gascony. He seems to have suffered a nervous breakdown, and to have become incapable of governing. There was much about his policies to admire. He encouraged the development of schools and colleges, and supported the Church. But people said he was indecisive and blamed him for the defeats in France.

The government was bankrupt, and the taxpayer had nothing to show for his money. In 1450 John Cade led an uprising and attacked the traitors who had lost France, left the south coast undefended, and wasted the king's treasures. Richard, Duke of York, became 'Protector of the Realm' during Henry VI's illness.

◁ *This map shows the sites of the main battles in the Hundred Years' War. By 1453 only Calais remained in English hands. The English dream of an empire in France was over.*

△ *Pictured here are Henry VI and his queen, Margaret of Anjou. Henry supported the church and education but he was blamed for the loss of an empire in France.*

Although they lasted for 30 years the Wars did not affect the whole country – just the areas of fighting. Since the retreat from France, England was disturbed by gangs of returning soldiers and by nobles who could no longer take part in their favourite occupation of warfare. But for much of England the middle and later years of the 15th century were a time of prosperity. The Wars did, however, kill off many leading nobles and infuriated the merchants and townsmen, whose trade was disrupted. Later kings played on these feelings when they set out to re-establish the Crown's control over the country.

THE WARS OF THE ROSES

When Henry recovered from his illness, Protector Richard decided to claim the throne for himself and his heirs. He was descended from Edward III's youngest son, the Duke of Clarence, and maintained he had a better claim to the throne than the Lancastrian Henry VI and his baby son Edward. From 1455 onwards the country faced the intermittent disruption of civil wars fought between the rival claimants, the Yorkists and the Lancastrians. These wars became known as the Wars of the Roses because they were fought between the followers of the red rose of House of Lancaster and the white rose of the House of York.

PEACE UNDER EDWARD IV

The Wars seemed over in 1471, when the Yorkist Edward IV seized the throne. Henry VI's only son was killed in battle, and Henry himself died in the Tower. Edward's power was unchallenged. His peaceful foreign policies encouraged trade abroad and kept taxes low. But trouble returned when he died in 1483. He left two young sons, 11-year-old Edward V and nine-year-old Richard.

RICHARD III BECOMES KING

The boys' uncle, who had been appointed Protector until Edward V came of age, was crowned Richard III (1483–1485). The boys were imprisoned in the Tower, where they were murdered, possibly on Richard's orders. They are remembered as 'the Princes in the Tower'.

Richard was challenged by a Lancastrian – the Welshman Henry Tudor, whose father was Henry VI's half brother. In 1485 at the battle of Bosworth, in Leicestershire, Richard III was defeated and killed. Though nobody then realized it, the Wars of the Roses were finally over.

LIFE IN MEDIEVAL TIMES

To a modern person, a medieval town would seem more like a large village. Apart from London, no town housed more than five thousand people.

TOWN LIFE
Medieval towns were walled for protection, but many people lived in the suburbs outside. They would retreat within the walls only in an emergency. Many of the townspeople had strips of land in the town fields outside the walls, and pastured animals outside on the town common. If any animals strayed from the common they were put in the town pound (lock-up) and their owners could only reclaim them by paying a fine.

Most streets in the town were narrow and the fronts of the houses hung over them. Garbage and chamber pots were tipped into the streets below.

▽ *This 13th century fortified bridge and gatehouse is at Monnon in Monmouth. At night the gate was shut and people could enter the town only with the keeper's permission.*

TOWN HOUSES

Medieval town houses were generally small, for it was rare to have more than two children. They were made of wood and wattle and daub, with thatched roofs. The most common danger the patrolling nightwatchman looked out for was fire. The only way of fighting a fire that had taken hold was to pull the house down.

By 1450, stone and brick houses became more common. Tiled roofs began to replace thatch. Large town houses, built with blackened beams and white plaster, with windows made of leaded panes, began to appear.

TRADE AND COMMERCE

Medieval towns were mainly lived in by people who manufactured and traded. They were often skilled craftsmen who, with their journeymen (workers) and apprentices, made a great variety of goods. Some were sold in the town and

△ *Illustrated here is a 14th century English port. Much English trade was carried on by Italian and German merchants. Eastern goods – such as spices and silks – were exchanged for English wool and cloth.*

surrounding countryside; others much farther away. Cloth, for instance, was the main British export to Europe for hundreds of years.

Among other important craftsmen were the goldsmiths. The blacksmiths, who made horseshoes, were often vets as well; the apothecaries (chemists) were the doctors of the time. There were also the bowyers who made bows, and fletchers who made arrows. Houses were built by carpenters, bricklayers, tilers and plasterers, and lit by the chandler who made the candles. Bakers, butchers, grocers and fishmongers provided food. Brewers brewed the townspeople's ale and the vintners made their wine.

CRAFT GUILDS

The craftsmen formed themselves into guilds, which guaranteed the quality of their members' work and kept up their prices. After an apprenticeship, which might last seven years, an apprentice qualified for membership of his craft by presenting his 'masterpiece'.

The merchants were men of the world and traded their goods by land and sea. Much medieval foreign trade was carried out not by English merchants but by Europeans living in English towns.

Each medieval town had its local fairs and markets. Some of these, like St Bartholomew's in London or St Giles's in Oxford, were gatherings of traders from all over Europe. Italians – particularly the Venetians – brought spices, silks, carpets, pearls and ivory from India and China, to exchange for English wool, cloth, shoes, boots, pewter and silver plate.

LIFE IN THE COUNTRY

The great majority of people lived in the countryside. Most of them were villeins and their families. As in Norman times the men worked on two farms, their own and that of their lord. Each village was surrounded by three large fields split into long, thin strips of land. Each villein owned a number of strips in each of the village fields. His total of strips normally added up to 12–15 hectares. The strips were located in different parts of the field so that each farmer would have his fair share of good and poor soil. The fields had no hedges. Wooden markers, called land marks, were used to divide one strip of land from another.

▽ *During the 15th century yeomen (free) farmers grew increasingly prosperous, particularly if they had flocks of sheep. Their farmhouses are much sought-after today.*

The crops to be grown in the fields were decided at the village meeting. This was held in the autumn, after the harvest had been gathered in. All strip-owners could vote on the crops for next year. The choice was limited – generally it would be wheat, oats, rye or barley. Root-crops, such as potatoes and turnips, were not yet known.

CROP ROTATION

The villagers had discovered from experience that if you grew crops over and over again on the same land, the soil grew dusty and the crops were poor. So one of the three fields was left fallow (unfarmed). The next year it would be used again and a different field would be left. On the fallow field, the villeins would graze their sheep and cattle, whose manure would enrich the land for the next year.

A VILLEIN'S RESPONSIBILITIES

The villein spent two or three days a week working on his lord's strips in the open fields or on the manor farm. When he was working for the lord, the villein was part of a team working under the manor foreman, the 'reeve'. He also had to spend extra time working on the lord's estate at harvest time or at haymaking.

The villein and his family had to give the lord some of their produce at certain times of the year, such as eggs, or honey from their own bees. The villein had to grind his corn in the lord's mill, at prices fixed by the lord. The villein's wife was supposed to bake her bread only in the lord's ovens and to pay for the service.

▷ *In medieval times the farmer and his wife began to live much more comfortably, with four-poster beds. Babies' cradles were passed down the family from generation to generation.*

The manor court, where the villeins' cases were heard, was supervised by the lord's steward. The villein had to get permission from this court if he wanted to sell his livestock at market, or let his daughter get married. When he died, the villein's son had to pay the court for the right to take over the land.

HOME FOR THE VILLEIN'S FAMILY

The villein's houses, still made of wattle and daub and thatched, contained one or two rooms. The windows were holes in the walls. The floors were of beaten earth, covered with straw or reeds. From the rafters hung a flitch (side) of bacon or some dried herbs. The family's beds were bags of straw, with blankets of rough wool, spun and woven at home from wool shorn off their sheep. Chickens and dogs would live in the same room as the family.

Caxton first saw printing, which was invented by the Chinese, at work in Germany in 1450. His books, chiefly written in English, were printed on paper – not parchment or vellum as earlier books had been.

FOOD

Meals were simple. Breakfast was eaten before dawn, before the men went to work in the fields. It consisted of rye bread and a cup of water. At midday, the men returned home for dinner, which was bread again, this time with cheese and a cup of watery beer. The evening meal, at the end of the working day, included thick vegetable soup and some salted meat or bacon, or fish caught in the local river.

The 15th century saw the final end of the old feudal system. Men rented their land for money and worked for wages. An increasing number of prosperous yeomen farmers were to be found all over England.

The thriving English wool industry had already become famous throughout Europe. By the end of the 14th century a flourishing cloth industry had also been established. The merchants who exported the cloth, whose company was called the Merchant Adventurers, were some of the richest men in England.

LANGUAGE AND LITERATURE

During the 15th century English began to be used in official circles at Court and in Parliament. The invention of printing helped to spread the use of a common English language instead of local dialects. These remained normal in spoken speech. Printing was introduced to England by William Caxton, who set up a printing press at Westminster in 1476. He used the English of the London area as the basic language for his books. English literature could now develop.

The medieval town on market day was a place of bustle and noise. All kinds of produce were sold, including fruit, vegetables, eggs, sheep, pigs and geese. A juggler and a dancing bear provided the entertainment. The shopkeepers lived behind the shops and stalls.

1486–1603
THE TUDORS

TIME CHART

* denotes events that occurred outside Britain and Ireland.

1486	Henry VII marries Elizabeth of York.
1492	*Christopher Columbus reaches West Indies.
1497	*Vasco da Gama rounds Cape of Good Hope.
1503	Henry's daughter Margaret marries James IV of Scotland.
1504	Statute of Liveries bans private armies.
1509	Henry VII dies. Henry VIII becomes king. Henry marries Catherine of Aragon.
1513	Henry lands in France and starts French wars again. Battle of Flodden.
1515	Cardinal Wolsey now Henry's chief minister.
1517	*Martin Luther starts Protestant revolt in Germany.
1519–1522	*Magellan sails round world.
1520	*Field of Cloth of Gold.
1530	Wolsey falls from Henry's favour and dies.
1533	Henry's marriage with Catherine is annulled and he marries Anne Boleyn. Elizabeth I is born.
1534	Act of Supremacy makes Henry head of Church of England. Thomas Cromwell becomes chief minister.
1536–1539	Monasteries are closed.
1536	Anne Boleyn is executed. Pilgrimage of Grace. Act of Union with Wales.
1537	Edward VI is born.
1540	Thomas Cromwell is executed.
1547	Henry VIII dies. Edward VI becomes king, at the age of nine; the Duke of Somerset assumes control as Protector.
1549	Ket's Rebellion. Duke of Northumberland becomes Protector.
1553	Edward VI dies. Mary Tudor becomes Queen.
1555	First English protestants burned.
1558	Mary dies. British lose Calais. Elizabeth I becomes queen.
1559	Act of Uniformity establishes Church of England.
1560	Treaty of Edinburgh is signed.
1568	Mary Stuart flees to England.
1568	*Revolt of the Netherlands.
1569	Rising of the North.
1570	*Pope excommunicates Elizabeth I.
1577–1580	Drake sails round the world.
1587	Mary Stuart is executed.
1588	Royal Navy battles with and defeats the Spanish Armada.
1590	First Shakespeare plays are performed.
1596	Irish rebellion.
1599	Irish rebellion is suppressed.
1600	English East India Company is formed. British slave trade from West Africa to West Indies is steadily growing.
1601	Queen Elizabeth's last Parliament. Poor Law.
1603	Queen Elizabeth dies.

THE POWER OF THE THRONE

England was changing at the end of the 15th century. The Wars of the Roses had made the barons weaker than at any time since the Norman Conquest. Out of the 60 leading families which dominated England at the beginning of the Wars, only about half now had an adult head. Most were bankrupt. Even the leading Yorkists were keen to make peace. When Henry VII married Elizabeth of York, daughter of Edward IV, in 1486, most Yorkist families were prepared to accept his rule. They were exhausted.

Twice Yorkist risings on behalf of 'Pretenders' to the crown were defeated. Lambert Simnel (1487) and Perkin Warbeck (1497) impersonated Yorkist claimants. Despite being supported abroad, both risings failed.

THE END OF PRIVATE ARMIES

From the beginning of his reign, Henry set out to ban private armies. These uniformed gangs of young men, called retainers, were the curse of the country. They had been recruited by powerful barons to fight for them in the Wars of the Roses. But now that the fighting was over they had nothing to do but pillage the countryside or pick quarrels with rival gangs. Their suppression was one of Henry's greatest achievements.

SUBDUING THE BARONS

Henry also undermined the power of the great barons in another way. Whenever he met with opposition from a noble family, he used every opportunity to declare the lord a traitor. Not only did this mean the lord might be executed; it also meant that his lands would fall into the hands of the king. In this way, Henry took over 138 estates during his reign. His marriage to Elizabeth of York brought him further lands. As he became more powerful, his 'overmighty subjects' weakened. He made a number of sound decisions about foreign and financial policies which further increased his power.

THE COST OF WAR

Throughout medieval times, English kings had been bankrupted by wars, particularly in France. Despite their costs and the unpopularity of the taxes raised to pay for them, the wars had proved popular. Warrior-kings like Richard I, Edward III and Henry V were heroes.

△ *Henry VII, who came from a Welsh family, reasserted the king's power over the barons who had threatened to tear England apart.*

△ *Royal judges travelled all around England to administer the common law.*

WAR WITH FRANCE

England still owned Calais, and Henry could have used the town as a base from which to renew the fighting with France. Fortunately he avoided the temptation. Although he was drawn into war in 1492, he soon ended it. He spent only £50,000 out of the £100,000 allowed to him by Parliament for the war. By the peace treaty the French paid Henry money each year to forget his claim to the French throne.

PEACE WITH SCOTLAND

Peace with France also brought peace with their allies, the Scots. Henry VII strengthened this by marrying his daughter to the Scottish King James IV. Frontier fighting was now confined to cattle raids.

Peace at home and abroad boosted the royal income. Customs duties on imports increased by about a quarter. As the amount of royal estates grew, so did the rents. Lords who broke the ban on private armies were fined heavily.

CONTROLLING GOVERNMENT

Henry also tightened his grip on government. He brought back Henry II's system of royal judges to administer the common law. The Privy Council used its own courts, such as the Star Chamber, to try barons who broke the law. When the barons tried to influence local juries the king transferred cases to the Privy Council courts in London which were under his control. Parliament was not called to meet very often, and when it was called, it voted Henry the taxes he wanted.

By the time of his death, Henry had re-established the king's power. For the next 100 years no English subject managed to challenge royal power. By then the danger had swung the other way. Monarchs were in danger of becoming dictators.

△ *Newark Castle, near Selkirk, is a Scottish border house built about 1450. It was fortified against English attack.*

EXPLORATION

Maps of the Middle Ages showed a flat world consisting of Europe and the north African and Eastern Mediterranean coastline. But in the 13th century people realized this was wrong. They had met Arabs who had long traded with the East.

NEW ROUTES TO THE EAST

In the second half of the 15th century the Turks refused to let traders cross their empire, which now stretched from Egypt to Istanbul. Geographers in Europe were asked by their kings to suggest new routes to the East. Some advised sailing south; others said to sail west. Both answers showed they knew the world was round.

▽ *Columbus used Toscanelli's map of the world. Its miscalculations led Columbus to believe he had discovered China.*

The Portuguese sailed south. They explored the west coast of Africa until Vasco da Gama rounded the Cape of Good Hope and reached India. Soon the Portuguese had a great trading empire.

COLUMBUS AND CABOT

The Spanish king was persuaded by an Italian sailor, Christopher Columbus, to let him try the western route. Columbus miscalculated the size of the globe. When he stumbled on the West Indies in 1492 he believed he was on the edge of China.

Another Italian, John Cabot, persuaded some Bristol merchants to finance his voyage to find a north-west passage round the north of America. Though he found no passage he landed at Newfoundland. His voyage led to the first English colony, and a thriving English trade in fish.

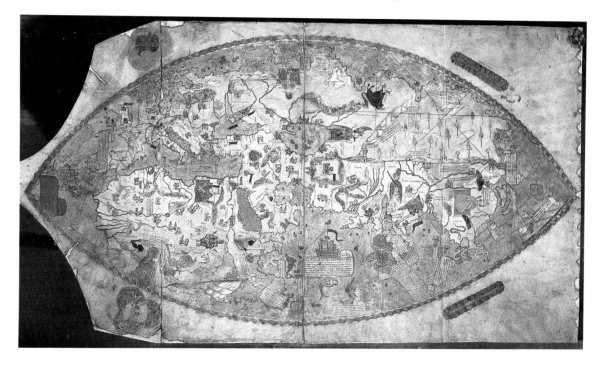

KING HENRY VIII

Henry VIII, who became king at the age of 17 in 1509, was determined to cut a glamorous figure at his court and in Europe. Whereas his father had been careful with money, Henry VIII was extravagant. Whereas his father avoided war, Henry VIII welcomed it. Within four years he was fighting in France. Soon the Scots were over the northern border. It was as if the lessons of the Hundred Years' War had been entirely forgotten.

THE YOUNG KING

Henry VIII had all the gifts which people then expected of a king. The Venetian ambassador reported to his government:

"His majesty is...extremely handsome... very accomplished, a good musician, composes well, is a most capital horse-man, fine jouster, speaks French, Latin and Spanish, and is very religious."[6]

HENRY'S FIRST MARRIAGE

A short time before his coronation, Henry married a Spanish princess, Catherine of Aragon. She had married Henry's elder brother Arthur in 1502. The marriage had shown how greatly respected England had become in Europe during the reign of Henry VII. For a marriage between members of the royal families was the usual way of creating an alliance between two nations. And Spain was one of the most powerful countries in Europe. Therefore when Arthur died Henry VII proposed that Catherine remarry his younger son. The marriage of a man to his brother's widow was against Church law and required special permission from the pope. The permission was eventually granted, but the marriage was to have an important effect on future events.

ENGLAND AT WAR AGAIN

Henry liked to think of himself as a warrior-king, and the pope encouraged him by calling him the rightful king of France. He landed in France in the summer of 1513 to take up the old struggle with the French once more. When he won some battles against the French it was as if Agincourt had come again.

The news from the Scottish border was even better. The Scottish army under King James IV was utterly defeated and the king killed at the battle of Flodden. The French king married Henry's sister Mary. Henry was on top of the world.

CARDINAL WOLSEY

All this success required a great deal of organization. The mind behind the campaign in France was Cardinal Thomas Wolsey's. Wolsey had become a priest because of his political ambitions rather than his religious beliefs. He had been valued by Henry VII because of his organizing skills and his attention to detail, and Henry VIII, in turn, came to rely on him more and more. While Henry hunted or danced or listened to music Wolsey devoted his time and energies to the paperwork.

▷ *The young Henry VIII had a romantic image. Flatterers exaggerated his gifts, but he was certainly a good horseman and a skilled linguist.*

△ *Henry VIII arrived at the Field of the Cloth of Gold with 5000 courtiers for the super-power meeting with King Francis I.*

▷ *Shown here is Henry VIII's armour. In later years the king was so heavy that when he wore armour he had to be winched onto his horse!*

THE FIELD OF THE CLOTH OF GOLD

In 1520 Henry had a meeting with Francis I, the young king of France. It took place near Calais and became known as the meeting of the Field of the Cloth of Gold.

For nearly a fortnight the kings and their courtiers feasted, jousted and danced. One day the two kings wrestled each other. Francis threw Henry and Henry's courtiers had to restrain their master from charging at his royal friend. The meeting ended with a solemn service sung by Wolsey.

HENRY WANTS A SON

Two years later France and England were at war again. The fighting dragged on. By 1530 England had nothing to show for all the fighting and flamboyant display. But by that time Henry's mind was on other matters, and in particular his marriage to Catherine of Aragon. At some time in the 1520s, Henry VIII decided to get rid of his wife. He had started a love affair with a lady at his court, Anne Boleyn, and, moreover, had become convinced that he must have a son to succeed him.

Catherine had given birth to seven children, but six died in childbirth or early in their lives. Only one lived – a girl, Mary – and it was thought that no woman ruler would be able to hold the country together after Henry died. The king convinced himself that his wife's misfortunes were judgements of God upon them for their marriage. The pope, he said, should never have agreed to let him marry his brother's widow in the first place. Now the new pope, successor to Clement VII, must admit his predecessor's mistake. He must cancel the ruling and declare Henry and Catherine to be no longer man and wife. Then Henry could marry Anne, who would give him the baby boy he wanted.

HENRY AGAINST THE POPE

Even if the pope had wished to do as Henry said, he was in no position to do so. Emperor Charles V of Spain, who was Catherine's nephew, had recently occupied Rome and taken the pope prisoner.

Catherine refused to give up her rights as queen, or her daughter Mary's rights to succeed her father. The emperor supported his aunt. Nothing that Wolsey could do would make the pope agree to carry out Henry's wishes.

THE BREAK WITH ROME

In 1530 Wolsey fell from Henry's favour. He died before the trial which the king had prepared for him, and so avoided a traitor's death. The new Archbishop of

Canterbury, Thomas Cranmer, was also unable to make the pope change his mind. By the end of 1532 Anne Boleyn was pregnant. Henry was now forced to decide. Either he would have to stay married to Catherine, which would mean that Anne's baby would be illegitimate and Mary would succeed him, or he could defy the pope and set up a new church under his own control. This church would legally separate Catherine and Henry, and marry Henry to Anne. He chose the second, and Cranmer obliged by secretly marrying the pair. Catherine and Mary were sent to a nunnery. In September 1533 Anne gave birth to a baby. It was a girl – Elizabeth, the future Elizabeth I. Then Henry set up a new Church of England and made himself head of it.

THOMAS MORE (1477–1535)

Of the few men who dared to stand up against Henry VIII the best known were John Fisher, Bishop of Rochester, and Thomas More. More, the son of a judge, was educated in the household of the Archbishop of Canterbury and at Oxford University. He soon became a brilliant barrister who devoted his spare time to literature and religious learning. With the great European scholar Erasmus, whom he first met when he was only 22, and John Colet, the Dean of St Paul's, More moved in a circle of learned Roman Catholics. They were determined to reform their religion and encourage the study of literature, Latin and Greek, astronomy and the sciences. Erasmus published an edition of the New Testament in Greek, so that people could learn what Jesus had actually said and taught. More published *Utopia* (which means 'no place'), an imaginary description of a perfect society.

MORE DEFIES HENRY

More became a close friend of Henry VIII's, who prided himself on his encouragement of the New Learning, and entered Parliament in 1504. He became Speaker of the House of Commons, and was with Henry at the Field of the Cloth of Gold. Although he was scornfully critical of abuses in the Church, he was a strong defender of Roman Catholic teachings against the views of Martin Luther. Following Wolsey's fall from Henry VIII's favour, More became Lord Chancellor in 1529, the highest political post in the land. Within three years he had resigned, being determined not to accept Queen Catherine's divorce from Henry. He refused to take any oath which would deny the pope's authority over the English Church. He and Fisher were arrested and found guilty of high treason. More was beheaded in 1535, and his head was exhibited on London Bridge. Four hundred years later the Roman Catholic Church made More a saint.

HENRY IS EXCOMMUNICATED

The pope did not take such an open challenge to the authority of his Roman Catholic Church quietly. Already, for the first time in western Europe for over a thousand years, a Christian leader had set up a rival Christian church. This was Martin Luther, whose Protestant Church was now the main church in northern Germany. Protestant Christianity was spreading quickly into Holland, France

▽ *Thomas More and his family are shown here in a painting by Holbein. Although he was once a friend of Henry VIII's, More was executed for refusing to accept Henry's new church.*

and Switzerland. There were increasing numbers of Lutherans in England. The pope was determined to put a stop to the spread of these rival churches. He 'excommunicated' Henry (expelled him from the Church), and called upon all Catholic Christians to have nothing to do with Henry's English Church.

THE CHURCH IN CRISIS

It seems extraordinary that, after a thousand years of membership, England should leave the Roman Catholic Church over a dispute about a marriage. But there were a number of reasons why many English people were prepared to give up their loyalty to the pope.

First of all there was the strength of Henry VIII himself. Henry had built on his father's success in establishing a firm control over his kingdom. He used his power ruthlessly. Anyone who challenged him faced execution.

The Church had been unpopular in England for a long time. Though people admired many of the local priests, who lived simply and tried sincerely to follow Jesus' teaching, they resented the Church's wealth. Nobody liked paying taxes to the pope. Some of the monks and friars lived unworthy lives, though no more so than in earlier times. Some ate and drank too much. Some were lazy. A few had secret lovers. Some people were secretly talking of the need for a new Christian start. They taught that the Roman Catholic Church was too corrupt to change its ways, and that only a new church could bring back the true worship of Jesus.

So it came about that only a few brave men refused to swear loyalty to the new Church of England. To most ordinary people it seemed that the old Church

continued, except that it was now ruled by the king and not by a foreign pope. It was only the monks and nuns whose lives were completely changed. The destruction of their monasteries was carried out by Thomas Cromwell, who now became Henry's main minister.

DISSOLUTION OF THE MONASTERIES

As the years had gone by, the monks had gained great estates. By the reign of Henry VIII they owned about a quarter of English farmland. Henry, who had wasted hundreds of thousands of pounds in the French wars, was keen to get his hands on their wealth.

Cromwell sent inspectors to investigate the monasteries and nunneries from 1535 onwards. They had little difficulty in proving that some of the monks were no longer leading the sort of lives which their founders had wanted them to lead. Some of the monasteries had few members, for not nearly as many men and women were joining the orders as had done in medieval times. They were not giving as much of their money to the poor or elderly or sick as they should have been.

There was nothing that could not have been put right by reform. But the king wanted the monasteries closed, and their wealth given to his government.

When there was a rising in the north in support of the monks – the Pilgrimage of Grace – it was suppressed. By 1540 it was all over. Christian communities that had been serving people for up to a thousand years were wiped away in five. It was not until Victorian times that monasteries and convents were allowed to be refounded.

Henry made some attempts to fill the gaps in the country left by the closure of the monasteries. Their schools were allowed to continue, so long as they took the name of their destroyer: Henry VIII School in Coventry and King's School in Canterbury are two of the old monastic schools which still thrive today. The monks who wanted to become clergy in Henry's Church were welcomed; the rest were given pensions.

HENRY REMARRIES – FOUR TIMES

Nothing could stop Henry now. From 1536 onwards he changed wives four more times. Anne Boleyn, who did not give Henry the son he wanted, was beheaded. She was supposed to have been unfaithful to him, although the evidence was false. Jane Seymour gave Henry his longed-for male heir, Prince Edward, but she died shortly after giving birth. Henry sent away his next wife, Anne of Cleves, soon after he married her.

Henry's fifth wife, Katherine Howard, was executed for being unfaithful to him. His last wife, an intelligent widow named Catherine Parr, survived him. She was the only one of his wives who knew how to handle him and calm his great rages. These were probably caused in part by the ulcers on his legs, which gave him great pain. In his later years, Henry grew very fat. When he was wearing his full armour he had to be winched onto his horse.

FIGHTING CONTINUES

Henry went on fighting in France nearly to the end of his life, even though the wars left the country bankrupt. His troops captured Boulogne in 1544 but Henry returned home because of a threatened French invasion. The French fleet fought the English in the Solent, but their crews were attacked by plague, and the ships returned to France.

TROUBLE WITH SCOTLAND

Before the final campaigns in France, England had faced the Scottish invasion of Cumbria. They had defeated the Scots at the battle of Solway Moss, north of Carlisle. Under the command of Jane Seymour's brother, the Earl of Hertford (later Protector Somerset), British troops invaded Scotland and burnt Edinburgh.

UNION WITH WALES

Wales and England were united by the Act of Union in 1536. Welsh counties were created along English lines and Welsh MPs attended the English Parliament.

ATTEMPTED UNION WITH IRELAND

Another early attempt at a union, this time with Ireland, was made by Henry VIII. In 1541 an Irish parliament was called in Dublin and proclaimed Henry king of Ireland. As Henry was head of the Church in England he claimed the same position for himself in Ireland, although the vast majority of Irish men and women were Roman Catholics. The English attempt to impose their form of Christianity on the Irish was to poison relations between the countries for hundreds of years.

THE KING DIES

By the beginning of January 1547 it was clear that Henry VIII was very ill. Soon the doctors knew he was dying, but dared not say so. (Six years earlier a lord had been executed for foretelling the king's death.) On 28th January Henry VIII died. His huge coffin was buried in the grave of Jane Seymour, the mother of Edward VI, who now became king at the age of nine.

▷ *This 16th century miniature gives an idealized picture of country life.*

CATHOLICS AND PROTESTANTS

Because Edward VI was only nine years old when he became king, his uncle, the Duke of Somerset, was appointed Protector to rule the country with a council until Edward was old enough to rule alone. Somerset ruled for two years until he was defeated by his rival, the Duke of Northumberland, who took over.

Although Edward's father, King Henry VIII, had quarrelled with the pope and founded a new Church of England, he had no intention of altering the basic beliefs of the Church or its customs. Henry ordered his clergymen to refer to the pope as the Bishop of Rome, but otherwise they were to continue as usual.

▷ *Edward VI was crowned in 1547 at the age of nine. Shown here is the coronation procession as it moved down Cheapside from the Tower of London. At this time, London has scarcely developed south of the Thames.*

Even so, some changes were introduced during Henry's reign. A translation of the Bible in English was placed in each church. It had to be read in the church and it was chained to the reading desk so no one could take it away. In 1545 the first English service was used in the Church of England. It was written by the Archbishop of Canterbury, Thomas Cranmer, whose hand Henry was holding when he died. For years Cranmer had been trying to make Henry more Protestant.

THE CHURCH BECOMES PROTESTANT

Protector Somerset and Edward, who had strong Protestant beliefs, were determined to make the English Church Protestant. With their support, Cranmer put together in 1549 a new service book in English – the first *Book of Common Prayer* – for all clergymen to use.

The priests were now allowed to marry. Churches were told to remove or destroy holy images (pictures or statues) – of Jesus' mother Mary, for instance, or of the

saints. This was because people were thought to treat such pictures as if they were holy in themselves rather than just illustrations of the Christian faith.

When the Duke of Northumberland became Protector, the English Church became completely Protestant. The second *Book of Common Prayer* had all traces of Roman Catholic belief, which was now called 'Popery', removed from it. A special Act was passed to order the removal of all images from churches. This led to a spate of destruction.

THE LOSS OF COMMON LAND

Since the 15th century, landowners and rich farmers had been changing from growing crops to farming sheep, particularly in the Midlands and East Anglia. English wool and cloth was in great demand at home and abroad. The sheep farmers took over common land and enclosed it (put fences round it) for themselves despite Tudor governments' attempts to stop them. Their enclosures hurt the poor most. They could no longer keep a cow, some sheep or a pig on the common and grew even poorer. Others became unemployed or lost their small plots of land.

In 1549 Robert Ket, a wealthy tanner, led a party of labourers in Norfolk. Believing they had government support, they pulled down fences that had recently been put up around commons. Soon they were joined by others and marched on Norwich. The Duke of Northumberland led an army that included about 1500 mercenaries to put down the rising. The labourers, most of whom were unarmed, were no match for the soldiers. Three thousand labourers were killed. Another popular rising had been cruelly put down.

THE GROWING PROBLEM OF THE POOR

Since the closure of the monasteries, the homeless, beggars, and tramps found it increasingly difficult to get food or a bed for the night. London, in particular, was crowded with beggars who clutched at the sleeves of passers-by and cried for help. Soldiers and sailors who lost a leg or an arm fighting for their country could claim no pension. They could not get work, so they were forced to beg.

Tudor governments were reluctant to help the poor but they realized that the presence of large numbers of desperate men was a threat to the country's peace and stability. It was not, however, until Elizabeth's reign that any effective policy was worked out to help the poor.

In 1547 Somerset had invaded Scotland and defeated the Scots at Pinkie, near Edinburgh. The Scots government sent their six-year-old queen to France, fearing she might be forced to marry Edward. The English withdrew most of their troops from Scotland, apart from some garrisons, and returned Boulogne to France.

The national finances were in chaos. Henry's French wars had bankrupted the country and Somerset's Scottish invasion made the situation worse. Rising prices were producing hardships and riots all over England. Northumberland had made inflation even worse by 'debasing' the coins – reducing the amount of silver and gold in coins.

QUEEN FOR NINE DAYS

Edward VI, who had never been very healthy, died in 1553 at the age of 16. The troubles during his reign made some people more convinced than ever that the country needed a strong ruler. The only person with a real claim to the throne was

Mary Tudor, daughter of Henry VIII and Catherine of Aragon. But as well as being a woman, she was a Roman Catholic. Before he died, Edward VI and the Duke of Northumberland conspired to give the crown instead to Lady Jane Grey, aged 16, who was quickly married to the Duke of Northumberland's eldest son.

Lady Jane Grey reigned for nine days. But court, Parliament and the people of London would have none of it. When Mary Tudor marched from Suffolk to London to claim her rights, support for Lady Jane Grey and Northumberland faded away. The gates of London were open to Mary and she was crowned queen. Northumberland and Lady Jane Grey were executed.

THE REIGN OF MARY I (1553–1558)
Mary I was a deeply convinced Roman Catholic. For many years, ever since Henry had left her mother Catherine, she had led an unhappy life. She had felt

△ *Beggars who were accused of refusing work were publicly whipped. They were then sent home to their birthplace.*

friendless and, in the last year of Edward's life, had been afraid that she might be killed to prevent her becoming queen. She was determined to be loyal to her mother's memory and to the faith which had comforted and supported both of them.

Mary united England once more with the Roman Catholic Church, brought back Roman Catholic services, stopped the marriage of priests, and even attempted to return the monks' lands, although Parliament would not allow it. She married the Spanish King Philip II. The marriage provoked a rebellion in Kent led by Sir Thomas Wyatt, which was suppressed without great difficulty.

Mary then decided to force English Protestants back to her Church by persecuting those who would not agree. About 300 people were burned alive during Mary's reign, 60 of them women. They were mostly ordinary people (Protestant nobles and clergymen could afford to flee abroad). Though religious persecution was then common, the burnings were never forgotten.

By the time of her death in 1558, at the age of 42, Mary had become a pathetic figure. Failures in the harvests and rising prices were looked on by her people as judgements of God upon her. She longed to have a child and heir, but she never succeeded. She adored her husband Philip, but he spent little time in England. When he knew she was dying, he did not come to her deathbed. She was jealous of her half-sister Elizabeth, Anne Boleyn's daughter, and feared a rebellion against her in support of Elizabeth. When, in 1558, the French captured Calais, Mary was deeply ashamed. Calais was the last piece of French soil which the English had held. Shortly afterwards she died.

THE REIGN OF ELIZABETH I

When Elizabeth became queen at the age of 25, in 1558, there was no reason to expect she would rule for long. Though Mary Tudor's persecutions had made her unpopular, many people, particularly of an older generation, still supported the traditional Catholic religion. As Anne Boleyn's daughter, Elizabeth I could never be recognized as the rightful monarch by any loyal Roman Catholic.

PROTESTANT COMPLAINTS

Nor were all Protestants satisfied with Elizabeth's new Church of England. The Puritans, the most extreme English Protestants, wanted the Church to be 'purified' of all its Catholic practices.

They wanted the priest's clothing to be simple and all statues and images to be removed from churches. They wanted to end the appointment of bishops by the monarch and demanded that all clergymen should be elected by their congregations.

OTHER THREATS

As well as these disputes over religion, Elizabeth had to deal with the troubles arising from unemployment, inflation and the Poor Laws. Then there were the threats from abroad. The Scots and the French were now closer allies than ever after Queen Mary Stuart's marriage, in 1558, to the heir to the French throne, Francis. They might unite to get rid of Elizabeth. More dangerous still was Spain, whose King Philip, a Protestant hater, had

just lost his power over England through the death of his wife, Mary Tudor.

To survive, Elizabeth would need tact and cunning, as well as courage and determination. She had all these qualities.

▷ *Queen Elizabeth I combined political skill with great determination.*

ELIZABETH AND RELIGION

First Elizabeth set out to settle the conflicts over religion. Although she was a Protestant, she did not like the Puritans and would not let them have their way.

Her new Archbishop of Canterbury, Archbishop Parker, stopped any further looting and destruction of churches. Bishops were still appointed by Elizabeth. Everyone had to attend the new Church of England, but the punishment for failing to do so was only a fine of a shilling a month. A few brave Roman Catholics would have nothing to do with it; everyone else accepted it.

MARY QUEEN OF SCOTS

The dangers from abroad soon grew less. In 1559 Francis II, aged 15 and an invalid, became King of France. Mary Stuart was now Queen of France and Scotland. But in 1560 Francis II died and Mary returned to Scotland. There she found that there had been a Protestant revolution, led by the preacher John Knox and supported by many of the nobles.

William Cecil, Elizabeth's Secretary of State who served her quietly and skilfully throughout her long reign, had shrewdly encouraged the Scottish Protestants and sent an English army into the Lowlands to support them. The French had been surrounded in their garrison at Leith, and blockaded at sea by the English fleet. In the Treaty of Edinburgh, in 1560, it was agreed that all French troops would be removed from Scotland.

From the moment that she returned to Scotland, Mary Stuart quarrelled with her Protestant government. There were rumours about her scandalous private life. Her second marriage, to the Earl of Darnley, was known to be unhappy. The

△ Shown here is Mary Queen of Scots and one of her courtiers in captivity. When she escaped from Scotland, Elizabeth kept her under house arrest for 19 years. She became the centre of many plots against Elizabeth.

couple made up their quarrel, and a son, James, was born. But then Darnley was murdered by a group of Protestant lords, led by the Earl of Bothwell. Rumours spread that Mary had been involved, though they were never proved. But when, shortly after the murder, Bothwell divorced his wife, and Mary married him, Mary's court and government could stand it no longer. She was imprisoned. In 1568 she escaped, fled across the border and threw herself on the mercy of her cousin, Elizabeth. For the next 19 years Mary was Elizabeth's prisoner.

During Elizabeth's long and peaceful reign, many new private houses were built. Here the Countess of Shrewsbury consults her architect, Robert Smythson, during the building of Hardwick Hall in Derbyshire. Her initials, ES (Elizabeth Shrewsbury), already cap one tower. Most materials, like the stone blocks, came from the Hardwick estate. The marble, used in fireplaces and mantelpieces, was quarried in Derbyshire. The family and state apartments were on the first and second floors, as the height of the windows shows. The servants' quarters were, unusually, on the ground floor. Great Elizabethan houses were unfortified. The centuries of barons' wars were over at last.

THE RISING OF THE NORTH

The year after Mary's flight into England, Elizabeth faced a dangerous rebellion – the Rising of the North. It was led by the northern Earls of Northumberland and Westmorland, who wanted a Roman Catholic ruler. They planned to release Mary Stuart from imprisonment and make her queen. She was to marry the leading English Roman Catholic, the Duke of Norfolk. The Spanish ambassador was involved in one of the plans, which became known as the Ridolfi Plot.

English spies heard of the plots and the rising was prevented. The Duke of Norfolk was executed. But Elizabeth, against her minister's advice, refused to put Mary Stuart on trial.

TROUBLE WITH THE POPE

In 1570 Pope Pius V excommunicated Elizabeth from the Roman Catholic Church. After that English Roman Catholic missionaries began to work secretly to reconvert people in England and Wales to the Roman Catholic faith. The missionaries were hidden by other Roman Catholics who risked death to give them shelter.

The government hit back hard against the Catholics. Fines for refusing to attend Church of England services were raised to £20 a month. This was a huge sum which would bankrupt all but the richest families. The government did not stop there. Nearly 300 Roman Catholics were executed for their beliefs, most of them in 1588. This was the year when the Spaniards set out on their campaign to invade Britain. The government looked on every Catholic as a friend of the Spaniards. This was certainly not the case (the commander of the English navy which defeated the Armada was himself a Catholic), but it explains the persecution, which was seen as protecting the country.

The Catholic Spaniards now hated the Protestant English as enemies of God. The English thought the same, from the opposite point of view.

SPANISH ATTACKS

In 1568 Sir John Hawkins was trading slaves from West Africa to the Spanish colonies in the West Indies and Panama. Spanish sailors attacked Hawkins and his men while their ships were lying peacefully in a harbour in Mexico called Juan d'Ulloa. Many were killed or captured and made slaves in the Spanish navy. Hawkins himself escaped with his young cousin, Francis Drake. From that time onwards they swore revenge on the Spaniards.

Though war had not been declared officially between England and Spain, English sea captains now did all they could to attack the Spanish empire and its bases in America and the West Indies.

In 1572 Drake seized a gold convoy in Panama and got away with £200,000 in the money of that time. Five years later he set off on a secret mission to sail round the world with five ships.

Only one of his five ships returned, the *Golden Hind*, along with 51 of the original 160 crew. But he came back with £1.5 million of gold and silver looted from Spanish South America. He was the first Englishman to sail round the world. Elizabeth I knighted Drake. The Spaniards were furious.

In 1568 Spain's colonies, Holland and Belgium, revolted against Spanish rule. The Dutch were the most Protestant and formed the heart of what came to be called the revolt of the Netherlands. They

△ *When Roman Catholic missionaries began to work secretly they were often hidden in 'priests' holes', such as this one under a fireplace.*

looked to Queen Elizabeth for help. At first her government refused to be involved, but many Englishmen went out to fight as volunteers with the Dutch armies. Finally, in 1585, an English army under the Earl of Leicester went to help the Dutch. War between Spain and England had been declared.

THE DEATH OF MARY QUEEN OF SCOTS

All this time various plots had been made to overthrow Elizabeth and put Mary Stuart in her place. In 1587 British spies reported that Mary had taken part in a plot to assassinate the queen. Mary was found guilty and condemned to death. Reluctantly, Elizabeth signed her death warrant, and she was executed at Fotheringay Castle in Northamptonshire.

THE SPANISH ARMADA

The execution of Mary Stuart made King Philip II of Spain decide to go ahead with plans to invade and occupy England. (Philip saw himself as the champion of the Roman Catholic faith.) The Spanish fleet prepared for an expedition in 1587. But while many of its supply ships were anchored in Cadiz, Drake led his men in a surprise attack on the harbour. He destroyed 30 ships and burned warehouses full of supplies. The Spanish invasion had to be postponed.

The Spanish had decided not to invade England directly. Although their ships were carrying large numbers of troops there were not enough to ensure a successful landing. So the plan was for the troops to be escorted in convoy by Spanish galleons through the English Channel to Belgium. Here they would join forces with Spanish troops who were fighting the Dutch and Belgians. The combined force of 30,000 men would then sail to the mouth of the Thames, land near Margate and march on London.

The English had been expecting a Spanish invasion ever since the summer of 1587. But Elizabeth had always refused to spend much money on defence. The English troops fighting in Holland were months behind with their pay. There was no proper army with which to defend the south coast. However, Sir John Hawkins, who was treasurer of the navy, had managed to persuade Elizabeth to strengthen her fleet.

The English navy, under the command of an English Catholic, Lord Howard of Effingham, had several advantages over the Spanish. The English ships were better suited to the rough seas of the English Channel and the Atlantic. The Spanish ships were top-heavy, for they stood higher in the water. They were too wide for bad weather and rolled in high seas. They were designed for sailing in the calmer waters of the Mediterranean. The English sea captains, such as Drake, Martin Frobisher and Walter Raleigh, were experts at handling their faster and slimmer craft. And they were fighting in their own waters.

THE ARMADA ATTACKS ENGLAND
Nevertheless, in July 1588, 132 ships left Spain in rough seas. An English warship sighted them off Plymouth on 14th July. The warning system of beacons sprang into action. From Cornwall to York beacons on hilltops gave warning that the invasion was finally coming.

▽ *The Spanish painted crosses on the sails of the Armada ships to give the expedition the look of a Christian crusade.*

The Spanish Armada, with the wind behind it, sailed up the Channel. In the middle of the fleet the troop ships wallowed in the waves. At the rear on each side sailed the big galleons, which convoyed the troop ships. Thousands of people lined the cliffs of the Isle of Wight to watch the Armada sail by. They cheered the English ships as they twisted in and out of range of the Spanish galleons, trying to isolate Spanish ships from the main fleet and destroy them.

On the night of 22nd July the Spaniards were anchored off Calais. The English sent eight fireships in among the Spanish ships. These were old merchant ships that had been crammed with bonfires and tar barrels. They had fully loaded guns aboard, which would fire when flames

reached the gunpowder. The crews of the fireships had a dangerous job. As they sailed straight for the anchored Spanish ships, they set fire to the bonfires and hurriedly took to their boats.

The arrival of the fireships caused panic in the Spanish navy, whose ships were anchored close together in military formation. In the general confusion the commanders cut their anchors and made for the open sea.

When the next day dawned, the English sailors moved in. Fighting began and continued throughout the day. The wind was driving the Spanish ships onto the sandbanks off Gravelines and Dunkirk. The English fired again and again from their cannons, sailing close to the Spanish ships. They sank one galleon. Two others ran aground on the sand.

THE SPANISH ARE DEFEATED

Next morning the wind changed direction and drove the Armada into the North Sea. The English ships followed as far as the Scottish coast, but finally had to give up through lack of ammunition. The Spanish struggled home, sailing north of Scotland and west of the Irish coast. The storm continued, and many of the Spanish ships sank or ran aground.

Of the 132 Armada ships that set sail, 53 never returned. The war continued, though by the time of Elizabeth's death, in 1603, both of the sides were beginning to think of making peace. However, her government could not bring itself to enter into peace talks with Spain, and it was left to the new government of James I to do so. As for the sailors whose skill and courage had destroyed the Armada, many of them were dismissed without pay as soon as the fighting ended.

ELIZABETH'S STYLE OF GOVERNMENT

Elizabeth never married. She preferred to dangle the possibility of her hand in marriage to foreign royalty, so their country would remain friendly. At home, particularly in the last 15 years of her reign, she and her court became the centre of national life. She continued the medieval practice by which the court, especially in summer, when London was most plague-ridden, went 'on progress' in the countryside. She would arrive at one of her courtiers' country houses with about 600 of her household and announce she would stay with him. The visit could last a month and the expenses would cripple her courtier financially. In an age of poor communications the progress carried her name far outside London.

Elizabeth loved to be flattered. She demanded the presence of her leading men at court. Politically this was a shrewd move as she could be certain they were not plotting against her. For always hanging over both herself and her government was the dread of the succession. She had no heir and refused to appoint a successor because of her fear that she might be queen in name only. The court, with her full approval, liked to call her 'Gloriana', the glorious one.

SHAKESPEARE AND THE THEATRE

Plays became popular during Elizabeth's reign, both at court and among the people. Men, women and children flocked over the Thames to visit the Globe Theatre in south London. Here a young actor, William Shakespeare, saw his first plays performed in the 1590s. The audience sat on the stage itself. They liked to show their feelings about the plays or the actors by cheering, booing or throwing refuse.

ELIZABETH'S EXPLORERS

Elizabeth's reign also saw a number of long distance voyages which were later to prove crucial in the development of the British Empire. The war against the Spaniards in their South and Central American empire went alongside the search to discover new lands or to plant British colonies.

John Cabot's son Sebastian believed that you might reach the Spice Islands by sailing north-east round Russia, and a voyage had been made in Edward VI's reign to test his ideas. In 1553 an expedition led by Sir Henry Willoughby, with Richard Chancellor as second in command, left London to sail round northern Russia. Willoughby and all his crew were frozen to death in Lapland, but Chancellor landed at Archangel on the White Sea. He was escorted to Moscow by horse-sleigh over the ice. Here he had an interview with the Russian emperor, Tsar Ivan the Terrible, who showed great interest in trading with England. The Russians wanted English cloth and weapons; the English desired Russian furs, hemp and tallow. The Muscovy Company was later founded in London to begin the first regular trade with Russia.

During the 16th and early 17th centuries a number of sailors tried to discover a north-west passage around North America. None succeeded. During James I's reign, William Hudson and his men sailed across the huge bay in Canada which bears his name today. But they found no passage to the Pacific and had to spend the winter in Canada. In spring Hudson's men mutinied and set Hudson and his ten-year-old son adrift in an open boat with just enough food and water for two weeks. They were never seen again.

BRITISH COLONIES ABROAD

The first British colonies were founded in America in Elizabethan times. Sir Humphrey Gilbert followed up John Cabot's voyage at the end of the 15th century and claimed official possession of Newfoundland in the name of Queen Elizabeth in 1583. Two years later settlers were landed on Roanoke Island, North Carolina, by Sir Richard Grenville. The settlement was later abandoned.

THE POOR LAW

In 1601 Elizabeth's government published their Poor Law, which was to remain the basis of governments' policies towards the poor for over 200 years. Overseers were appointed in each area to help the poor. They could make each householder pay a yearly rate (a small local tax) which was to be used to help the poor. Each area was responsible only for its own poor.

The needy were divided into three groups. Those who were too old or ill to work were to be housed and looked after. Those who could work and were prepared to do so were to have work found for them by the overseers. If they could not afford to live at home, they must live in specially built workhouses. Their children would be apprenticed to local employers.

The third group were to be treated ferociously. They were people who were able to work but refused to – the 'sturdy beggars'. The act said they must be whipped "until his or her body be bloody" and put in "houses of correction".

PROBLEMS WITH PARLIAMENT

Elizabeth had such absolute authority that she could largely ignore criticism from Parliament. But she left an explosive problem for her successor.

The problem lay with the House of Commons. Despite its name, it did not represent the common people. Only one man in 30 (and no women) could vote.

MPs were rich and powerful. Some were involved in trade. Others owned land. Their great houses ruled over the local districts as the castles had done before. They owned most of the farms round them and employed the local labourers.

Elizabeth, like her father, tried to ignore the views of Parliament and call it as rarely as possible. Parliament's job was to give her advice if she asked for it and to vote her taxes unquestioningly. She would not even allow religion to be discussed in the House of Commons. Some MPs were imprisoned in the Tower simply because of their Puritan opinions. At other times, Elizabeth stopped debates in Parliament and reprimanded those she disagreed with.

Elizabeth believed that anyone who criticized her was a traitor. MPs who claimed the right of 'free speech' – the right to say what they believed to be true

▽ Elizabeth I died on 24th March 1603. Her funeral procession, with its magnificent horses drawing her coffin draped in purple velvet, must have been a splendid sight.

– were told that they could only express their opinions when the queen asked for them. But whether she liked it or not she was forced to rely to some extent on taxes which only Parliament could vote. In particular, the war with Spain was costing her government more than it could afford.

Elizabeth, shortly before she died, could only quell Parliament's criticism by calling the MPs and Lords to her and appealing to their loyalty. "Though God hath raised me high," she is reputed to have said, "yet this I count the glory of my crown, that I have reigned with your loves".

REBELLIONS AGAINST THE QUEEN
The Armada was not the only Spanish attempt to invade England. In 1596 they took advantage of the most serious Irish rebellion in the 16th century when the Irish chieftains O'Neill and O'Donnell led a rising against the English colonists and demanded Irish independence.

Elizabeth's main favourite, Essex, made peace with the chieftains and soon led a rebellion against his mistress which was to lead to his execution. Lord Mountjoy defeated the Irish and their Spanish allies, who returned home. Ireland was now quiet again, for the time being.

1603–1714

THE

STUARTS

TIME CHART

*denotes events that occurred outside Britain and Ireland.

1603	James VI of Scotland becomes James I of England and begins English Stuart line.	1649	Charles I is executed. Britain becomes a Republic. Oliver Cromwell goes on expedition to Ireland.
1604	Peace is made with Spain.		
1605	The Gunpowder Plot.	1653	Cromwell becomes Protector.
1607	Colony of Jamestown (Virginia) is founded.	1655	Jews allowed to settle again in England.
1611	Authorized (King James') version of Bible is published.	1658	Oliver Cromwell dies.
		1660	Restoration of Charles II.
1611–1621	Parliament meets for only three weeks.	1664	British acquire New York.
		1665	Great Plague.
1618	*Thirty Years' War begins in Germany.	1666	Great Fire.
		1667	Dutch burn English fleet.
1620	Pilgrim Fathers land in North America.	1670	Treaty of Dover.
		1673	Test Act.
1623	English East India Company begins trading in India.	1678	'Popish Plot'.
		1679	Habeas Corpus Act.
1625	James I dies. Charles I becomes king.	1685	Charles II dies. James II becomes king.
1628	Petition of Right is signed.	1688	'Glorious Revolution'. James flees.
1629–1640	Charles I rules without Parliament.	1689	William III and Mary II are joint rulers. Bill of Rights. Toleration Act.
1632	Strafford is Deputy in Ireland.		
1633	Laud is Archbishop of Canterbury.	1690	Battle of Boyne.
1640–1660	The Long Parliament.	1692	Massacre of Glencoe.
1641	Strafford is executed.	1701	William III dies. Anne becomes Queen. Britain enters War of Spanish Succession.
1642	Attempted arrest of Five Members.		
1642–1645	First Civil War.	1704	Battle of Blenheim. British take Gibraltar.
1643	Solemn League and Covenant.	1707	Act of Union with Scotland.
1644	Battle of Marston Moor.	1713	British make separate peace at Utrecht.
1645	New Model Army is formed. Battle of Naseby.		
		1714	Queen Anne dies. George I becomes king, starting Hanoverian line.
1648	Second Civil War.		
1648	*Thirty Years' War ends.		

STUART RULE IN ENGLAND – JAMES I

Any ruler who took over from Elizabeth was bound to face great difficulties. MPs and others, who had been prepared to wait till her death and the end of the war with Spain before making demands, would certainly not hold back afterwards. And James I, who became king at the age of 37 in 1603, made things more difficult than they need have been. He had been King of Scotland since the age of two.

THE DIVINE RIGHT OF KINGS

James believed in a theory which became known as the 'divine right of kings'. This theory stated simply that as God was the ruler of the world, the king ruled on behalf of God. Therefore a monarch could not be disobeyed, just as God could not be. He could rule as he saw fit, and his people must never criticize him.

As well as objecting to this attitude, the English disliked James I merely because he was a Scotsman. James did not make it any better by bringing with him a crowd of Scottish courtiers, greedy for positions at court and English lands.

James was as wily a politician as Elizabeth, but he never commanded the respect which she had. This was unfair, for he was often wise and far-seeing. He ended the war with Spain at the start of his reign. He hoped to make Scotland and England properly united. He arranged for the best-known English translation of the Bible – the Authorized Version or King James' Bible. Until modern times it was often the only book in many homes.

THE GUNPOWDER PLOT

In 1605 a group of Roman Catholic conspirators planned to blow up James and his ministers at the opening of Parliament on 5th November. A Catholic soldier called Guy Fawkes stacked gunpowder and firewood in the cellars of the Houses of Parliament for months. He was acting under orders from Richard Catesby and other Catholic nobles.

News of Fawkes' plot leaked out, and the conspirators were rounded up. They were horribly tortured before being executed as traitors.

△ People laughed at James I but he was a shrewder king than he seemed. One man called him "the wisest fool in Christendom."

△ *Guy Fawkes and his fellow conspirators plotted to assassinate James I. Fawkes stacked firewood and gunpowder under the Houses of Parliament. He planned to set fire to them when the king came to open Parliament.*

DISPUTES WITH PARLIAMENT

The troubles with Parliament started with James I's first Parliament in 1604 and continued until his death. Behind them lay the government's financial troubles.

The king soon ran into debt. The cost of government was rising but much of the government's income remained the same. Rents from royal lands, for instance, could only be raised when a tenant's lease ran out. Customs taxes could only be raised if Parliament agreed.

The House of Commons decided that if the king wanted more money from them he would have to put their grievances right – and give them more say in government. The conflicts that led to the outbreak of civil war in 1642 were beginning.

James' financial difficulties grew worse, partly due to the extravagance of his court and the thousands of pounds he spent on his favourites. The appointment of the extravagant Duke of Buckingham as leading minister made things worse. Parliament therefore refused to grant the taxes James demanded.

THE KING GETS HIS WAY

James replied with defiance. He and his ministers won an important victory in the Bate's Case (1606) when the judges ruled that the king was entitled to increase customs duties without the approval of Parliament. Landowners were made to become knights, whether they liked it or not, and to pay the king for the privilege.

Soon James I gave up calling Parliament altogether. Between 1611 and 1621 he called only one Parliament and that only lasted three weeks before he closed it.

James planned to make a lasting peace with Spain by marrying his heir, Charles, to a Spanish princess. The marriage would have enraged Parliament, but the plan broke down. Relations improved between James and Parliament. He agreed that monopolies were illegal. He dropped his opposition to Parliament's impeachment of his Treasurer, Lionel Cranfield. Then suddenly James died in 1625.

EXPLORERS AND SETTLERS

The success of the Spanish in finding gold in South America encouraged many British adventurers. Sir Walter Raleigh was sure a kingdom of Gold, 'El Dorado', existed in the Guiana highlands in South America. He tried to find it but failed. On his return to Britain he was executed for disobeying James I's orders not to fight the Spanish. Raleigh's execution was always held against James.

▽ *In 1620 a number of English Puritans, persecuted for their Protestant faith, set sail in the* Mayflower *in search of a new life. They landed in Cape Cod, Massachusetts. Thousands followed. The hard work and modest ways of these settlers deeply influenced American life.*

SETTLEMENTS IN NORTH AMERICA

During the 17th century, 13 separate British colonies grew up along the North American coast. By the end of the century a million colonists had settled there.

The colonies were of two very different types. Those in the north – known as New England – were dominated by their Puritan leaders. Like the Pilgrim Fathers themselves, many had fled from England because James I and Charles I had persecuted them for their Puritan beliefs. They were religious, independent and hardworking. They lived strict private lives. None of them was aristocratic and they did not believe in having different social classes as in Britain.

The southern colonies were mainly founded by large British landowners. Their great estates of cotton, sugar and tobacco were modelled on the big estates in Britain. Labourers were transported across the Atlantic free in return for signing an 'indenture', or contract, promising to work for an employer for five years or more. When the landlords or their tenant farmers found they could not attract sufficient labourers they turned to importing slaves who would do the heavy work on the plantations.

THE SLAVE TRADE

The transportation of slaves from West Africa to the West Indies had been started by Portuguese and Spanish traders in the 16th century. By the reign of Charles II English, Dutch and other European slave traders were carrying slaves from West Africa to the West Indies, and the southern American colonies. Within one hundred years more than 100,000 slaves a year were being carried across the Atlantic, half of them in British ships. It was one of the richest trades known.

△ *The first American colonists settled in the woods of New England. Their houses are made of wood, though the chimneys are made of stone. Curious Indians have crept up to the clearing to have a look at their new neighbours.*

CANADIAN SETTLEMENTS

French explorers had founded the first Canadian colonies along the St Lawrence River at Quebec and Montreal. In the reign of Charles II, British fur traders around Hudson Bay in Canada developed a profitable trade and took over a large area of land. This led to competition with France. The competition was to lead to war in the 18th century.

TRADE WITH INDIA

The East India Company had been formed in 1601 to trade with the Spice Islands of modern Indonesia. But the Dutch would not share the trade, so the English turned to the Indian trade instead. By the end of the 17th century, trade, particularly in tea and cotton, was making the East India Company one of the world's richest trading companies.

THE PARTING OF THE WAYS
(1625–1642)

Charles I accepted kingship as a duty but he never enjoyed it. Like his father, he too believed in the 'divine right of kings'. He made an alteration to his coronation oath. He swore to maintain the liberties and laws of England only in so far as they did not clash with his royal prerogative (rights).

His disagreements with Parliament began immediately. An expedition to fight the Spaniards in Holland was a disaster. Parliament blamed the government and particularly Buckingham. Charles replied that Parliament should have voted more funds for the expedition, and dismissed it.

CHARLES' CATHOLIC QUEEN
Before his next Parliament was called, in 1626, Charles I married a French princess, Henrietta Maria. She was a Roman Catholic, and the English court became a centre for Roman Catholics, many of them French. Their lifelong love is moving to recall. She and Charles were devoted to each other. But Henrietta's religious and political influence on her husband was disastrous. She encouraged him to defy Parliament and to rule as a royal dictator.

After the failure of the expedition to Holland, Buckingham planned a raid on the Spanish port of Cadiz. The sailors who landed there got drunk. The raid was another failure. The year after, Buckingham organized a raid in Brittany to give support to French Protestants in their civil war with the Catholics. It proved the third failure in three years.

Such failures cost money. Parliament refused to increase taxes, so the government ordered 'forced loans'. Taxpayers had to 'lend' the government the amounts they would have paid if Parliament had passed the taxes Charles demanded. Many influential men refused to pay. Some were jailed. When Charles called Parliament in 1628, both Houses presented him with a petition to sign.

THE PETITION OF RIGHT
This petition, the Petition of Right, is one of the foundations of Britain's liberties. Its first two clauses were the vital ones:

1. No man should be forced to pay a tax which has not been passed by Act of Parliament.
2. No man can be imprisoned without a reason which has been clearly shown.

The king accepted the Petition of Right, but it made little difference to his behaviour. When Buckingham was severely criticized by the House of Commons, Charles dismissed the MPs.

After more disputes with Parliament in 1629, Charles dismissed both Houses. From 1629 to 1640 he ruled without once calling Parliament. During those 11 years he governed by himself with a small group of ministers. His Treasurer, Sir Richard Weston, was so successful at finding methods of taxation which did not involve Parliament that by 1635 Charles was no longer short of money.

ARCHBISHOP LAUD

Another statesman on whom Charles I relied was his Archbishop of Canterbury, William Laud. He and Charles believed that the Church should use every means to teach people about the Christian faith, just as the medieval Church had done. Stained glass, images, statues and music were encouraged. Laud aimed to stop all Puritan influence in his church. Because of his persecution some Puritans emigrated to the colonies in North America. But those who remained behind in England became more and more certain that at some point they would have to stand up to Charles and defend their beliefs.

STRAFFORD AND IRELAND

The most powerful of Charles' ministers was a wealthy Yorkshire landowner, Thomas Wentworth, who later became Earl of Strafford. In 1633 he was appointed Lord Deputy of Ireland.

By 1633 English government in Ireland had become thoroughly corrupt. It did not even provide Charles with much money. Strafford was determined to 'clean up' the English government in Ireland and make the colony profitable. He ensured that the rich paid more tax. He improved roads and bridges, helped the Irish industries producing woollen and linen cloth, and encouraged the breeding of horses by the Irish, for which they became famous.

Strafford also began a 'plantation' scheme, which the governments of Oliver Cromwell and William of Orange were later to follow. In the northwest – Sligo, Mayo and Galway – he expelled Roman Catholic landlords and 'planted' loyal Protestant English in their place. These policies made Strafford hated by the Irish and feared by MPs in England.

WAR WITH SCOTLAND

Charles I's personal government was at last brought to an end by the Scottish war. The ruling group in Scotland were Puritans who belonged to the Presbyterian Church. Many of their services were written by the most respected of their early leaders, John Knox. When Charles ordered that clergymen in Scottish churches should use the English prayer book, a defiant Scottish army was raised. They were known as the Covenanters, as they covenanted (promised) to end Charles I's religious changes.

Charles marched north to face the Scottish forces. He called on his English subjects to elect a new Parliament, which would pass taxes to pay for a war.

Parliament met in the spring of 1640, but lasted only a few weeks before Charles dismissed it. That summer the Scots occupied Newcastle. The king had no army capable of defeating them. He entered into peace talks in which the Scottish leaders demanded the removal of Strafford and Laud from Charles' council. From now on the Scots and the MPs who opposed the king worked closely together. Charles was forced to call another Parliament in the autumn of 1640. It was to meet on and off for the next 20 years and to earn the title 'the Long Parliament'. As soon as it met, its leader John Pym introduced a bill accusing Strafford of treason. Charles signed the death warrant and Strafford was executed. Charles was to blame himself for the rest of his life.

PARLIAMENT GETS ITS WAY

Throughout the summer of 1641 Pym and his supporters made the most of the advantage they had gained. Acts were passed which ordered that Parliament must meet at least once every three years and could not be dismissed without its own agreement. Parliament was to have control of customs duties. The king signed them all in a daze. Archbishop Laud was imprisoned, and later executed.

But not all MPs supported Pym. Many disagreed when he proposed to abolish bishops. Then Parliament demanded the right to control the army being raised to suppress an uprising in Ireland. Soon it claimed the right to appoint the king's council of ministers. Half of Parliament thought Pym was going too far.

▽ *This famous picture, by the Dutch portrait painter van Dyck, depicts King Charles I from three different angles.*

Charles decided he would give up no more of his power. On 3rd January 1642 his Attorney accused five leading MPs, including Pym, of high treason. Next day Charles I, urged on by the queen, marched down to the Commons with 400 guards. He demanded that the five members be handed over. No previous king had ever entered the House of Commons. But news of his plan had been 'leaked' and the MPs had left the House earlier.

Charles' failure to seize the five MPs made civil war inevitable. The queen fled abroad with her children. Parliament and the king began to organize their armies. On 22nd August 1642 Charles raised the royal standard at Nottingham. He called on his subjects to bear arms in his defence.

THE CIVIL WARS

The Civil Wars of 1642–1645 and 1648 involved a tiny proportion of the population. Yet both sides knew they were fighting to resolve one question: 'Who is to rule the country – king or Parliament?'

Both sides had solid support. The king could rely on the great landowners, Oxford University and the church leaders. Parliament had most followers in London, and the support of the Puritans. Both sides knew they would win if they could get the Scottish armies to fight for them.

CHARLES MARCHES ON LONDON
Parliament had control of London, so the Royalists had to recapture it quickly. Charles marched on London in the autumn of 1642 and Parliament's men marched out to meet him. They met at Edgehill near Warwick. After the battle no side could claim victory. Charles went on to London but was checked at Turnham Green. He spent the winter in Oxford. In 1643 his men tried again to march on London but were stopped at Newbury.

One of the Parliamentarians at Edgehill was the MP for Cambridge, Oliver Cromwell. He took no part in the battle, but watched it closely. He decided that the Parliamentarians needed a better army, so

▽ In 1645 the Parliamentarians confronted the Royalists at the Battle of Naseby. The Royalists were thoroughly beaten and peace talks began.

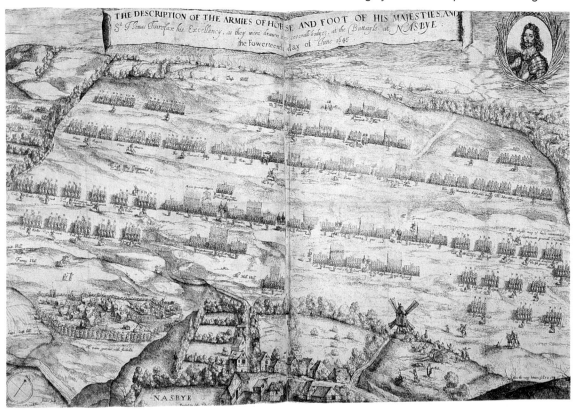

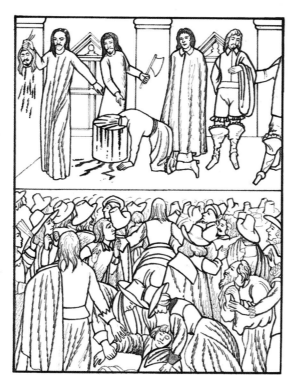

△ *Charles I's execution took place on a bitterly cold day. Charles wore two shirts to avoid shivering and appearing frightened. His dignity impressed the crowd, some of whom fainted.*

he went home to East Anglia to see if he could produce one. Within a year, his new Eastern Association had 15,000 well-disciplined men, led by Sir Thomas Fairfax, the Earl of Manchester, and Cromwell himself. Cromwell's cavalrymen developed into a formidable fighting force.

THE SCOTS ENTER THE WAR

During the winter John Pym completed an agreement with the Scots, known as the Solemn League and Covenant of 1643. The Scots agreed to enter the war on Parliament's side. Next summer Scottish armies marched on York. They fought the Royalists at Marston Moor on 2nd July 1644. The result was a complete victory for the Scottish and Parliamentary armies.

In the winter of 1644–1645 Cromwell and Fairfax ousted the faction in Parliament who wanted peace. They formed a new army called the New Model Army. It was the first national rather than local army – professional, disciplined, regularly paid and uniformed. Many of the men were deeply convinced Puritans.

On 14th June 1645 the king's forces met Parliament's New Model Army at Naseby in Leicestershire. The Royalist forces, outnumbered and ill-equipped, were utterly defeated. The first Civil War was over and peace talks began. But little progress was made, for the king refused to surrender any of his power. And though Parliament favoured a settlement, the Army's leaders were adamant. They would not compromise over the religious and political principles for which they had fought, and they did not trust Charles.

THE SECOND CIVIL WAR

In 1648 Charles I escaped from Hampton Court, where the Army held him under house arrest, and took refuge in Carisbrooke Castle on the Isle of Wight. Here he made a secret pact with the Scots. When Cromwell heard this the second Civil War, of 1648, started. It did not last long. The Scots were defeated by the New Model Army at Preston. Royalist risings in Kent and Essex were easily suppressed.

On 20th January 1649, Charles I was tried for treason and found guilty. On 30th January he was executed on a scaffold outside Whitehall Palace. A man who saw the axe fall wrote that he would always remember the sound that broke from the watching crowd:

"Such a groan as I never heard before, and desire I may never hear again."[7]

CROMWELL AND THE COMMONWEALTH (1649–1660)

After Charles I's death, Britain became a republic, a country without a king. Those MPs who hadn't been expelled by the Army leaders became known as the 'Rump' Parliament. The Rump abolished the House of Lords and declared Britain a 'Commonwealth'. No attempt was made to hold new elections.

The Commonwealth had many enemies. France, Spain and Holland declared war on Britain. Royalist warships roamed the Mediterranean and the Atlantic, hunting Commonwealth ships. The Scots were at war with the new government; the Irish had risen against it.

At home those MPs who had been expelled by the Army plotted revenge, as did the Royalists. Popular groups in the Army such as the Levellers, who wanted all men to have the vote, were suppressed. Democratic ideas were scarcely heard in Britain again for the next 150 years.

CROMWELL IN IRELAND

Cromwell was now accepted in practice as the most powerful man in Britain. In the summer of 1649 he led the New Model Army's expedition to suppress the Irish. Ireland had raised savage rebellions against the hated English settlers since Strafford's time as Lord Deputy of Ireland had ended in 1639. The Commonwealth decided to send an army to Ireland to restore order and to take revenge.

In a swift and ruthless campaign, Cromwell completely suppressed the rebellion there. The methods he used were to make his name still hated in Ireland today. As a result of them one third of the Irish population died. From that time onwards the Irish never stopped hating English occupation of their country and looking for ways to become independent.

Strafford's policy of 'plantation' had tried to replace Roman Catholic landowners in Ireland with English Protestants. Cromwell's government in Ireland continued this policy. Two thirds of Irish lands were confiscated and given to English landowners and farmers. Cromwell thought the gift of an Irish farm was a good way to reward his Puritan soldiers. It also had the advantage of being cheap. Irish landowners were banished to Connaught. Roman Catholic worship was now forbidden. Priests were killed or transported to colonies, when they could be found. They went into hiding, and secret services were held in the fields.

CROMWELL SHOWS HIS STRENGTH

In 1650 Cromwell defeated the Scottish army at Dunbar. In 1651 he won a total victory against Prince Charles' army at Worcester. Charles, the 20-year-old son of Charles I, fled into exile in France. Cromwell returned to London in triumph. A grateful Parliament gave him Hampton Court to live in.

By the end of 1652, France and Spain were suing for peace, though the Dutch were still at war with the Commonwealth. The Irish rebellion had been suppressed, the Scots defeated.

△ This contemporary engraving shows Cromwell expelling the Rump Parliament. The Speaker is surrounded by soldiers. Written on the wall is "This house is to let".

CROMWELL EXPELS THE RUMP

Many Puritans and soldiers now wanted Cromwell to take action against the Rump Parliament. The Rump had said it would reform the Church and the law, and seek peace with the Dutch. Nothing had been done and taxes were high. Above all MPs seemed curiously reluctant to call an election to choose a new Parliament.

In April 1653 Cromwell, who was an MP as well as Army Commander, could stand it no longer. He marched down to the Parliament building, turned out the Speaker from his chair and ejected the MPs. So ended the rule of Parliament.

PROTECTOR CROMWELL (1653–1658)

After Cromwell had dismissed the Rump Parliament, he was not sure what to do next. He was reluctant to become a military dictator. For a few months, Britain was ruled by a new Parliament, elected by members of the Puritan churches. They planned to change the Church of England and the legal system totally. They even proposed that Army leaders should set an example to the country by serving for a year without pay. Such proposals horrified the Army leaders and divided the MPs themselves. In December the new Parliament surrendered its power voluntarily.

In 1653 Cromwell was declared Lord Protector and held the position until his death five years later. His rule was known as the Protectorate.

Cromwell treated his Royalist opponents generously. He allowed local church congregations to elect their own clergymen and leaders. Christians of different beliefs, including Roman Catholics, were tolerated in England, though members of the Church of England were not allowed to use their traditional services. Cromwell also permitted Jews to live in Britain for the first time in 350 years.

Parliaments were called during the Protectorate, though Cromwell dismissed them in much the same way as Charles I had done. At one point Parliament even urged him to become king himself – its views had altered strangely since Charles' time. But Cromwell would have none of it.

The most unpopular thing about Cromwell's Protectorate was that he tried to make people obey 'godly' – in other words Puritan – laws. Swearing, drunkenness and cockfighting could be punished by death, though in fact no one was ever convicted. Sunday was strictly observed. No shops or public houses could open, and no work could be done.

Many justices of the peace disagreed with these laws and did not enforce them. In desperation Cromwell decided to divide the country up into districts. Each was to be supervised by a major-general, who would enforce the 'godly' laws. Cromwell soon abandoned the idea.

Although the Army was gradually reduced in size, taxes remained high, chiefly to pay for Britain's defences.

Britain's military power under Cromwell came to be feared on the Continent. Peace was made with Holland on good terms. Jamaica, in the West Indies, became a British colony. In 1658, one hundred years after Mary Tudor's loss of Calais, the Army won Dunkirk from the Spanish.

THE END OF THE PROTECTORATE

On 3rd September 1658 Cromwell died. At the time of his death his power as Lord Protector was unchallenged. The Royalists had given up all hope of overthrowing his government. Prince Charles was still in exile, wandering from one European country to another and permanently bankrupt. Yet within 18 months the Protectorate system fell apart.

Oliver Cromwell's son Richard was neither well respected by the Army nor well liked by Parliament. He became Protector on his father's death, but by the spring of 1659 he had resigned.

After that there were further rapid changes of government. The Rump was restored. Then the Army disbanded it again. The Army itself split up into separate sections led by Generals Lambert, Fleetwood and Monk. Finally General Monk, who was in charge of the forces that were occupying Scotland, marched his soldiers down to London, which he took over in early 1660.

Monk was a professional soldier and, unlike earlier leaders of the New Model Army, he did not want the Army to be permanently involved in governing the country. He therefore organized new Parliamentary elections.

The new Parliament issued an invitation to Prince Charles, who was in Holland, to return to his kingdom. Charles showed no signs of behaving like his father. He promised to be tolerant in religion and to share political power with Parliament. In May 1660 he landed at Dover, knelt down and kissed the stony beach. Looking around him at the cheering crowds, Charles was heard to wonder why, if he was so popular, he need ever have gone on his travels in the first place.

THE MONARCHY RESTORED – CHARLES II (1660–1685)

Shortly before he returned to England to become Charles II, Prince Charles had issued a statement of his policies. He made it clear that he did not plan a return to the 1630s, when Charles I had ruled without Parliament. Taxes had to be raised through Parliament. Parliament could not be dismissed except with its own consent. Charles was happy to work with Parliament. The elections of 1660 had produced a large majority of Royalist MPs. The House of Lords was restored, along with the Church.

REVENGE AND PARDONS

At first things went smoothly. Charles, who did not bear grudges against his opponents, announced that he would offer them a general pardon. Parliament was not so generous. It proposed the execution

△ Many Londoners preferred to travel by boat rather than along the crowded streets. Great houses had their own riverside quays, and boatmen offered a taxi service.

of all those who had signed Charles I's death warrant (the Regicides). Twenty-eight men were to meet a traitor's death by hanging, drawing and quartering. Ten of them did so. Charles reprieved the remainder. The New Model Army was paid off and disbanded.

The religious differences remained. Roman Catholics were persecuted, though Charles tried to help them.

In 1661 Parliament passed the Corporation Act, which said that all members of town councils had to take Holy Communion in the Church of England. Parliament tried to make the lives of Puritan clergy difficult by saying they could not live within five miles of a town. The Society of Friends (Quakers) were cruelly persecuted.

Soon the king and Parliament were arguing over taxes. Charles said he needed a minimum payment of £1,200,000 a year to govern the state during peace time. Parliament rarely gave him as much as £800,000 a year.

WAR WITH HOLLAND

In 1664 the country drifted into another war with the Dutch. They were rivals over the slave trade from west Africa, and over colonies in North America.

One of the most humiliating events in English history occurred in 1667. The Dutch sailed up the Thames estuary and turned south into the River Medway. They brushed aside what defences there were, broke the chain across the entrance to

Chatham harbour and sailed in. They attached their tow lines to the royal flagship, the *Royal Charles*. They then set sail for Holland, where they moored the flagship off Amsterdam.

Soon afterwards the Treaty of Breda was signed between England and Holland. The English gained the Dutch colonies at the mouth of the Hudson River in North America. New Amsterdam became New York, named after Charles II's brother, James, the Duke of York.

After the disgrace of the *Royal Charles*, the king decided that things must change. He dismissed his chief adviser, the Earl of Clarendon, who had served him loyally.

A DEAL WITH FRANCE
Using his sister Henrietta, who was married to a French duke, as a go-between, Charles made a secret treaty at Dover with the French king, Louis XIV. The French agreed to give Charles money, and even, if necessary, French troops with which to suppress any trouble in Britain. In return Charles would cancel the laws against English Roman Catholics without consulting Parliament and help France in their planned invasion of Holland.

When news of the secret terms leaked out there was uproar in London. English prejudices against Roman Catholics and

△ *In 1667 Dutch ships sailed up the Medway and attacked the British fleet as it lay at anchor. To add to the humiliation, they also towed away the royal flagship and took it back to Holland.*

the French blazed up all over again. Had not Guy Fawkes and his treacherous cronies tried to blow up Parliament and did not all loyal Englishmen remember their crimes every 5th November? Were not rumours circulating that French spies had started the Plague by poison and had planned the Great Fire of London? In 1672 Charles dismissed Parliament and abolished the laws against Roman Catholics. People feared that the king was about to become a Roman Catholic dictator, like Louis XIV in France.

CHARLES GIVES IN
But Charles II was not Charles I. Faced with such determined opposition, he reinstated the laws against Roman Catholics and recalled Parliament. He even signed the Test Act in 1673, which decreed that no man, unless he was a member of the Church of England, could hold any position in the government of the country or even attend university.

From 1673 to 1678 Charles II co-operated with Parliament. He agreed to the marriage of the Duke of York's daughter by his first marriage, Mary, to William of Orange, the Dutch king, who was now regarded as the 'Protestant champion' of Europe. Then suddenly both king and Parliament were caught up in the explosion of the 'Popish Plot'.

THE POPISH PLOT

For several years two men, Titus Oates and Israel Tonge, had been trying to convince anyone who would listen that a Catholic group at court was plotting with the French to overthrow the king and Parliament and put James, Duke of York, on the throne. (Charles II and his wife, Catherine, had no children.) Then James, a Catholic, would rule without Parliament and force everybody to become Roman Catholics. But nobody took the two men seriously because of their untrustworthy characters. Finally, in the autumn of 1678, Oates and Tonge were called in front of the Privy Council and cross-examined.

Charles himself questioned Oates and caught him out in some lies. This convinced him that nothing Oates said was true. But the council was not so sure.

Then one of London's best-known magistrates, Sir Edmund Berry Godfrey, who had been hearing Oates' accusations, was murdered. It was said that Catholics were responsible. Within a few days London was swept with waves of anti-Catholic hysteria. Lord Chief Justice Scroggs, urged on by the Commons, sentenced 21 Catholics to death.

Parliament gave Oates the title 'Saviour of the Nation', along with apartments in Whitehall, a salary of £1200 a year and an armed bodyguard. The capital buzzed with reports of French spies and of French troops secretly landing in the Thames estuary to advance on London.

SHAFTESBURY TESTS HIS POWER

The government was now dominated by the Earl of Shaftesbury. He believed passionately in a strong Parliament. He demanded that the Duke of York be removed from Charles' government, and excluded from ever becoming king.

At this point, Charles II took his stand. He said James was his only rightful heir. He dismissed Parliament and called for new elections. Charles' supporters were called Tories. Those who followed Shaftesbury were known as the Whigs.

In 1680 London raged. Innocent men, chiefly Catholics, were executed for treason. Crowds marched through London, carrying images of the pope. Charles waited for Shaftesbury to go too far. This he did when he named Charles' illegitimate son, the Duke of Monmouth, as the next king. The new Parliament proposed a bill to exclude James from the succession, and Charles returned to his father's ways. He dismissed Parliament.

THE END OF CHARLES' REIGN

For the last four years of his reign Charles ruled without Parliament. He had timed its dismissal shrewdly. The day after he dismissed it money from Louis XIV arrived. Overseas trade was thriving and customs duties provided sufficient taxes for Charles to rule England, with secret French money, for the next few years. Shaftesbury and Monmouth fled abroad. It was left to James, when he became king, to take revenge on Titus Oates. He was twice whipped through the streets of London, and then imprisoned.

In 1685 Charles II died. He had outwitted his enemies and died peacefully (a last-minute convert to the Roman Catholic faith) in his bed.

THE GREAT PLAGUE OF 1665

During Charles II's reign England's capital city suffered two disasters. The first was the Great Plague. London had not changed basically since the Black Death, though it had grown much bigger. (Its population was half a million, compared with 350,000 in Paris and 25,000 in York.) The roads were just as narrow, overhung and filthy as they had been in medieval times. The water supply was just as scarce. The fleas which spread the plague were now more plentiful, for the black rats who carried them came in the holds of ships trading from Europe, and London had become the largest trading port in northern Europe.

The total death toll from the Great Plague is believed to have been about 70,000, though nobody can be certain. Many other parts of England were

▽ *This engraving shows the Fire of London as seen from Southwark, south of the Thames. St Paul's was destroyed but the Tower of London, near Samuel Pepys' house, was spared.*

stricken, but London's suffering was the worst. Such plagues never returned to England. Streets became wider, lighter and cleaner. The water supply was improved. Most importantly, brown rats migrated to Britain and drove out the black rats who spread the plague.

We know many details about the Great Plague of 1665 because of an eyewitness account – the diary of the civil servant, courtier, man-about-London and gossip, Samuel Pepys. Pepys' diary also provides information about the other event that devastated parts of the capital – the Fire of London.

THE FIRE OF LONDON

Fires were part of town life. The only hope of putting out a fire in crowded streets of wooden houses, many of which were still thatched, was to detect it early. Fire-fighting equipment consisted of pumps, tanks and buckets. Once fire caught hold of a house, the only way to prevent it spreading was by blowing up all the houses round about with gunpowder.

In September 1666 a fire began in a baker's shop in Pudding Lane to the east of London Bridge and spread with appalling speed. It had been a hot summer and the flames were spread by high wind.

On 4th September St Paul's Cathedral, which had towered over the capital for centuries, became engulfed by the flames. The lead from the roof streamed down dangerously and the building was completely destroyed.

About five-sixths of the old city were destroyed in the Great Fire: 13,000 houses were burned and 100,000 people made homeless. The capital was quickly rebuilt, though now in brick and stone. There were more tiles on the roofs, and wider streets. The new city had drains in it and a system of refuse collection. Water was now piped from the Thames to the streets through wooden pipes. Fire plugs set into the pipes could be opened with a key which was kept by the parish officer, and water would then – it was hoped – gush out. In future London was to experience many serious fires, but none of them were as bad as the Great Fire.

ADVANCES IN THE SCIENCES

Charles II's reign also saw some important developments in science. At the height of the Civil Wars, a group of men interested in mathematics and the sciences organized weekly meetings to discuss matters connected with their subjects. After the Restoration they made their headquarters in the capital. In 1662 Charles, who was interested in the sciences, gave them a royal charter. They were called The 'Royal Society of London for the advancement of Natural Knowledge'. The 'Royal Society' is still one of the most distinguished scientific societies in the world.

Probably its most famous president was the great mathematician Sir Isaac Newton, who presided over the Society's meetings from 1703 to 1727. Newton's theory of gravity became the basis of modern physics and of people's ideas about the universe. He also taught scientists the importance of the scientific method – that every scientific theory has to be proved before it can be treated seriously.

Other scientists who altered whole ways of thinking were William Harvey (physician to Charles I), who discovered how the blood circulates round the body, Robert Boyle, who became known as 'the Father of Chemistry', and the astronomer Edmund Halley.

THE END OF STUART RULE

The new king was James II. His reign opened with a meeting of Parliament in 1685. The MPs showed their confidence in the king, although he was a Roman Catholic, by letting him have all the money from customs to spend as he wished for the rest of his life. Customs duties formed a large proportion of the taxes that were needed to govern the country. No Stuart king had ever been in so strong a position.

MONMOUTH'S REBELLION

A few months later, the Duke of Monmouth landed in Dorset to lead a rebellion against James. James' army had little difficulty in defeating Monmouth's troops – many of whom were armed only with scythes and pikes – at the battle of Sedgemoor. Monmouth was beheaded and 150 supporters were hanged. Eight hundred more were transported to the colonies as slaves.

TROUBLE WITH PARLIAMENT

James' easy victory made him too sure of himself. He immediately asked Parliament to give him special sums of money to pay for his victorious army of 20,000 men, who were now camped on Hounslow Heath outside London. He had to keep them stationed there, he said, in case other rebels followed Monmouth. He also proposed the immediate repeal of the Test Act. Parliament had seemed likely to give James little trouble, but it turned down both of his suggestions. He therefore dismissed it. Parliament was never to meet again during his reign.

JAMES RULES ALONE

The king then set out on the familiar Stuart road of government by king alone. He ignored the Test Act. He began steadily to increase the number of Catholics in important positions both in government and the army.

James knew that Puritans had been as unfairly treated by the governments of Charles I and Charles II as Catholics. He wanted to help. In return, he hoped for their support if it was needed. In 1687 all acts which harmed either English Catholics or Puritans were cancelled. By 1688 three-quarters of the local justices of the peace – the magistrates who governed in the towns and villages – had been dismissed. In their place Catholic and Puritan justices were appointed.

RESENTMENT GROWS

These actions horrified the local squires and merchants who were the day-to-day rulers of the country. James was radically altering the country's government and religion without consulting Parliament. Once again people feared the king was becoming a dictator.

Seven leading bishops in the Church of England attacked James' policies and were put on trial. They were found not guilty.

AN HEIR IS BORN

Shortly before the verdict in the bishops' trial, James' second wife, Mary of Modena, gave birth to a baby boy. She and James had been married for 15 years without having children, and it was assumed they would never have any. For

△ *Everyone who hoped to be noticed at court or in high society in the 17th century had to be sure to dress in the latest fashion.*

this reason, many influential men who feared James' policies had been quietly waiting for his death. They were confident his daughter by his first marriage, Mary, with her 'Protestant champion' husband, William of Orange, would then take over.

But now all that was changed. With the birth of a Catholic male heir, England might be ruled by Roman Catholic dictator-kings for ever. To prevent this happening a group of leading Englishmen therefore wrote to William of Orange in Holland and asked him to invade Britain.

WILLIAM AND MARY RULE ENGLAND

On 5th November 1688 William landed at Torbay in Devon with an army of 24,000 men. James was deserted by his Commander in Chief, John Churchill (later the Duke of Marlborough), and by his second daughter by his first marriage, Anne. James fled to France and was never seen again in England.

After James' flight, William and Mary were declared joint rulers. During their reign (William III was king from 1689 to 1701, but Mary II died in 1694) a series of Acts were passed, which were known as the Revolution Settlement. Between them they established by law a number of important rights.

THE REVOLUTION SETTLEMENT

One of the most important of these acts, the Habeas Corpus Act, had first been passed in Charles II's time in 1679. Kings and queens had for centuries imprisoned their enemies without trial if they did not have enough evidence to charge them with any crime. They often left them in prison for years. Under the act – *habeas corpus* means 'you must have the body' – people had to be arrested by a warrant giving reasons for their arrest. Moreover, they must then quickly be brought to trial.

The Bill of Rights (1689) laid down that no Catholic could become king or queen of Britain. Nor could a British king or queen marry a Catholic. The bill also said that future monarchs must not simply ignore the law and claim to be above it, as James II had done. They must obey the law, like everyone else. Nor were they to raise taxes without Parliament's consent.

The Mutiny Act (1689) decreed that Parliament had to decide every year whether or not to go on keeping an army in peace time.

Under the Toleration Act (1689), Puritans were free to worship as they chose, though neither Puritans nor Roman Catholics could be appointed to hold responsible positions in government or attend universities. Catholics were still not allowed to worship freely, although in practice the authorities left them alone.

By the Act of Settlement (1701) judges could not in practice be dismissed. In 1695 the royal power of press censorship was quietly dropped.

These acts ended a battle for power that had begun in Tudor times. Kings could no longer rule as they liked. They could now only govern if Parliament agreed with their policies.

REBELLION IN IRELAND

In 1689 James II landed in Ireland with a French army, calling on the Roman Catholic Irish to rebel in support of him. Not surprisingly, many of them did so. James' combined army of Frenchmen and Irishmen then besieged the Protestant garrison at Londonderry. The siege lasted 105 days and during that time 15,000 men, women and children starved to death before the English fleet came to their rescue. But the next year, William himself landed in Ireland. At the battle of the Boyne, James' forces were utterly defeated. James then fled back to France where, in 1701, he died.

The treatment of the Irish by their English conquerors now grew even worse. Half a million hectares of land belonging to Catholics – particularly in Ulster in the north – were confiscated and given to Protestant English or Scots as a reward for their services to William of Orange. Ever since, the descendants of these 'planters' have been known as Orangemen. Roman Catholic priests were still forbidden to hold services or go about their duties and no Catholic could carry arms, teach in an Irish school or serve as town councillors. The majority of the Irish, who were Catholics, remained second class citizens in their own country.

WAR WITH FRANCE

William III's life work was to defend his native Holland against Louis XIV's France. Over and over again, the French, who had the greatest army in Europe, threatened to overrun Holland. But they never managed to do so, any more than the Spanish before them. In taking over the British crown, William had gained the support of the British army and navy in

△ *Queen Anne was the younger daughter of James II and his first wife, Anne Hyde. She had 15 children, 14 of whom died in infancy, and one aged 11. She was the last of the Stuarts.*

his battle against France. From 1689 to 1697 British troops fought alongside the Dutch, while British and French ships clashed in the Channel.

QUEEN ANNE'S REIGN

After William's death in 1701, James II's younger daughter, Anne, carried on the wars against France. Under her great general, the Duke of Marlborough, British armies won a number of victories against France, of which the battle of Blenheim, in 1704, was the most remarkable. Britain even seized a piece of European territory – the rock of Gibraltar – which it took from Spain and has held ever since.

But the war in Europe known as the War of the Spanish Succession dragged on. Though Marlborough with his international army won several battles, such as Ramillies (1706), which led to the capture of Antwerp from the French; and Oudenarde (1708), which led to the fall of Lille, the first French base to fall, there was no sign of French national defeat. After the last great victory at Malplaquet (1709) the path to the invasion of France seemed clear. It never came. The countries that had combined together to fight French power in Europe had no wish, now that France had been checked, to invade and occupy her.

The Whigs, the British political party which had been waging the war, lost the general election of 1709. The victorious Tories withdrew the British armies from the continental alliance and dismissed Marlborough. They made a separate peace with the French at the Treaty of Utrecht. The British gained some French colonies in North America, including those around the Hudson Bay with its valuable fur-trapping trade. Spain gave them the monopoly right to trade slaves with South America. The British kept Gibraltar.

Holland was saved from occupation by the French, but had exhausted itself in the long struggle for national survival. During William and Anne's reigns British overseas trade had increased while Holland's had declined. In the 18th century Britain was to be unchallenged as the greatest European trading power.

Queen Anne died childless in 1714, and George – who was Elector (king) of a German state, Hanover – was the next in line. He was James I's great-grandson and a Protestant. He was 54 and could not speak English when he took the throne.

1700–1801
THE EIGHTEENTH CENTURY

TIME CHART

*denotes events that occurred outside Britain and Ireland.

1700 onwards	Root crops used in farming.
1707	Act of Union with Scotland.
1713	Treaty of Utrecht
1714	Queen Anne dies. George I becomes king and starts Hanoverian line.
1715	Jacobite Rebellion in Scotland (the Fifteen).
1720	South Sea Bubble.
1721–1742	Walpole is main (Prime) Minister.
1727	George I dies. George II becomes king.
1731	Jethro Tull publishes Horse-Hoeing Husbandry.
1733	Kay invents Flying Shuttle.
1738	John Wesley starts Methodist revival of Christianity.
1740 onwards	Bakewell pioneers better stock breeding.
1740–1748	*War of Austrian Succession.
1745	Jacobite Rebellion in Scotland (the Forty-Five).
1746	Battle of Culloden. Highland Clearances begin.
1750–1800	Private Enclosure Acts enclose most land in southern England and the Midlands.
1753	First national race meeting is held at Newmarket.
1755	Dr Johnson publishes the first English dictionary.
1756–1763	Seven Years' War.
1757	*Battle of Plassey. British gain control of Bengal, India.
1759	*Battle of Quebec. British gain control of Canada.
1760	Watt develops steam engine.
1760 onwards	Turnpike Trusts improve roads.
1760	George II dies. George III becomes king.
1763	*Treaty of Paris.
1764	Brindley completes his Bridgewater canal in Lancashire.
1768–1771	*Cook surveys coasts of New Zealand and eastern Australia.
1771	Arkwright opens his cotton-spinning factory at Cromford, near Derby.
1773	*Boston Tea Party.
1776	*13 North American colonies declare independence from Britain.
1779	First cast-iron bridge completed at Coalbrookdale.
1780	Gordon Riots.
1781	*Battle of Yorktown.
1783	*American colonies secure independence.
1789	*George Washington becomes first President of United States. French Revolution starts.
1793	*French king and queen are executed.
1793–1802	British join Revolutionary Wars against France.
1796	Jenner develops vaccination against smallpox.
1797	Naval mutiny.
1798	Irish Rebellion.
1801	Act of Union with Ireland.

SCOTLAND

English governments had been afraid for centuries that the Scots would take advantage of an English war with France to attempt an invasion of England. At the height of the Spanish Succession War the fear of invasion became even stronger and led to the union of England and Scotland. But even when the Act of Union was signed in 1707, many people doubted that it would last for long.

Under the act, customs barriers between the two countries were removed and there was to be a common currency. The Scottish parliament at Edinburgh was closed and Scottish MPs sat in the House of Commons at Westminster. But the Presbyterian Church of Scotland remained the national church, with Queen Anne at its head. Scottish law continued to apply in Scotland, as it does today.

JACOBITE RISINGS

Many Scots refused to accept George I as their king and rebelled in support of James II's son James Edward, who was known as the 'Old Pretender'.

The first of these Jacobite risings – Jacobus is Latin for James – occurred in 1715, and is known as the Fifteen. It was suppressed fairly easily. English Jacobites were defeated at Preston. James Edward's son Charles (known as the Young Pretender or 'Bonnie Prince Charlie') led a much more formidable rising in 1745 (the Forty-Five). He captured Edinburgh, and his troops reached as far south as Derby. He then retreated into Scotland, where the Scottish defeat at the battle of Culloden finally ended the rebellion.

THE HIGHLAND CLEARANCES

The British government was determined to teach the Highlanders a lesson. For three months British troops, led by George II's third son, the Duke of Cumberland (known as the 'Butcher' in Scotland), hunted fleeing Jacobites through the Highlands. (Charles fled abroad and died in 1788.) They shot prisoners, burned villages and tortured suspects.

The government then introduced changes which attacked the clan system. Highland chieftains were similar to feudal barons, kings of their own districts. Now the chieftains were banned from holding their own courts of law and from raising their own private armies of clansmen. The king's judges and sheriffs implemented Scottish law in the Highlands. English was taught in Scottish schools. The wearing of the kilt and tartans was forbidden. The Highlands were opened up by the building of modern roads.

The 'clearances' of the Highlands were also caused by Scottish landlords, known as 'lairds', who wanted to improve their farms by introducing modern agricultural methods. They were unable to do this on the tiny rents they received from their tenants. Much the most profitable way of using the Highland estates was by sheep-farming, which employs few men. So the lairds began to evict their tenants, and employed fewer labourers. Some of those who were evicted found employment in the new iron, coal and cotton industries which developed in southern Scotland. Many left Scotland to start a new life in a British colony overseas.

AGRICULTURAL AND ECONOMIC CHANGES

Britain was ruled during the 18th century by its country gentlemen and rich merchants. The typical image of 18th-century Britain was the great house. Great country houses were worlds of their own. Local farmers paid their rents to the noblemen or their bailiffs. On the noble's own farms – the home farms – the latest agricultural methods were tried out.

NEW FARMING METHODS

In the medieval three-field system one field was always left fallow (unfarmed) every three years. Thus the goodness was restored to the field. For a long time, however, people had been trying to think of ways to avoid such a waste of productive land.

In 1731 Jethro Tull published *The New Horse-Hoeing Husbandry*. In this book he described methods which made a fallow period unnecessary. He invented a horse-drawn hoe which penetrated deeply into the ground while crops were growing, so the roots were kept moist and the weeds destroyed. He also invented the horse-drawn seed-drill. Seeds were sown in straight lines and covered up. This meant land between the rows could be hoed, and the seeds were protected from birds.

The Dutch had started to use root crops, such as swedes and turnips. These could be grown on land which would otherwise have been left fallow, because they restored fertility to the soil. Root crops could be stored in the winter and fed to the animals. It was no longer necessary to slaughter the animals at Christmas time. An 18th-century Foreign Secretary, Lord Townsend, particularly encouraged his farmers to use root crops, and earned the nickname 'Turnip Townsend'.

The supply of winter food made the careful breeding of animals possible. Robert Bakewell was one of the first to breed better sheep and cattle. Soon farmers produced much heavier animals, and sheep with much thicker fleeces.

ENCLOSURES

New methods meant new farms. At the start of the 18th century the three-field open system of farming was still used over much of England, though it had never been practised in the west and north. By the end of the century it had gone. The old system could not adapt to the new farming methods. The demands for higher food production, caused by the growth of population in the industrial towns and the wars with France, could not be met. Land was enclosed – divided up among the villages' farmers, with the farms' boundaries marked by hedges or walls.

Before village land could be enclosed, an act of Parliament had to be passed. This could be easily arranged by the large landowners, since Parliament represented their interests. Once the act was passed, Parliament appointed commissioners to arrange the enclosure of the land.

The commissioners allotted land according to how many strips a man held in the village fields. The small farmers

△ *This painting shows farmers inspecting Robert Bakewell's famous rams. Winter food enabled Bakewell and others to breed larger sheep, with thicker fleeces. The average weight of sheep sold at London's Smithfield Market doubled during the 18th century.*

were offered farms that were so small they would be hard put to finance the necessary hedges, let alone make the farm pay. They would sell their farms to the large farmers and go to work for them as labourers. They also lost their rights in the common land and were compensated, if at all, with just a tiny plot of land. By the end of the French wars the English countryside was divided up into private farms, whose labourers owned no land, apart from their gardens, and had only their labour to sell.

THE GREAT HOUSE ESTATES

The estate of the 18th-century great house was self-sufficient. The owner's workers produced all the crops needed and brewed the beer. The laundry-maids washed and ironed the clothes. The dairymaids churned butter from the home farm's prize herd of cows. The estate even levelled out its own football and cricket pitches, for its own home-produced teams.

The country noblemen competed with each other as to who could produce the finest houses and estates. Some of them employed the celebrated landscape artist Lancelot 'Capability' Brown. He designed not only beautiful formal gardens, but also striking vistas (views). Lakes were often built in the grounds.

The lesser landowners, the squires, modelled their lives, houses and estates on those of the nobility.

The estate workers lived in cottages provided by their employer. Their wages were very low but their children were employed on the estate, they received some food and fuel free from the great house, and their dependents were supported in old age.

THE ROLE OF WOMEN

At all levels of society, the life of a married woman was determined by her husband's position. The nobleman's wife entertained guests with her husband. The squire's wife supervised the work of her cooks and maids. The labourer's wife cooked for her family and worked in the fields, and in her garden. Or she spun and wove at home.

An unmarried woman would often spin or weave as a full-time job. New machines – John Kay's flying shuttle loom and James Hargreaves' 'spinning jenny' – doubled the output of British weavers and spinners. Both were used in the home.

▽ *For centuries the woollen industry was carried out in the home. Here the farm worker's wife spins the wool while her daughter winds it off the spindle into a ball. The wool was taken to the weavers' cottages to be woven into cloth.*

TRADE AND POLITICS

The style of life enjoyed by the great English merchants was the envy of their fellows all over Europe. During the reign of William III, the Bank of England had been set up, based on the national bank in Holland. The directors of the bank and the heads of the great trading companies lived like kings. Indeed one Frenchman wrote in 1727:

"Some English merchants are certainly far wealthier than many sovereign princes of Germany and Italy."

INVESTING IN TRADE

The nobles and squires were deeply involved in the ventures of English overseas trading companies, which now roamed all over the world. Many a squire invested heavily in the activities of companies such as the East India Company or the Royal African Company, which organized the slave trade, in return for huge profits. For both squires and nobles were liable to live above their income, and over them hung the fear of debt. For some, gambling on 'the exchange' became a mania.

The South Seas Company was formed in 1711 to promote trade in the Pacific Ocean. The success of the company led to wild speculation in its shares and those of other operations promoting Pacific trade. In 1720 the shares slumped, the 'South Sea Bubble' burst, and hundreds of speculators were instantly ruined. The Duke of Chandos, for example, lost the enormous sum of £700,000 (in money of that time) in the financial crash.

The bursting of the 'Bubble' produced a political crisis. Sir Robert Walpole, the First Lord of the Treasury, restored financial confidence and proceeded to dominate British politics in the 1720s and 1730s. He was the leader of the Whig Party, which was the ruling political party during the reigns of George I and George II (1714–1760). As both kings spent much time in Hanover, government was concentrated on the senior group of the king's ministers, called the Cabinet. Their leader was now called the Prime Minister. They controlled the House of Commons, which had become the most powerful of the two Houses of Parliament.

NEWSPAPERS

People were able to learn about political events through the more widespread availability of newspapers. After the Restoration royal censorship had prevented the publication of newspapers. Instead, newsletters, written in London and circulated to country subscribers, described the main events in the capital and at Court and touched on sporting and literary affairs. With the ending of censorship in the 1690s, the first newspapers appeared. (The first daily newspaper was the *Daily Courant* in 1702; the first evening newspaper was the *Evening Post* in 1706.)

Newspapers were read at the popular coffee houses of the day, above all in London. The papers generally consisted of four pages and contained news of foreign wars, party politics and, increasingly, of business affairs.

18TH-CENTURY HIGH SOCIETY

The wealth of the aristocracy and the great merchants was expected to be displayed as well as invested. Successful men patronized the leading architects of the day to build great new country houses or to adapt the homes of their ancestors by building new wings.

Young gentlemen, before they settled down on their estates, were expected to go on the 'Grand Tour' of Europe for one or two years. They came back with a taste for Italian styles of architecture, particularly styles based on the buildings of ancient Greece and Rome, the so-called 'classical' and 'Palladian' styles.

TOWN HOUSES

Successful people were expected to have a town house as well as a country house, which the family would visit when the Court was in residence or Parliament was in session.

Eighteenth century houses and squares can be found in all British towns, some of the finest being in Edinburgh and Dublin. The houses are beautiful because they are simple. The windows are straight-lined and well proportioned. A growing number of middle class families lived in them – fashionable doctors and lawyers, and successful seed merchants and shopkeepers (though there was a snobbish contempt for those who had made money 'in trade').

During the 18th century many of the wealthy men and more of the rich women liked to be seen in the right places. Apart from the Court and London, Bath became the best known of such places, where 'the Quality' loved to congregate.

BATH – THE FASHIONABLE SPA TOWN

Bath had been famous for the healing properties of its waters from Roman times. Not only was bathing in the baths thought to cure diseases, but drinking the spring water in the Pump Room was believed to be good for health. This was true of other 'Spa' towns such as Buxton, Leamington, or Tunbridge Wells, but Bath became the centre of fashion. Anyone who was anyone was expected to visit Bath during the summer season, to take the waters, to gamble, and to dance the night away in the Assembly Rooms.

Bath was at its height as a fashionable centre around 1760. Its streets were rebuilt to make the town worthy of the company it was now accommodating for much of the year. Even in 1801, when the first official census was carried out (before then all population figures are intelligent guesswork), the population was 30,000, ninth in size among English cities. The town's terraced houses and its Royal Crescent (built in 1775) remain superbly dignified examples of 18th-century architecture, long after its fashionable visitors have vanished.

FASHIONABLE LIFE

It was absolutely essential to a man or woman of 'Quality' to be well dressed and in the latest fashion. When Richard Nash, known as 'Beau' (Handsome) Nash was master of ceremonies in Bath's Assembly rooms he laid down what clothes were in fashion, as well as what constituted good and bad manners. Upper-class men wore full-skirted coats and embroidered waistcoats with lace at the neck, knee breeches and stockings. The women wore underskirts and looped back overskirts of richly embroidered silks which reached down to their ankles. They wore tight bodices with low necks, and their sleeves ended in voluminous lace. Both men and women wore high wigs. The men wore buckled shoes; the women's shoes were moderately high-heeled.

COFFEE HOUSES

In London the coffee and chocolate houses were centres of fashionable social life. In Queen Anne's reign there were nearly 500 houses registered, mostly in London. There were houses for the supporters of political parties – Tories in the Cocoa Tree Chocolate House, Whigs in St James' Coffee House. White's Chocolate House in St James Street was highly fashionable, which is why so many gamblers played there. The stakes were high.

▽ Pictured here is Heveningham Hall in Suffolk, a typical 18th-century great house, with a lake and huge grounds.

Alcoholic drinks were not served in the coffee houses, but pipe smoking was universal. ('Beau' Nash forbade smoking in the public rooms at Bath, as it was disrespectful to ladies.) Also popular was the taking of snuff, which caught on during Queen Anne's reign. Tea drinking, which had started in Charles II's reign through imports from the East India Company, became universal. Tea was drunk even in the poorest homes during the reign of George III.

THE ARTS

Wealthy men loved to patronize fine craftsmen, particularly furniture makers, such as Thomas Chippendale, and later Hepplewhite and Sheraton.

The gentry also patronized artists, such as Sir Joshua Reynolds and Thomas Gainsborough, and original members of the Royal Academy, which was founded in 1768. These artists were paid well for their portraits of leading men and women of the time. It was left to the painter and engraver William Hogarth to show the wealthy how the poor lived.

Playwrights in the 18th-century liked to portray the manners and peculiarities of the upper classes. Their plays, such as Sheridan's *School for Scandal* (1777) and Goldsmith's *She Stoops to Conquer* (1773), contained ingenious plots which were enjoyed by packed audiences in London and the provinces. Fashionable towns were considered to be incomplete without a theatre.

SPORT

The gentry took the lead in patronizing sport on their estates and villages. Their interest in sport helped to bridge the gap between themselves and their tenants and estate workers. A form of cricket was played earlier, but the game became more organized in the 18th century and bets were placed on the results. The first major cricket match was that between All England and Kent in 1744.

△ *Thomas Rowlandson's painting* The Pump Room at Bath *pokes fun at fashionable society. The singer is finding it difficult to attract the attention of the audience, who are either deep in conversation with one another or have fallen asleep out of boredom.*

The first boxing fights were held with boxing gloves around this time. Before then they had been bare knuckled, as they continued to be for many years, and must have been savage occasions.

Cock-fighting was equally savage and just as popular. The fights took place in pits, round which the intent spectators sat, placing their bets on the birds, which then fought to the death.

Horse-racing, which was followed by numbers of spectators on horseback running alongside the competitors, was organized locally. The first national race meeting was at Newmarket in 1753.

THE BRITISH EMPIRE

The Treaty of Utrecht (1713), which brought the War of the Spanish Succession to an end, led to the struggles between Britain and France about trade and colonies. (It was not until the 19th century that the British looked on colonies primarily as places where settlers could start a new life, though in North America they had planned colonies with settlements in mind from Elizabethan times.)

Two long wars, the War of the Austrian Succession (1740–1748) and the Seven Years' War (1756–1763), led to British troops fighting French troops in Europe. Apart from other causes George II was involved in these wars as Elector of Hanover. But it was the rivalry between Britain and France for colonies which was to have the greatest influence in the long run. From this struggle the British were to emerge as the masters of the greatest empire in the world.

THE STRUGGLE FOR COLONIES

The struggle was to be fought in three areas – the West Indies, India and Canada. The competition in the West Indies was concerned with the sugar trade from the plantations and the right to supply slaves to the plantation owners. Here the Spaniards were also involved. In India the French and English East India companies were competing for trade, trading bases ('factories') and influence over the Indian princes. In Canada the French settlers and fur traders were being challenged by the growing numbers of English settlers in the New England colonies. The French responded by building a line of forts along the St Lawrence and Mississippi rivers as far south as their colony of Louisiana at the latter's mouth. By these means they hoped to prevent the English moving west over the Appalachian Mountains into the mid-west and west of the modern United States. These lands were then only occupied by scattered North American native tribes.

TRADE WITH THE WEST INDIES

By the Treaty of Paris (1763) the British gained from France the West Indian islands of Grenada, Dominica, St Vincent and Tobago. These gains, when placed alongside the islands, such as Jamaica, which the British held already, were to make them the strongest power in the West Indies. At the time the West Indian trade was more coveted in Europe than the Indian or North American trade. This section of the treaty was therefore particularly welcomed by the fabulously rich English merchants, among them the slave traders, now operating from the fast-growing port of Liverpool.

THE END OF THE MOGUL EMPIRE

The opportunities for trade in India were greatly increased when the last ruler of the Mogul Empire to control most of India died in 1707. The emperors had controlled the Indian sub-continent from their capital at Agra, home of the magnificent Taj Mahal monument. Now the empire began to fall apart and the French and English East Indian trading companies moved in to fill the vacuum.

THE BRITISH IN INDIA

At first the French were the most determined and successful. In 1741 Joseph Dupleix became Governor of Pondicherry, the French base in South East India. He dreamed of creating a French empire in India. In 1746 French forces captured Madras, the British base to the north of Pondicherry. A young British clerk, Robert Clive, was in Madras when it was besieged by the French. At the age of 26 he raised a force which went on to dominate South East India. Dupleix was recalled to France in disgrace in 1754. Three years later, at the battle of Plassey, the British defeated a large Indian force and seized the city of Calcutta. The French were expelled from their nearby base at Chandernagore. The rich province of Bengal in North East India was under British control. The foundation of the British Indian Empire had been laid. The English now made huge fortunes in India from tea, diamonds, jute and cotton.

VICTORY IN CANADA

Behind the British campaigns in the Seven Years' War lay the ambitious planning of the war minister, William Pitt the Elder. He is generally called the Earl of Chatham to distinguish him from his son William Pitt the Younger who was later to become British prime minister. Chatham entrusted the command of the Canadian campaign to General James Wolfe, aged 33. Wolfe's men were transported up the St Lawrence River to the French base at Quebec by Admiral Saunder's ships. The navigation of the waters was a highly skilful and dangerous task. It was carried out by a young ship's master, James Cook, who thereby established a reputation for brilliant seamanship.

Quebec fell to a daring night assault led by Wolfe himself. His 5000 men struggled up a steep cliff path to surprise the French. Wolfe was killed in the attack. Next year the other main French base in Canada, Montreal, fell to the British.

By the Treaty of Paris all Canada became British. Most of the French settlers stayed. Their descendants are still French-speaking today. All lands east of the Mississippi river, except Louisiana at its mouth, became British.

CAPTAIN COOK'S VOYAGES

Captain James Cook was 31 years of age when he successfully piloted Wolfe's men up the St Lawrence River. Nine years later the Admiralty gave him the command of a boat of 368 tonnes, called the *Endeavour*. Over the next 11 years Cook was to lead three expeditions to the Pacific. The purpose of these was to map one of the last unknown areas of ocean in the world, which Cook and his men did expertly.

Cook's first voyage (1768–1771) was his greatest. He sailed south of South America, visited the island of Tahiti, and then sailed round New Zealand, surveying its coastline as he went. He then sailed along the previously unknown eastern coast of Australia and through the Torres Strait, which lies between Australia and New Guinea, narrowly avoiding being shipwrecked off the Great Barrier Reef. From now on the coastlines of New Zealand and eastern Australia were known to Europeans. Colonization of the 'new' lands was to follow later. Cook himself, who normally had excellent relations with native peoples wherever he travelled, was killed in a fight with the islanders of Hawaii during his third expedition in 1779.

THE AMERICAN WAR OF INDEPENDENCE

The removal of the French from Canada by the Treaty of Paris in 1763 had an important effect on the 13 British colonies in North America. They had long been dissatisfied with the British government's treatment of them. But they relied on the British army to protect them from the French, who had ideas of building a New France which would stretch from their colonies around the banks of the St Lawrence to their colony of Louisiana at the mouth of the

Mississippi. Now that the French had no power to fulfil their dream, British Americans wanted to stand on their own feet for the first time.

GROWING RESENTMENT
The Americans disliked the way British governments interfered in their trade and made them pay unreasonable taxes. The British expected their colonies to send their valuable raw materials to Britain, where they were turned into finished products in British factories. The products were then exported back to the colonies.

The British disliked the colonists trying to develop their own industries. They forbade them to use non-British ships for their trade, even if these provided a better

▽ *The Declaration of Independence was signed by the 13 American colonies at their Continental Congress in 1776. It stated that the people of a country had the right to decide how and by whom they are governed.*

and cheaper service, as the Dutch did, for example. Moreover, if the Americans imported goods from European countries, they had to pay British taxes on them.

TROUBLE OVER TAXATION

The British government also tried to prevent American colonists travelling west to open up their country. (Up to now they had lived only along the eastern seaboard of the modern United States.) If they did so, the British argued, an army would be needed to defend them from attacks by Frenchmen, Spaniards or Indians. And who would pay for that?

The wars with France had left the British with a national debt of £140 million. They were determined that the colonists should

pay at least some of the cost of the wars. After all, the British said, it was the Americans who had gained from the removal of the French from Canada.

DEMANDS FOR REPRESENTATION

The Americans replied with the strongest of their arguments in the dispute. They insisted that if they were to be taxed, they should be consulted. Taxes were passed by the British Parliament, in which the

▽ The last battle in the American War of Independence was at Yorktown, Maryland, in 1781. American soldiers, helped by French soldiers and sailors, stormed the British troops and forced them to surrender. The way was now clear for the creation of the United States.

Americans had no representatives. There should be, in the words of their slogan, "No taxation without representation".

The troubles started when the British Parliament passed a Stamp Act, which said all legal documents in the colonies had to carry a stamp. This was really a tax – the money for the stamp was to go to the British government. When the Americans protested, Parliament withdrew the act, but instead imposed small taxes on American imports of tea, paper, glass and other articles. The colonists replied by boycotting (not buying) those goods. Again the British withdrew the taxes, on all imports except tea.

THE BOSTON TEA PARTY

In December 1773 a cargo of specially cheap Indian tea, to be taxed at threepence a pound, entered Boston harbour in Massachusetts. A group of Americans, with blackened faces and dressed as American Indians, boarded the three tea ships at night. They threw the 342 chests of tea into Boston harbour. This event became known as the 'Boston Tea Party'.

Boston had been the centre of trouble for several years. In 1770 an incident occurred which became magnified until it was known as the 'Boston Massacre'. A group of young Americans had been taunting and snowballing British soldiers. In the end the soldiers could stand it no longer. They fired without orders into the crowd and killed five civilians.

THE DECLARATION OF INDEPENDENCE

After the Boston Tea Party, the British closed the port of Boston. They then declared that the whole colony of Massachusetts was in revolt. Fighting broke out and the 13 colonies issued their famous Declaration of Independence in 1776. They declared themselves to be the 13 United States of America. The Declaration sums up the principle of democracy – that countries should be governed according to the wishes of their people. Their justification of their break with Britain has been taught to American school children ever since.

After seven years of fighting, the war ended with the battle of Yorktown in 1781. With the surrender of the British army, the first British Empire ended, and independence of the former British colonies was granted in 1783.

THE COLONISTS

The first British empire was built by trading companies, landowners or persecuted individuals and groups. All sorts of people believed the colonies offered the chance of a new and better life. They included persecuted Puritans, the jobless and poorly paid farm labourers. Governments followed the companies and individuals, and protected them, grudgingly, with a few ships and soldiers.

The loss of the American colonies made many English leaders doubt the value of acquiring an empire. What was the point of setting up colonies if they then broke away and became independent? Nevertheless, during the 19th century more and more ordinary English men and women – desperate with poverty, frustrated by snobbery, or penalized for political beliefs – sold all that they had and sailed off to start a new life.

The British learnt a lesson from the loss of their American colonies. Never again, once it became clear that one of their colonies wanted independence, did they try to keep it under their control for long.

REVOLUTIONS IN INDUSTRY AND TRANSPORT

The changes that occurred in Britain between the end of the 18th and the middle of the 19th centuries altered the whole nature of life for millions of British people. Instead of a country largely empty of people, Britain became overcrowded. For the first time more people began to live in the towns than in the country. There they earned their living mainly by working in factories rather than by farming. These changes are known as the Industrial Revolution.

Between 1780 and 1851, the population of Britain grew from 13 million to about 27 million. One of the reasons for this great increase was that safer methods were now used by the midwives who delivered the country's babies. Far fewer children died at birth or in the first year of their life. And people were beginning to understand the importance of cleanliness, and to wear more washable cotton clothes. Cleanliness meant better health. People began to live longer.

CHANGES IN THE CLOTH INDUSTRY
Although buildings which were called industrial factories had existed in the cloth industry for 200 years, they were no more than large spinning and weaving sheds where the work was done by women working at separate machines. It was not until Richard Arkwright built his first cotton-spinning factory at Cromford near Derby in 1771 that the old domestic methods of production in the textile industry began to change.

Arkwright built his factory over the River Derwent so that the waters of the river moved wheels which provided the power for his machinery. The use of water power for cotton factories soon spread to South Lancashire and Clydeside. As the factories resembled mill-houses which had long ground flour by water power they were called mills.

STEAM POWER
For many years steam pumps had been used in coal and tin mines to prevent flooding. In the 1760s James Watt developed the ideas of inventor Thomas Newcomen, and designed a steam engine. With money from a Birmingham businessman, Matthew Boulton, Watt built engines which could drive machinery with steam produced from boilers heated by coal. By 1800 Boulton and Watt's machines were being used by any factory owner who could buy coal cheaply. From now on industry moved to be near the coalfields, and no longer relied on fast-running streams and rivers. The cotton-spinning factories were largely steam powered by 1800.

Two other inventions helped modernize the cotton industry. Firstly, in 1785 Edmund Cartwright invented a loom that could be driven by Watt's steam engine. Secondly, in 1793 Elias Whitney invented a machine for cleaning cotton produced on the plantations of the United States. This meant far more cotton was now available to British factories.

△ *James Brindley built a canal from Worsley to Manchester, a distance of 10 kilometres, to carry coal. The picture shows the aqueduct on the canal, called the Bridgewater canal, after Brindley's master the Duke of Bridgewater. The canal boats were pulled by horses.*

In the same period similar developments were taking place in the woollen industry, which was now concentrated in Yorkshire. Production of wool more than doubled during the 18th century.

THE FIRST CANALS

Transport improved greatly in the 18th and 19th centuries. This was achieved by building canals and improving roads.

The pioneer of canal-building was the Duke of Bridgewater, who had large supplies of coal on his estate at Worsley, 10 kilometres from Manchester. He wanted a better way of moving coal than strapping it on the back of packhorses, which was the method of the day. The Duke employed James Brindley, an engineer of genius who never learned to read and write properly, to build a canal from Worsley to Manchester.

It took Brindley five years, from 1759 to 1764, to build the Bridgewater Canal. With its ten-metre aqueduct over the river Irwell, it was one of the wonders of the age. Later Brindley extended the canal for 60 kilometres to the Mersey, so that Manchester was linked with Liverpool. One horse pulling a barge along a canal could transport more coal than 60 packhorses. The cost of carrying cotton from Liverpool to Manchester was cut by a massive 83 per cent.

The Bridgewater Canal proved to be an example which local groups of landlords, farmers, manufacturers and bankers were quick to follow. By the 1770s all Britain's main rivers were linked up by canal to form a vast network of waterways.

One manufacturer who took advantage of Brindley's Grand Trunk Canal was Josiah Wedgwood. He invested a lot of money in the scheme and was well rewarded for his foresight. He built a pottery works on the banks of the canal at Stoke. Not only could he receive china clay by canal, but his delicate pottery could travel by canal barge to Liverpool or Hull instead of risking breakages on the backs of packhorses. His china was exported all over the world.

THE STATE OF THE ROADS

In the early 18th century journeys by coach on Britain's bumpy roads were unpopular because they were long, uncomfortable and expensive. And they were dangerous, for coaches were easy targets for highwaymen.

As for trade, fleets of packhorses transported baskets of coal or bales of wool or cotton by road. Cattle and sheep were driven by drovers along the roads from the farms to market.

TURNPIKE TRUSTS

Improvements to the roads came through groups of enterprising squires, bankers and businessmen. They banded together to form groups called turnpike trusts, which were given the right to improve stretches of road by acts of Parliament. The trust provided the money and hired the engineers to survey and build the road. Then they charged people a regular toll (tax) for using the road.

ROAD ENGINEERS

One of the most remarkable road engineers was the blind John Metcalfe. He used jagged broken stones, not pebbles, for his surfaces as they crushed better.

Another road builder who laid great emphasis on his road surfaces was the Scotsman John Macadam. They were made up of thousands of small chipped stones of standard shapes and sizes which

△ *The first iron bridge was built by Thomas Telford in 1779. It spans the river Severn at Coalbrookdale in Shropshire.*

packed tightly together when they were rolled. Prisoners or people from the workhouses broke the stones into the required shapes with a hammer. Later the 'Macadamized' surfaces were sprayed with tar to make 'Tarmac' roads.

But the most famous road engineer, who also designed canals, docks, lighthouses and bridges, was Thomas Telford, another Scot. Like the Romans, he believed that a road must be well drained and built on a solid foundation of stone blocks laid by hand. He built more than a thousand kilometres of roads. His Caledonian Canal linked northern Scotland from coast to coast. His suspension bridge over the Menai Straits, linking Anglesey to the Welsh mainland, is still in use.

URBAN POVERTY AND PROBLEMS

The fast rise in the British population left its worst effects in the towns. Thousands were living in extreme poverty, crammed into old buildings overflowing with people. This was particularly the case in London. Country people who left home to find a job joined thousands of unemployed men and women whose main means of earning a living was crime.

CRIME, LAW AND ORDER

There was no police force, though there were men called the 'Bow Street runners', who tried to maintain some sort of law and order in the capital under the control of the Bow Street magistrates.

One of the worst problems was caused by drink. There were no licensing laws and public houses were open all day and all night. Drunks were seen everywhere,

among them children. Publicans of the time advertised the popular spirit, gin, with the slogan: "Drunk for a penny, Dead drunk for twopence."

There was no street lighting. Servants escorted their masters, carrying strong cudgels to protect them. A boy would accompany them, holding a 'link' (flare) to light their way. Street gangs carried out muggings without much difficulty. All men who possessed any wealth carried a sword in London.

The crowds of unemployed men and women could always be organized into an angry 'mob' by unscrupulous men who wanted to use them for their own purposes. A mere rumour or cry – about Catholic shopkeepers, for instance – would start a stampede by thousands of chanting, angry people, smashing shop windows and burning property.

THE MOB

The most terrifying example of the London mob on the rampage occurred in 1780. Two years earlier a law had been passed by Parliament which allowed Catholics to own land and permitted Catholic priests to enter Britain. Protestants petitioned Parliament to

◁ Hogarth's famous engraving Gin Lane (1751) warns of the dangers of drinking gin. The baby falls from its drunken mother's breast, and a man and a dog gnaw on the same bone next to her. The skeletal-looking man at the bottom of the picture and the man who has hung himself at the back show that, where poverty is, death is never far behind.

repeal the act. For a week a huge mob, led by Lord George Gordon, ran wild through the streets of London, shouting anti-Catholic slogans, burning, smashing and looting. When the crowd destroyed a gin distillery, men and women rushed in to loot the burning building. An eyewitness described how:

"They rushed down the stone steps into the cellar and came up choking with blackened faces and bloodshot eyes, carrying untapped casks of gin, or pails and jugs, bowls and even pig troughs overflowing . . . Soon the gin came gushing up into the streets and ran in warm streams in the gutter . . . The people knelt down and dipped their faces in the river of fiery spirits . . . Men and women lay down prostrate in the streets, incapably drunk; some of the women had babies in their arms."[8]

More than 800 people were killed during the week of the Gordon riots.

CALLS FOR REFORM

There were no legal ways for people's grievances to be expressed. John Wilkes, who became an MP in 1768, campaigned to make the House of Commons more representative of the people. Wilkes became Lord Mayor of London and was influential in allowing the press to report Parliamentary debates. At one time he was the hero of the city. But the wealthy classes were afraid of reformers, or radicals, and his influence faded away.

EVANGELICALS START CAMPAIGNING

Towards the end of the 18th century, groups of serious minded and generally wealthy Christians, who came to be called evangelicals began to campaign for reforms. They helped to found schools for the poor, such as the National Schools, the only schools there were for the majority of village children. They attacked the use of child labour in factories. And they began the campaign against slavery, which the Quakers had long been attacking. In 1772 a slave was declared free when he landed in England. Now the campaign was directed against slavery in British colonies.

THE CHURCH OF ENGLAND

Although the great majority of English people belonged to the Church of England, and attended church each week, many people were half-hearted about Christianity. Many clergy did good work. They taught the beliefs of their founder, visited the sick, helped the poor, and educated the cleverest of the local children. But they were appointed by local landowners, and were thought of often as being in their pockets.

The 18th-century church had little contact with the poorest people in the towns and lacked an awareness of the increasing urban problems. Industry was growing, along with the towns, and new churches were not built in the new areas of work and living. It was in these areas – coal-mining areas such as Kingswood, outside Bristol, or tin-mining districts such as those in Cornwall – that the great 18th-century preacher John Wesley gained some of his strongest support.

JOHN WESLEY

Wesley was a clergyman of the Church of England and never had any intention or desire to leave it. He and his brother Charles tried to bring the church to life for the ordinary people.

△ Hogarth's Polling at the Elections *(1754)*
catches the mood of an election in the middle
of the 18th century. Elections were occasions
for drunkeness and rioting until well after the
first reform bill of 1832. The few men who were
entitled to vote did so publicly on a platform.

John Wesley set out to travel the country preaching wherever he went, like Jesus and his disciples. He preached on the village commons or in the open spaces of the towns. He drew great crowds. He and his preachers were howled down, jeered at, stoned and thrown into ponds. Their meetings were highly emotional. Men and women who heard the words and teachings of Jesus for the first time would shout out, weep and groan.

Whenever he left an area, Wesley left behind him a little group of keen Christians. He kept in touch with them by letter and organized them 'methodically' into groups by areas. They would 'methodically' study the Bible together, pray, and work to bring the Christianity of the local church to life. The movement therefore became known as 'Methodism'.

THE METHODIST CHURCH
Finally, against Wesley's wishes, Methodism became a separate Christian church, distinct from the Church of England. In the next century it was to reach thousands of working people whose lives had previously been untouched by the Church of England.

SUPPRESSION OF POLITICAL REFORM

In 1789 there was a revolution in Paris. The rule of a small group of nobles, supported by the monarchy and the Church, was overthrown. The middle class, who felt excluded by the old forms of government, took the lead in the revolution which took a moderate form. At first the British welcomed the French Revolution. The French people were admired for their determination to establish in their country the liberties which the British themselves had long been enjoying.

FRANCE THREATENS BRITAIN

But within three years the revolution took a more violent turn. The chaos which the revolution had caused led the Prussians and Austrians to invade France. The French threw the invaders back and advanced into Belgium, which they showed no signs of evacuating. The British government under William Pitt the Younger was alarmed by their presence. There were massacres in Paris. The French revolutionary leaders executed the French king, Louis XVI, and his Austrian wife, Marie Antoinette. The executions were greeted with horror in Britain. On 1st February 1793 the new French Republic declared war on Britain.

By now British enthusiasm for the Revolution had turned to revulsion. The government played on popular feelings and were quick to call those who supported any type of reform 'Jacobins' – extreme French revolutionaries. In the 1780s it had seemed possible that Parliament might be reformed without a struggle. Those who were not members of the Church of England began to hope that the acts which prevented them from taking any part in the government of their country would be repealed. All such hopes were now forgotten.

Societies which had been founded to support reform were threatened. Some of the reformers were convicted as traitors and transported to the colonies. No meeting of more than 50 people could be held without obtaining permission from a magistrate. Mobs ransacked the houses of some well-known radicals. Trade unions, which were beginning to be formed so that working men could fight for better pay and conditions, were banned by the Combination Act of 1800, and the Habeas Corpus Act was suspended.

REFORMS IN IRELAND

The wars with France had a particularly bad effect in Ireland. In 1783 Ireland still had its own Parliament, though its members had to be Protestants in a country where over 80 per cent of the people were Catholics. But, under the leadership of Henry Grattan, Parliament secured a number of improvements in the Catholic position. Catholics were allowed their own schools and could own more property. In 1793 they were allowed to vote at Parliamentary elections if they possessed the property qualifications that were necessary.

WOLFE TONE'S REBELLION

The French Republic's declaration of war on Britain changed the whole nature of Irish politics. The Society of United Irishmen had originally been formed to unite Protestants and Catholics in a movement for the reform of Parliament. Now, under a young leader, Wolfe Tone, the society set out to establish an independent Irish Republic, and looked to the French for support. The government in Dublin responded by turning on Catholics in different parts of Ireland. Its soldiers committed atrocities. Catholics attacked Protestants. In Ulster the Protestants talked of driving out the native Catholics.

In 1798 a Catholic rebellion was put down, and Wolfe Tone, taken prisoner on a French ship sailing to help the rebels, committed suicide. A French force landed but was defeated at Ballinamuck.

By the Act of Union in 1801 the Irish Parliament was abolished. The Irish sent one hundred MPs to the Westminster House of Commons – but none of them were allowed by law to be Catholics.

THE EFFECTS OF THE FRENCH WARS

The French wars, which lasted till 1815, with a year's break from 1802 to 1803, were the first foreign wars which really affected the lives of the British people. All previous wars had been fought by small groups of soldiers raised by mercenary commanders, who recruited men from all over Europe, to fight under their command for pay. (The so called 'British army' was certainly not composed solely of Britons when it was engaged on active service.) Casualties were usually minute. When news reached London in 1709 that 600 British soldiers had been killed in the battle of Malplaquet against the French there was a public outcry. But between 1793 and 1815 one sixth of the adult male population of Britain was in the armed forces and 210,000 fighting men died.

In 1802 the British and French made peace at the Treaty of Amiens. The terms left the French in complete control of western Europe. It was clear, however, that the peace would not last.

◁ *After the new French Republic declared war on Britain in 1793, a young general, Napoleon Bonaparte, led a French army to Egypt to cut British trade links with India. Napoleon later became Emperor of France and during the early 19th century he conquered most of western Europe, although he never managed to invade Britain.*

1801–1901
THE NINETEENTH CENTURY

TIME CHART

* denotes events that occurred outside Britain and Ireland.

1801	First official census: British population numbers about 10 million.
1802	Peace between Britain and France. Thomas Telford begins building roads through the Highlands.
1803–1815	British join wars against Napoleon.
1803	Caledonian Canal is started.
1804	Pitt is prime minister.
1805	French plan invasion of England; it never happens. Battle of Trafalgar: Nelson dies defeating French.
1807	British ban slave trade.
1812	*Napoleon's Russian campaign. Main streets of London are lit by gas.
1815	*Battle of Waterloo. *Congress of Vienna.
1819	Peterloo Massacre. Britain gains Singapore.
1820	George III dies. George IV (former Prince Regent) becomes king.
1824	Combination Acts are repealed.
1825	First railway is opened, from Stockton to Darlington.
1828	Test Act is repealed. County Clare by-election. Catholic emancipation.
1829	Metropolitan Police formed.
1830	George IV dies. William IV becomes king.
1832	Reform Act.
1833	Slavery abolished. Factory Act.
1834	Poor Law Amendment Act.
1837	William IV dies. Victoria becomes queen.
1838–1848	Chartists.
1840	Britain acquires New Zealand.
1845	Irish potato famine.
1846	Corn Laws are repealed.
1848	Public Health Act.
1851	Great Exhibition.
1854–1856	*Crimean War. *Florence Nightingale at Scutari, Turkey.
1859	Darwin publishes On the Origin of Species.
1861	*US Civil War.
1867	Second Reform Bill.
1870	*Suez Canal opened. Education Act.
1872	Ballot Act.
1875	First council houses built.
1877	Victoria becomes Empress of India.
1879	Irish Land League.
1884	Third Reform Bill.
1886	*Nigeria is colonized. First Home Rule Bill.
1889	London dock strike.
1894	First motor cars manufactured.
1896	Daily Mail newspaper begins publication. Marconi demonstrates the wireless.
1899–1902	*Second South African war.
1900	Labour Party is formed.
1901	Queen Victoria dies. Edward VII becomes king. Population of Britain numbers about 40 million.

THE FORCES OF INDUSTRIAL CHANGE

During the first half of the 19th century Britain became the greatest industrial power in the world. A price was paid to gain such an enviable position. It was paid by those who worked in the new factories and lived in the industrial towns.

URBAN OVERCROWDING

Men, women and children crowded into the new mining villages, mill towns and industrial cities in a manner which had never been known before. Builders never kept up with the demand for small houses, built back to back, with outside earth toilets and one street pump to serve the row. So families crowded into the old buildings, which were now let to them by floors or even single rooms. The only place where children could play was in the

▽ *In the coal mines, boys and girls – some as young as four years old – were made to work for an average of 12 hours a day.*

street, which was made of crushed earth and ash. A man, woman and three or four children crowded into one room, and slept together in one bed.

POLLUTION

By day, the air was thick with smoke belching out of the factory chimneys. By night the only light came from the fires of the factories or iron works.

CHILD LABOUR

Children, aged six upwards, worked in the new factories and mines. Often they risked injury. The hours were long and accidents were caused when children fell asleep. They did what they were told. Many were orphans, with no parents to defend them. Children had always worked in the fields. To many people there was nothing to choose between employing children on farms or in factories. Most people thought little about the factory children.

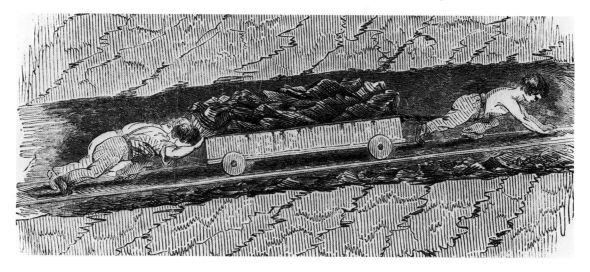

THE NAPOLEONIC WARS

Fighting between Britain and France resumed in 1803 after the previous year's Treaty of Amiens. The French emperor, Napoleon Bonaparte, then began to make preparations for the invasion of southern England. He established his headquarters at Boulogne, where on clear days he could see across the Channel to the white cliffs of Dover and Folkestone, and collected an army of 100,000 men. The shipbuilders of western Europe were set to work to make their warships.

The British began to make frantic preparations. Troops were massed along the south coast. A military canal was dug along the coast of Romney Marsh. Mothers terrified their children by telling them that 'Boney' (Napoleon) would deal with them unless they behaved themselves.

But the French, like the Spaniards at the time of the Armada, knew they could never invade England unless they controlled the Channel.

In 1805 the French navy tried to lure squadrons of the British navy across the Atlantic to the West Indies. The Channel, they hoped, would then be clear for an invasion of southern England. They were joined by their allies the Spaniards.

NELSON'S GREAT VICTORY
After sailing great distances to the West Indies and back, British ships caught up with the French and Spanish fleet off the south-west coast of Spain. They were commanded by Admiral Nelson, the most daring and popular of British naval commanders. The Battle of Trafalgar was a decisive British victory. A total of 18 out of 33 French and Spanish ships were taken. Nelson himself was shot dead just when his men's victory was clear.

Napoleon in fact had given up any idea of invasion before he heard the news from Trafalgar. He thought no more of invading England and led his troops into Austria and Prussia. Soon Napoleon's France controlled Europe from the Atlantic to the Russian border, and from Spain to the Adriatic Sea.

The first crack in the building of Napoleon's European empire occurred in Spain, when the Spaniards rebelled against French occupation in 1808. Sir Arthur Wellesley (later the Duke of Wellington) landed with British troops in Portugal and then advanced into Spain. Napoleon took personal charge of the Peninsular War but, in the face of defeats, left Spain.

In 1812 Napoleon tried to occupy Russia. By October his men had advanced as far as Moscow. But faced with the coming of the terrible winter, Napoleon ordered them to retreat. Hundreds of thousands froze to death or died of exhaustion. Napoleon left his men to their fate, as he had done earlier in Egypt and in Spain. His grip on Europe was broken.

British troops, allied with Spanish guerillas (fighters), drove the French out of Spain. Britain, Russia, Prussia, Austria and Sweden formed a coalition. In March 1814 their troops entered Paris. Napoleon abdicated and the allies exiled him to Elba, an island in the Mediterranean.

He escaped from there the next year.

He entered Paris in triumph, but his Hundred Days of freedom ended in defeat

△ *Admiral Nelson is shown here with a midshipman. Nelson was loved by his men because, unlike many naval commanders, he cared for them. Apart from the battle of Trafalgar he won outstanding victories off Copenhagen (1801) and the Nile (1798).*

when allied forces, chiefly British and Prussian under Wellington, defeated the French at Waterloo in Belgium. This time Napoleon was exiled by the allies to the island of St Helena in the South Atlantic. He died there in 1821, at the age of 52.

THE CONGRESS OF VIENNA (1815)

In 1815 ministers from the victorious coalition of countries that had defeated Napoleon met at the Congress of Vienna. They divided the lands they gained from France between them.

The British were interested in acquiring colonies and bases outside Europe. In the Mediterranean they gained Malta. They took Mauritius in the Indian Ocean from France, along with the rich sugar islands of St Lucia and Tobago in the West Indies. They bought the tiny Dutch settlement at the Cape of Good Hope from Holland for £6 million. The Dutch colony of Sri Lanka also became British.

PRESS GANGS

The British naval victories were all the more remarkable when one remembers the sailors' conditions. Many of them had been kidnapped in the first place by the 'press gangs' or naval recruiting parties. The navy's sailors were generally fishermen or others with experience of the sea who were seized when they walked along the streets or quaysides of their own home port. Or they would be ambushed when they reeled out of a pub at closing time. They would be rushed straight to the quayside and then rowed to ships which were on the point of sailing.

LIFE IN THE NAVY

Discipline in the navy, as in the army, was maintained only by savage floggings. Some of these punishments were so severe that the sailors died as the result of them. The pay of these men who were toasted by the nation for their 'hearts of oak' was very poor, amounting to three pence a day for ordinary seamen, and three and a half pence for able seamen. The meat was often rotten with maggots, the ship's biscuits running with weevils.

MUTINY

With conditions such as these it was no wonder that the main squadrons of the fleet mutinied in 1797. The mutiny was quelled, its leaders hanged, and the ships sailed out to defeat the Dutch fleet off Camperdown (Holland).

THE MONARCHY AND THE PEOPLE

George III (1760–1820) was the first Hanoverian King whose interests were entirely English. He was popular with many of the public. He developed Windsor Castle and turned some of the Great Park into a model farm. He loved sea bathing. He liked to walk out of his bathing machine on Weymouth beach while the band played Rule Britannia. Politically his reign was far less happy. He earned much of the blame for the loss of the American colonies. He did all he could to exclude Fox, the Whig leader, from office. And he would not allow Irish Roman Catholics to become MPs in the Act of Union between Britain and Ireland (1801), although over 80 per cent of Irishmen were Catholics.

REGENT, THEN KING

George IV (1820–1830) had been king in fact long before his coronation. His father had suffered from bouts of mental illness with increasing frequency until finally, in 1811, his unpopular son became Prince Regent. (His years as regent are called the Regency). Both as regent and later as king, George opposed all reforms. His court was composed of the most selfish and dissolute of aristocrats. But he loved the arts – an unusual taste for one of his family. He patronized some of Britain's greatest architects, such as John Nash. He worked with him in the building of Regent's Park and Carlton House Terrace in London. He loved Brighton, where his Chinese Pavilion stands as his memorial.

AN ENGLISH REVOLUTION?

During the 15 years after the end of the Napoleonic Wars Britain was closer to revolution than at any other time since the execution of Charles I. In 1815 half a million men were demobilized all at once from the army. Many of them could not find work. Thousands of desperate men and women faced starvation. Bad harvests made matters worse.

The Corn Law of 1815 prevented the import of foreign corn until British corn reached the high price of £4 a quarter. British farmers were protected but bread prices were kept high. Townspeople hated the Corn Law because it made bread expensive when hundreds of thousands were starving. (Robert Peeel finally repealed the Corn Law in 1846, following years of campaigning by the Anti-Corn Law League.)

A PLOT AGAINST THE GOVERNMENT

In what later became known as the Cato Street Conspiracy, Arthur Thistlewood hatched a wild scheme to assassinate all the leading members of the government and run down the Strand in London with their heads displayed on silver platters.

INDUSTRIALIZATION AND POVERTY

Many workers responded to the introduction of new machinery, which threatened their livelihood, with violence. In Nottingham gangs of workers were going around smashing stocking factories in which the employers had installed new machinery well before the end of the war. They said they were commanded by a secret general named Ned Ludd and they became known as Luddites. In 1830 farm labourers took to smashing the new threshing machines in Kent and Sussex in much the same way. They claimed to be led by a mysterious Captain Swing, whose emblem was the figure of a man swinging from the gallows. Farmers were threatened. In the end the troops were called out. Four labourers were executed and 52 transported to Australia.

Magistrates, fearing that their towns might be overrun by rampaging mobs and that the new mills in the north would be set on fire, turned to the local troops to provide security. An army of 12,000 soldiers was put on standby in the north of England in case of trouble.

The march of the Blanketeers in 1817 employed peaceful means to draw the government's attention to the condition of the unemployed. Carrying a blanket to sleep in they set out from Manchester for London but had reached no further than Macclesfield when they were forcibly dispersed by troops.

EMIGRATION

Many desperate men and women decided that Britain had nothing to offer themselves and their families. They decided to emigrate to the British colonies of Australia, New Zealand, Canada and South Africa. Here they were able to start new lives. Many died in the struggle to make a living in a strange land. But many prospered in a way they could never have achieved in Britain.

▽ *Many children worked in the cotton mills, such as this one in Manchester. The hours were so long and their work so exhausting that children fell asleep at work and suffered serious injuries from moving machinery.*

Fares on the emigrant ships were cheap and emigrants might be helped to pay them by future employers. Some Poor Law authorities paid fares for young men, who faced permanent unemployment in their home areas, as a means of keeping down the rates. But the conditions on the long voyages were often appalling.

Men, women and children were crammed together in appalling conditions. Many died of disease. When they landed, many found that nothing came of the job or farm they had been promised.

THE 'PETERLOO' MASSACRE

On 16th August 1819, a large radical meeting was held outside Manchester in St Peter's Fields. Unlike the Luddite rioters, the crowd of about 70,000 men and women were well-disciplined and peaceful. They had come to hear William Hunt, a radical, demand a reform of Parliament.

△ *Cruikshank's painting* Massacre at St Peters or Britons strike Home *is a bitter portrayal of what happened when the cavalry was sent in to break up a peaceful meeting. The Peterloo Massacre hastened the drive for reform.*

Hunt had hardly started speaking when the local magistrates ordered soldiers to disperse the people. They rode into the crowd with drawn swords. Within a quarter of an hour the fields were empty, but 11 men had been killed, and 500–600 people seriously injured. The event was called the 'Peterloo' Massacre in sarcastic memory of the battle of Waterloo.

Peterloo changed the government's policy. Before 1819 the Conservative government's leaders believed that brute force would prevent a revolution. After Peterloo they moved slowly towards the reform of the conditions which were causing such demonstrations.

PEEL'S REFORMS

One of the new group of Conservative reformers was the Home Secretary, Sir Robert Peel. Peel carried out several important reforms in the 1820s. At this time you could be hanged for 200 different offences, including shoplifting and sheep-stealing. So rather than sending shoplifters or sheep-stealers to their deaths, juries were just letting them off altogether. Peel reduced the number of capital (hanging) offences by half. Public hangings continued for the other hundred offences. They were watched by large, jeering, drunken crowds.

The state of British prisons was a scandal at this time. If you had money, or could persuade your friends and relatives to help you, you could live fairly comfortably in your prison cell. But if you could not afford to pay for decent conditions, you were locked in a dark and filthy room, given foul water to drink, and half starved on a diet consisting of bread and potatoes.

Peel was greatly impressed by the reports compiled by Christian men and women, such as Elizabeth Fry, a Quaker, who visited prisons regularly for 30 years, and reported what she saw. Such reports led him to start a slow improvement in prison conditions.

Peel faced bitter opposition when he proposed to set up a British police force. But Parliament realized that the Peterloo Massacre had shown what happens when soldiers are asked to control great crowds. They were not trained for such work, and could not fairly be blamed if they lost their heads and attacked the crowd. In 1829 Parliament agreed to set up a police force in London only – the Metropolitan Police Force – so long as it was unarmed. Within 30 years similar police forces had spread to every part of Britain. The nickname the police were given – 'bobby'– was taken from the name of their founder.

Other reforms were also passed in the 1820s. For the first time trade unions were allowed. Their power was at first very limited. A group of local farmers and landowners managed to find a loophole in the law and used it to prosecute six farm labourers at Tolpuddle in Dorset merely for organizing a trade union. These men, who were transported to Australia, became known as the 'Tolpuddle martyrs.' Reforms, such as the repeal of the Test Act, made it possible for all wealthy Britons, whatever their religious beliefs, to take part in governing the country. Catholics and nonconformists had been able to vote for many years.

PARLIAMENTARY REFORM

But the most important reform – the reform of Parliament – was not even considered by the Conservatives, who dominated Parliament for 15 years from 1815. In 1830 the opposition party, the Whigs, at last formed a government under Lord Grey. The outbreak of another French Revolution and of disturbances in Kent and Sussex alarmed them.

Lord Grey's Whig government decided that it was time to introduce moderate reforms of Parliament. They feared that if they did not do so there were real possibilities of widespread violence.

They decided to make the constituencies more up to date. They also decided to give more men the vote (but they did not extend it to women). Their reform proposals were passed in the House of Commons by 345 votes to 246, but they were rejected by the House of Lords.

A huge gathering of 150,000 people attended a meeting in Birmingham to show their support for the Reform Bill. The windows of the Duke of Wellington's house in Piccadilly were smashed. Bristol's city centre was vandalized. The House of Lords was advised to pass the bill. If it refused, the king, acting on the advice of the government, promised to create enough new peers who were supporters of the bill to make its passage through the House certain. In the end the Lords agreed and the bill became law.

There was nothing extraordinary about the 1832 Reform Act. The new industrial towns were now properly represented. But the balance was still too much on representing the rural areas at the expense of the urban. Only one man in 20 now had the vote. Voting was still carried out in the open, so everybody knew how you voted. But the 1832 act in time led to further changes. By 1918 all men over the age of 21 could vote.

CONTROLLING CHILD LABOUR
The Reform Act was followed by two other vital reforms. Sir Robert Peel's father, a wealthy cotton manufacturer, had been responsible for the Factory Act of 1819, which had banned the employment of children under nine in cotton mills. But the act had had little effect because no inspectors had been appointed to enforce it. In 1833 an act was passed which again banned the use of children under the age of nine, and extended the ban to all textile mills. Children aged nine to 13 could not work more than nine hours a day, and those from 13 to 18 not more than 12 hours a day. Government inspectors were appointed to make the act work. It was

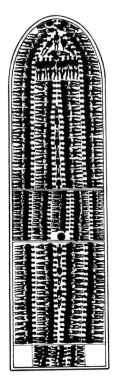

◁ This horrific drawing shows the interior of a slave ship. The slaves had to lay shoulder to shoulder, chained to each other below decks, during the long, rolling passage all the way from West Africa to the Americas. The drawing was part of the evidence William Wilberforce presented to Parliament in his campaign to end the slave trade. Slavery was finally outlawed in the empire in 1833.

later followed by other acts limiting working hours for women and children and improving working conditions. Such acts were extended to all factories.

Two Christians who had long campaigned for acts which would limit child labour in factories were the Earl of Shaftesbury and Richard Oastler. Another Christian who tried to end a great injustice was William Wilberforce.

THE END OF THE SLAVE TRADE
William Wilberforce spent much of his life campaigning against slavery. In 1807 Parliament banned all trading in slaves by British ships. After the end of the Napoleonic Wars the British navy patrolled the Atlantic attempting to stamp out the trade still continued by ships of many other nationalities. In 1833 slavery was ended by law in all parts of the British Empire. Wilberforce died shortly before the law was passed.

THE VICTORIAN AGE BEGINS

In 1837 William IV, who followed his brother George IV as king in 1830, died childless. He was succeeded by his 18-year-old niece. Queen Victoria was to reign for 64 years, until her death in 1901. When she was 21 she married Prince Albert from Saxe-Coburg in Germany. He died of typhoid 20 years later, in 1861. His death devastated Victoria and she withdrew into private life. She spent much time at Balmoral in Scotland.

THE GREAT QUEEN

Several years later, Victoria emerged from her seclusion and went on to become one of the most popular and successful British monarchs ever. She was hard working and serious. Her court may have been dull, but it was respectable and not expensive. By the time of her magnificent funeral in 1901 she was regarded as the symbol of the nation, though without great political power. Her long reign gave the British monarchy new life. No longer were suggestions that Britain might prefer to become a republic taken seriously.

THE RAILWAYS

One of the greatest changes Victoria's rule saw was the growth of the railways. The first railed ways were in the mines. Trucks were pushed and hauled along metal lines by horses or people, often children.

In 1804 a high-pressure steam engine invented by Richard Trevithick drew five wagons of coal, a coach and 70 passengers along 15 kilometres of track in South Wales. In 1825 George Stephenson's *Locomotion* travelled along 40 kilometres of track, pulling 12 wagons loaded with coal and 21 open passenger cars. The 'railway age' had begun. Soon a group of Lancashire businessmen had formed a company to carry both goods and people to and from Manchester and Liverpool.

▽ The Manchester–Liverpool railway carried sheep, cattle and goods as well as passengers. Notice how even the passengers' carriages were open to all weathers.

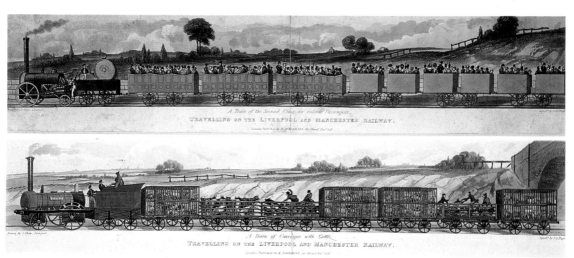

In 1830 George Stephenson and his son Robert designed the *Rocket*, a 'locomotive steam engine' which reached a top speed of nearly 50 kilometres per hour.

THE RAILWAYS GROW

Over the next 20 years railways spread all over Britain. By 1850 almost all the main modern lines had been laid, and a fast service provided. Because the fares were too dear for ordinary people, Parliament decreed that every railway company had to provide at least one train a day in each direction which stopped at all stations. Passengers must be given a covered seat – at first they sat in the open – and charged not more than a penny a mile.

RAILWAY NAVVIES

There were about 250,000 workmen – many of them Irish – building railways in 1850. They were known as 'navigators' or navvies. They lived in shanty towns, which they built along the line of the track as they went. They liked to wear sealskin caps, or white felt hats whose brims they would turn up. They wore rainbow waistcoats and moleskin trousers. They waved brightly coloured handkerchiefs.

The navvies were well paid, by the standards of those days. They spent much of their cash on food and drink. Indeed it was said at the time that the railways were built at the cost of £1000 a mile on drink. However, their casualties were very high. During 21 months' work on the Great Western Railway 131 seriously injured men were taken to Bath Hospital.

Isambard Kingdom Brunel, chief engineer of the Great Western Railway, was the greatest engineer of his day. His iron ship, the *Great Eastern*, weighed 18,000 tonnes – an unheard-of weight in

△ *These navvies are walking along the new railway they have just laid. If companies planned lines near great country houses, the owners tried desperately to move them.*

those days. His bridge over the Tamar was as famous as Telford's bridge across the Menai Straits. Brunel's tunnel on the London-Bristol line at Box Hill was three kilometres long. He designed it on such an incline that the rising sun shone right through it on his birthday (9th April).

THE PENNY POST

One of the greatest gains brought by the railways was the introduction of the penny post in 1840. Before then it was the receiver of a letter, not its sender, who paid for it. Charges were based on weight and distance and were high. Rowland Hill had the simple but revolutionary idea of charging a penny per half ounce letter to anywhere not just in Britain but in the British Empire. The government-run Post Office soon showed a profit.

THE TWO NATIONS

The nation over which Victoria reigned for so long was deeply divided. One of her prime ministers, Benjamin Disraeli, referred to Britain as a country of two nations in one of his novels – rich and poor. In fact there were many more divisions – between the landed aristocracy who controlled Parliament, and the middle class whose wealth came from trade and industry, for instance. Or between the skilled working class, known as artisans, who were in regular work, and the very poor, who were in and out of work and lived in the slums.

WORKHOUSES FOR THE POOR
Before Victoria became queen the law establishing what we call Victorian 'workhouses' had been passed. The old Elizabethan Poor Law had led to people becoming dependent on help from the poor law authorities. It had also

encouranged employers to pay low wages, as the worker's wage was supplemented out of the poor rates if he had a wife and family. The Poor Law Act of 1834 now swung to the other extreme. Anyone who wanted help from public funds had to enter a workhouse to get it. Here husbands and wives were separated. The food was scarce and of the poorest quality. The inmates slept on hard beds in great dormitories, and had to work very long hours on monotonous work like breaking stones for the roads. The workhouses were so feared and hated than many people preferred to starve to death or to turn to crime, rather than enter them. If you had a job, you worked to keep it at all costs. If you were unemployed, you went anywhere, however low the wages, in order to find work.

THE END OF THE CORN LAWS
Businessmen hated the Corn Laws. They depended on exporting abroad. When the government protected British farmers, foreign governments restricted the entry of British goods into their countries.

All over Britain anti-Corn Law meetings were held and anti-Corn Law adverts were placed in newspapers. In 1846 the businessmen converted the Conservative prime minister, Robert Peel. The Corn Laws were repealed.

◁ *The process of industrialization created some depressing scenes. Factories often developed in old established towns which they polluted with their smoking chimneys. Workers were forced to live nearby.*

THE CHARTISTS

The 1832 Reform Act was a great blow to millions of men. Their hopes of gaining the vote had been dashed. (As for women, only a few dreamers were talking of giving them the vote as yet.) In 1838 the campaign to make Parliament properly representative of the people began again. The aims of a group of campaigners called the Chartists were stated in the six points of their charter. They wanted all men to have the vote. They wanted voting to be secret. They wanted all constituencies to be of roughly the same size, and general elections to be held each year. They said that any man should be able to become an MP, whether or not he owned property, and that MPs should be paid.

The Chartists were split between those, like William Lovett, the main author of the Charter, who relied on persuasion to make their case, and those who were prepared to use force. The times were desperate, and in 1839 there was a riot in Newport, Monmouthshire, in which 24 miners were shot dead by troops.

THE 'PLUG PLOT'

In 1842, during the 'Plug Plot', when half of Bolton's workers were unemployed, the workers in many Lancashire cotton mills damaged their own factories so they could not operate.

THE CHARTISTS ARE HUMILIATED

In 1848 a huge meeting was called to present a petition for the reform of Parliament, which had been signed, the Chartist leaders said, by six million people. Half a million men and women were expected to meet on Kennington Common in south London. The government took no chances and raised 170,000 special constables to keep law and order. They need not have bothered. Only 20,000 people turned up for the meeting. Only two million signatures were found on the petition, and many of them were forged. The Chartists were made to look ridiculous, and they never managed to regain wide support.

Although the Chartists had aroused great public support, particularly in the north, they were scorned and feared as wild and dangerous men by those who had wealth and power. However, we see now that the Chartists were among the founders of our democratic system. In time their points were accepted. All their demands, apart from annual general elections, are now British law.

△ *Women selling fruit and vegetables were a common part of Victorian street life.*

△ *Charles Dickens wrote many of the outstanding social novels of the Victorian Age.*

IMPROVEMENTS FOR THE POOR

Towns had always been centres of disease. In 1851 the national census showed that if you lived in Manchester or Liverpool you were lucky if you lived past 25 years of age. The terrible epidemics hit poor and rich alike. But such diseases as typhus, typhoid fever and cholera always started in the areas where overcrowding and ventilation were worst, where there were no proper drains and no running water – that is, in the poorest areas. In such areas the sewage was dumped in the streets or thrown in the nearest river or pond. The only water pump was 50 metres away and would often have run dry by the time you reached it with your bucket.

Edwin Chadwick had long been heading enquiries into the causes of epidemics. He pointed out that far more British people died from filth each year than from wars.

Chadwick's Public Health Act of 1848 set up a Board of Health in London with power to set up local boards where death rates were exceptionally high. They organized street cleaning, the building of pavements and, above all, proper sewers. Many of their tasks were later taken over by local Medical Officers of Health. Decent sanitation, public water supplies and street lighting were now to be found even in the poorest areas of Victorian cities. But it took a long struggle against the ignorance of the poor and the selfishness of the rich before these benefits were secured. The Mines Act of 1842 stopped the employment of women and children in coal mines. Here women had often been employed dragging trucks along railway lines for 12 hours a day in the dark. In 1844, 28 Rochdale weavers opened a shop in their town from which they and the shoppers shared the profits. The cooperative movement spread from this experiment and did much to improve the lives of working people.

VICTORIAN WRITING

Victorian writers portrayed the social injustices of the times in vivid detail. One of the best-loved authors was Charles Dickens. When he was a boy of 12 his own father was imprisoned for debt and Charles was forced to go out to work in a factory, labelling bottles.

Fired by these experiences and by what he saw around him, Dickens became an author, writing newspaper articles and then novels that showed what life was like in the workhouses, factories and prisons. His most popular books include the *Pickwick Papers* (1836), *Oliver Twist* (1839), *The Old Curiosity Shop* (1841) and *David Copperfield* (1850).

IRELAND – FAMINE AND EMIGRATION

Slowly English governments began to right some of the worst of Irish wrongs. In 1793 Irish Catholics won the right to vote; in 1828 they could stand for Parliament and for local town councils. They could also now worship freely.

POPULATION EXPLOSION
The Irish population had doubled between 1800 and 1845 – from 4,500,000 to 8,500,000. Millions emigrated to England or the United States. Of those who stayed, many were poor. The main crop grown by farmers was potatoes, and about half the population ate them as their main food.

In 1845–1846 blight killed three quarters of the potato crop. Thousands starved. Thousands more just survived on relief, much of it from Britain. As a result millions of people left Ireland, mostly for the United States. By 1926 the population had dropped to 4,500,000. The famine and the exodus convinced many Irishmen they must achieve greater independence. An independent Ireland would never have allowed its people to suffer so much.

▽ During the 19th century, English landlords evicted thousands of Irish farmers and destroyed their cottages with battering rams.

THE MARCH OF PROGRESS

During the 19th century many lives were saved by medical discoveries and innovations which revolutionized people's expectation of life. One of the most important of these developments was Edward Jenner's discovery of vaccination.

VACCINATIONS

Jenner was a country doctor. Many of his patients held the old country belief that if you caught cowpox – a mild disease common among milkmaids – you would not catch smallpox. (One in ten people died of smallpox at this time, most in childhood.) After careful experiments, Jenner became convinced of the truth of the belief. He began injecting his patients with the virus of cowpox to prevent them catching smallpox. This is known as vaccination, from the Latin *vacca* (cow).

In time his methods caught on. In 1840 free vaccination was made available to everyone in Britain. Forty years later smallpox was almost unknown in Britain.

ANAESTHETICS

From the earliest times the usual anaesthetics, or painkillers, available to doctors were alcohol and opium. Sometimes men – particularly soldiers – were just knocked hard on the head and made unconscious before undergoing an operation. The first proper anaesthetics to be used were 'laughing gas' and ether. In 1800 Humphry Davy managed to make himself unconscious by inhaling gas. His pupil Michael Farady used ether to the same effect 20 years later. Both methods were unsatisfactory, as the effects wore off too soon to be used in long operations, though dentists took to using gas for their patients. It was James Simpson (1811–1870) who first used chloroform as an anaesthetic. Now surgeons could operate without their patients writhing in agony. Meanwhile Joseph Lister worked to overcome the danger of wound infections.

△ Joseph Lister insisted that everything coming into contact with a patient must be disinfected before use. Anaesthetic was given through a cloth soaked in chloroform.

Because of the filthy conditions of wards and operating tables, a surgeon could never carry out an operation without the cuts he made getting infected and turning septic. Joseph Lister realized through reading the work of Louis Pasteur, the great French scientist, that infections came from germs. If you killed the germs, you killed the infection. He insisted that the surgeon's hands, clothes and instruments should be disinfected before use. Carbolic acid was used to disinfect the wound as well as anything which might come into contact with it. Death from infected wounds now virtually ended.

FLORENCE NIGHTINGALE

The great improvements in the nursing profession at this time are always associated with Florence Nightingale. Before her, nurses were thought of as dirty, lazy and often drunken. She saw what happened to wounded soldiers in hospitals during the Crimean War of 1854–1856. Everywhere was filthy. Soldiers lay on blood-stained beds which were never washed. Their excrement lay in unemptied buckets on the wards. Their bandages were never changed.

Florence Nightingale began to clean things up when she was sent to improve the soldiers' hospitals in the Crimea. After six months, instead of 420 patients dying out of every 1000 soldiers admitted to hospital, only 22 died.

After the war was over, Florence Nightingale founded the first training school for nurses at St Thomas' Hospital in London. She supervised a strict method of training nurses which lasted from two to four years and ended with a final examination. Her methods were adopted by every hospital in the land.

ADVANCES IN SCIENCE

In the 18th century it had been discovered that electrical signals could be sent along wires. But it was not until the arrival of the railway age that the first telegraph wires were set up. They ran between Euston and Camden Town stations in London. In 1851 a cable was laid across the Channel. Messages could now be sent from London to Paris. In 1866 the first transatlantic cable was laid. In 1896 an Italian, Guglielmo Marconi, gave the first public demonstration of wireless communication. The British Post Office decided to support his research and he succeeded in transmitting a signal across the Bristol Channel. In 1899 he communicated with France across the Channel and in 1901 he sent the first radio signals across the Atlantic Ocean.

Transmission of speech by telephone was first made by an American, Alexander Graham Bell. The first British telephone exchange was built in 1879, the first automatic exchange in 1912. Despite its obvious advantages, the telephone was not quickly adopted even in business life because of its cost.

The main British railway network was in place by 1850. The thousands of miles of track that were laid in the second half of the century were laid for branch lines. By the year of Victoria's death (1901) the most remote British villages had their own railway stations.

Travel in large towns was by horse-drawn buses and cabs. The first London underground railway tunnel (1863) was built only a few feet below the surface, and was full of thick, swirling smoke from the steam-engines. The first 'tube' line (1890) was 40 foot deep and electrified. The tubes soon ran all over London.

EXPLORATION AND EMPIRE

It was not until the later years of the 19th century that the British Empire was deliberately planned. Bases were given in peace treaties, or seized by force because they were useful to traders or needed by the navy in its task of patrolling the world's waters. British people went to settle in new continents because they were restless or ambitious or desperate at home and wanted to make new lives.

▽ Sydney in Australia had originally been a convict settlement. By the early 19th century it had become an established empire town and was set to play a major role in the development of the country's wool trade.

AUSTRALIA

The British had originally used Australia as a settlement for convicts. The beginnings of sheep-farming in New South Wales and the discovery of gold in Victoria and Western Australia turned it into a prosperous country.

Although it still belonged to Britain, Australia took more charge of its own affairs as the century progressed. Millions of British people boarded the packed emigrant ships, which regularly sailed from Britain to Australia, to start a new life. Wool, wheat and meat became major exports. Sydney and Melbourne developed into great towns.

△ *Canadian fur trappers developed a profitable trade around the Hudson Bay.*

NEW ZEALAND

New Zealand had been taken over by Britain in 1840, when France was reported to be interested in establishing colonies on the islands. As in Australia, sheep-farming made the country prosperous, while the export of butter to Britain became a thriving trade.

CANADA

Canada had become a British colony after 1763 but the English and French-speaking communities lived very different lives. The Canadian Pacific Railway, which was finished in 1885, helped link the vast areas between the Atlantic and the Pacific together. In 1867 Canada became a dominion, a self-governing member of the empire – the first to do so.

INDIA

Until 1857 India was controlled by the British East India Company rather than the British government. But in that year there was a serious mutiny of Indian troops against their British masters. After it was suppressed, the British government decided to make India an official colony. Their power was soon firmly established – as it was too in Burma and Malaya.

AFRICA

When the British bought Cape Colony at the southern tip of Africa they took over a Dutch colony. The British and Dutch – or Afrikaner – settlers soon quarrelled. The British tried to make English, not Afrikaans, the official language in South Africa and refused to allow the Afrikaners to continue keeping slaves. The Afrikaners now 'trekked' (travelled) north in the Great Trek of 1835 and established their own states.

THE SUEZ CANAL

With the British developing not only India, Burma and Malaya but also Hong Kong (which they had seized from China in 1842), British interest in a canal linking the Mediterranean and Red Seas became strong. In 1870 a French firm finished building the Suez Canal and after that all British ships bound for India sailed down the canal from the Mediterranean to the Red Sea and into the Indian Ocean. The canal was owned by several companies, but from 1875 onwards the British government owned the largest share.

POLITICAL REFORM AND EDUCATION

In the middle of the 19th century a new British political party was formed by the Whigs and those Conservatives who followed Peel and voted to reform the Corn Laws. This party was called the Liberal party, and its leader was William Gladstone. His first government (1868–1874) set out to free Englishmen from unfair restrictions and to give them more opportunities.

GLADSTONE'S REFORMS

Voting for Parliamentary elections still took place openly in market squares or similar public places. Voters raised their hands for their chosen candidates, and could be victimized by their employers if they were seen voting for candidates the employers disliked. The Liberals passed the Ballot Act of 1872, which made all voting in Parliamentary elections secret.

CHANGES IN THE ARMY

Another act was passed which said that men could no longer become officers in the army simply by paying for their positions. Instead they had to show they would be good at the job. At the same time flogging in the army was abolished.

EDUCATION

The most important of all the reforms passed by Gladstone's first government was the Education Act of 1870. The majority of British children still did not go to school, though in most districts there were schools, run by the local churches.

Gladstone's government set up elected authorities, School Boards, in each area. The authorities had to build schools for children up to the age of 13 in any district which did not already have a church school. Where a church school existed, the government subsidized (paid money towards) the school. The boards got money from local taxpayers to build schools and pay the teachers. Schools were not yet free and children did not have to go to them. In practice the great majority now attended school without being made to do so. Twenty years later it was made compulsory for children to attend school up to the age of 13, and it became free.

HIGHER EDUCATION

The monopoly of university education by Oxford and Cambridge was broken when London University was established in 1836. Birmingham, Manchester, Liverpool, Leeds and Sheffield universities were founded around 1900. Bedford College for Women was opened in 1848. The London School of Medicine for Women opened in 1874 for training women doctors. Twenty-five years later there were over 300 women doctors.

TRADE UNIONS

Gladstone and the Liberal Party were not supporters of trade unions. However, Gladstone did pass a Trade Union Act which guaranteed trade unions the right to exist and go about their business. But it did not allow them to picket.

PICKETING

When an employer and his workers completely disagree – over wages, for instance – the only power the workers have, which can balance the employer's power to sack them, is to go on strike. A strike can only work if all the workers are united and remain on strike together. If some return to work or if new workers are taken on, the strike is bound to fail. The best way of maintaining unity among the strikers is by picketing. Pickets are workers – generally strong union men or women – who stand at the entrance to the factory or mine and try to persuade their fellow workers not to work until the strike has finished.

A NEW GOVERNMENT

In 1874 Gladstone's government was defeated at the general election. A new Conservative government, with Benjamin Disraeli as its prime minister, took office. Disraeli was more sympathetic to the trade unions. He allowed picketing, so long as it was peaceful.

DISRAELI'S REFORMS

Disraeli believed that over matters of public health it was a government's duty to interfere. His Public Health Act of 1875 decreed that all houses had to be supplied with clean water and proper drains, and that streets had to be regularly cleaned. The councils responsible for this also had to ensure that the food which was sold in the shops was clean and fit for human consumption and that the beer sold in pubs had not been watered down.

▷ *In 19th-century schools children of all ages were taught in one room. The children in the front seem to be doing exercises.*

BETTER HOMES FOR THE POOR

Another act encouraged councils to pull down the worst slums in their districts. They could replace them by their own council-built houses, which were cheap to rent and built to high standards of light and ventilation. Later, 20th-century councils did this on a large scale.

Although many people were desperately poor, the conditions of other working-class families began steadily to improve at the end of the 19th century. Many a working family now rented a well-built, warm house in a terraced street.

THE RIGHT TO VOTE

Many more men, though still no women, were now entitled to vote. In 1867 most working-class men in the towns could vote. In 1884 the vote was extended to farm labourers. Universal male suffrage had to wait till 1918, but the Chartists' dream was now much closer.

THE EMPIRE AT ITS HEIGHT

During the last quarter of the 19th century more and more colonies were established by Britain. The Conservative governments began to develop a policy known as 'imperialism'. Hundreds of thousands of working men and women, most of whom had friends or relations in Australia, New Zealand, Canada and South Africa, were proud to belong to the 'mother country' of the greatest empire the world had ever seen.

THE RACE FOR COLONIES

Britain was not the only nation interested in establishing overseas colonies. From 1870 onwards France, Belgium, Portugal, Germany and Italy all joined in the race for colonies.

British governments were particularly concerned to take over large parts of Africa before the French, Belgians and Germans got there before them. This competition between the European countries became known as the 'scramble for Africa'. The British managed to establish colonies on the coasts of both west and east Africa. On the west coast, they colonized Gambia, Sierra Leone, the Gold Coast and – the richest prize of all – Nigeria. On the east coast, they colonized Uganda and Kenya.

Great areas of India, Burma and Malaya were now ruled over by British district officers. Often young Englishmen, the officers were in sole charge of the lives of many thousands of people in their districts. They could never have been so successful if their rule had not been quietly accepted by the people they governed.

SOUTH AFRICA

In South Africa after the Great Trek of 1835, the Afrikaners set up their own states of Transvaal and the Orange Free State. Here they lived their own lives, and the British left them alone.

But trouble arose again when fabulously rich gold mines were discovered near Johannesburg, the capital of the Transvaal. The two groups of white colonists – ignored by most of the black population – went to war.

THE BOER WAR

The South African War (1899–1902), which the British insultingly called the Boer War – from the Afrikaans word *boer*, meaning peasant – was a bitter war. The British were shocked when, to begin with, the Afrikaners won some important battles. How could the highly trained and well-equipped soldiers of the great British Empire be defeated by a tiny group of settlers? Eventually the British managed to win the war and the South African colonies became part of the British Empire. However, in 1909 the South Africa Act was passed, making South Africa a dominion with equal rights for Britons and Afrikaners. The two white communities, however, continued to distrust each other.

NEW DOMINIONS

British governments always remembered how they lost their American colonies. When Australia and New Zealand wanted to become dominions like Canada they gladly agreed.

IRELAND'S MOVES FOR INDEPENDENCE

After the famine of 1845–1846 many Irish people believed that Ireland should be independent. Some thought that independence could only be achieved by force. From the 1850s onwards violence occurred all over Ireland. Bombs were exploded, cattle belonging to British landlords were maimed and hayricks were burnt. Landlords and their agents were murdered. In 1858 Irish Americans founded the Fenian Brotherhood. Its aim was to bring about an Irish Republic, by force if necessary. At the turn of the century, the Irish Sinn Fein party was formed. Sinn Fein means 'ourselves alone'.

REFORMS IN IRELAND

Gladstone made Irish affairs a priority for his government. He set up courts to fix fair rents for small Irish tenant farmers and protect them from being exploited by their landlords. (Many of these men lived in Britain, and never even visited Ireland.) Successful schemes were introduced to let Irish tenant farmers borrow money at cheap rates from the British government. With it they bought their own land. By 1914, 250,000 Irish farmers had joined the scheme.

HOME RULE

Gladstone tried twice to give Ireland its own parliament – or Home Rule. In 1886 and again in 1893 his Liberal government had proposed a plan to set up an Irish parliament in Dublin which would be in charge of Irish affairs. Matters of general United Kingdom concern, such as foreign policy and defence, would still be decided in the House of Commons. However, a group of Liberal MPs, led by Joseph Chamberlain and calling themselves Unionists (because they supported a united Britain, including Ireland), joined the Conservatives. The Conservatives had never agreed with Home Rule. Between them, Unionists and Conservatives defeated the first Home Rule Bill. The House of Lords turned down the second. The last attempt at achieving Home Rule occurred just before the First World War. In 1912 Asquith's Liberal government introduced another Home Rule Bill. It passed Parliament and was due to become law in the very month war broke out – August 1914.

But the bill caused an outcry among the people living in the six counties in the north of Ireland known as Ulster. These Ulstermen were strongly Protestant. They distrusted the Catholic south and wanted to go on being governed by Britain.

The Ulster Unionists, under Sir Edward Carson, were supported by the British Conservative Party, then in opposition. The Conservatives encouraged the Ulstermen to stand firm, and seemed to turn a blind eye to the way that Carson was secretly arming his Ulster Volunteer Force of 100,000 men. Carson's Catholic opponents, the Irish Volunteers, were also arming themselves. Ireland was on the point of civil war, when the First World War broke out.

THE BIRTH OF THE LABOUR MOVEMENT

Towards the end of the 19th century more and more working men joined trade unions. Many were skilled workers such as engineers. The unions were not only concerned with wages. In return for a weekly payment, the union would help a working man to pay for a doctor when he or his family were ill. It would organize sick pay for him and provide him with a decent funeral. Or it would keep the family going during unemployment.

▽ *This is the membership certificate of the National Union of Gas Workers and General Labourers, one of the mass organizations formed in the 1880s.*

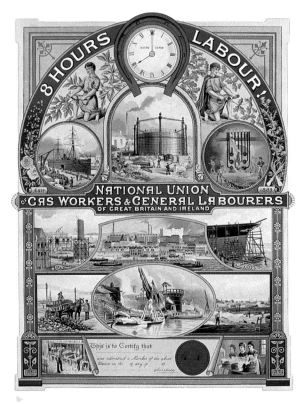

THE GROWTH OF TRADE UNIONS

In the London dock strike of 1889 the dockers closed down the greatest port in the world for six weeks and won their demand for a basic wage of sixpence an hour. This was a major victory for the union movement and led many unskilled labourers to join unions. But unions could not improve conditions by themselves. They needed a voice in Parliament.

THE LABOUR PARTY

One of the union leaders who realized the need for working people to be represented in Parliament was Keir Hardie. He had had a hard upbringing and from the age of ten had worked in the mines. He educated himself at night school, learned public speaking on temperance platforms and became an active trade unionist. In 1888 he founded the Scottish Parliamentary Labour Party. In 1892 he was elected as an Independent Socialist MP for West Ham and a year later he started the Independent Labour Party.

In 1884 another group had been founded that wished to see ordinary working people represented in Parliament. It was known as the Fabian Society and its members included writers such as the Irish dramatist George Bernard Shaw.

Before long, the trade unionists, the Independent Labour Party and the Fabian Society realized they had a better chance of achieving their aims by joining forces than by remaining separate. In 1900 they merged and the Labour Party was born.

THE END OF AN ERA

Queen Victoria died in 1901, aged 82. Her funeral was a great national and international event. Even at the time the occasion seemed to mark the passing of an age. Never again would the British seem, both to themselves and to foreigners, to be so powerful and confident.

ELECTRICITY
In the late 19th century a second Industrial Revolution occurred. Coal and iron remained basic British industries, but they were overtaken by steel, electricity, oil and chemicals. Now that electricity provided the power for industry, modern factories became much cleaner. No longer did their chimneys pour out filthy smoke.

▽ *One of London's first power stations was built in Deptford, south of the river Thames. At first, electricity was used to light the streets and drive factory machinery. Later, it was used in the home to power electrical appliances.*

INCREASED LEISURE TIME
For many British people conditions had improved noticeably since the early 1880s. Wages were slowly improving and working people at last had some leisure. Early-closing days became compulsory for shopkeepers. Fewer people worked on Saturday afternoons. Thousands of men regularly attended football matches, standing in their thousands on draughty terraces to cheer their local club. Long before Queen Victoria's death men – though not yet women – were sport mad. Notts. County, the first professional football club, had been founded as early as 1862. The F.A. Cup competition started in 1871, the Football League in 1888. First class rugby football, lawn tennis and cricket all started in the 1870s but none was so widely popular a sport as football. Parliament ordered regular bank holidays to be observed. If the banks were shut, businesses were shut too. This meant that

everybody had at least a few days off – such as Christmas Day, Easter and August Bank Holiday. The family week at the seaside – if you could afford it – had been popular since 1850 or before. Now the day at Blackpool, Margate or a multitude of other seaside resorts was added to it. During the 19th century, growing numbers of people worked in commerce - in banks, insurance offices and on the Stock Exchange. For them the bicycle - some of which were 'bicycles made for two' – spelt freedom. By 1900 townspeople, particularly young people, were bicycling from the town into the countryside at weekends.

NEWSPAPERS FOR ALL

More and more men and women travelled to work by bus, tram, tube or train. As they jolted their way along they loved to read magazines and newspapers. Indeed the Englishman's love of newspapers, whatever his social class, became as famous as his love of sport. There was now a great market for the popular press since most people could now read. The *Daily Mail*, the first daily paper written for ordinary people and not the well-to-do, first appeared in 1896.

CHRISTIANITY

Wider opportunities of leisure led to fewer people attending church on Sundays. Many working people in particular did not want to spend their precious Sunday mornings in church. The habit of regular church going, which had been part of Victorian country life, was not to be found in the towns and cities, or at least not in their poorer districts.

Hundreds of thousands of people lost touch with Christianity. But the Methodist Church was well attended in the industrial towns and had a considerable influence on the lives of working people. Many of the first Labour leaders were Methodists. The Salvation Army did particularly devoted work among the poor. They would be found at work in the poorest areas of big towns – especially London – and provided shelters for the thousands of homeless men and women who would otherwise sleep rough on the streets.

The National Society for the Prevention of Cruelty to Children and the Church of England's Children's Society helped thousands of orphan children who would otherwise have been homeless.

Christian missionaries took their faith to Africa, India and many other areas of the British Empire.

A CHANGING DIET

When recruitment for the amy was at its height during the First 'Boer' War, 35 per cent of applicants were being turned away. They failed to reach the fairly low standards of physique demanded because of their poor diet.

But by the end of the century, ordinary people were eating more meat. Cheap meat was imported into Britain on refrigerator ships from Australia and the Argentine. For the first time the 'roast beef of England', which was always supposed to be the national British meal, was now available to most British families. The Sunday joint – hot at midday, cold in the evening, and served up in various forms during the week – became a national institution. People were drinking more tea, and ladling into it more sugar, than ever before. They were also drinking more beer and smoking more tobacco, now generally in the form of cigarettes.

1901–1992
THE TWENTIETH CENTURY

TIME CHART

* denotes events that occurred outside Britain and Ireland.

1901	Edward V becomes king.
1905–1914	Reforming Liberal governments in power.
1904–1905	*Russo–Japanese War.
1908	Suffragette movement gathers momentum.
1910	George V becomes King
1911	Parliament Act.
1912–1914	Ulster Crisis. *First World War begins (1914).
1916	Conscription is introduced. Easter Rising in Dublin, Ireland.
1917	*Communist revolution in Russia. *US enters war.
1918	*First World War ends.
1918	Women gain the vote.
1921	Irish Free State is created.
1923–1924	First Labour government.
1924–1929	Conservative government.
1926	General Strike.
1931	Economic crisis and slump.
1933	*Hitler and Nazis take over in Germany.
1936	George V dies. Edward VIII becomes king but later abdicates. George VI becomes king.
1938	*Munich Conference.
1939	*Second World War begins.
1940	Battle of Britain follows fall of France. Churchill heads coalition government.
1941	*Germany attacks USSR. *Japan attacks US.
1942	*Battle of Stalingrad.
1944	*D-day landings.
1945	*Germany surrenders. Atomic bomb dropped on Hiroshima, causing Japan to surrender.
1945–51	Labour governments.
1947–1962	*British Empire breaks up.
1948	*NATO is formed. National Health Service begins.
1951–1964	Conservative governments.
1952	George VI dies. Elizabeth II becomes Queen.
1953	Television ownership grows.
1956	Suez crisis. Steady immigration into Britain.
1960 onwards	Home ownership grows.
1964–70	Labour governments.
1965	Britain finds oil and gas in North Sea.
1968	Ulster 'troubles' begin.
1970	Equal Pay Act and, later, Equal Opportunities Act give women more equality.
1970–1974	Conservative government.
1973	Britain joins the Common Market (now the EC).
1974–1979	Labour government.
1979–1990	Conservative governments under Margaret Thatcher.
1982	Falklands War.
1984–1985	Miners' Strike.
1989	*Soviet Union collapses and Cold War ends.
1990	John Major replaces Margaret Thatcher as Prime Minister.
1991	*Gulf War.
1992	Conservatives win election under John Major. Channel Tunnel nears completion.

POLITICAL REFORM IN BRITAIN

In 1905 a new Liberal government won a large majority in the general election. They promised reforms and were supported by the new Labour Party. The first thing they did was to change the law so that employers could not sue trade unions for profits lost during strikes.

IMPROVEMENTS FOR CHILDREN
They started the school meals service, and gave free meals to pupils whose parents could not pay for them. Hundreds of thousands of children now ate a good meal each day for the first time in their lives. A free school medical service was started. Many children now saw a doctor and a dentist for the first time.

OLD-AGE PENSIONS
The Liberals, with Asquith as their Prime Minister and Lloyd George as their strongest personality, introduced old-age pensions for the first time in Britain. They were only paid to the poorest men and women, but they were a welcome start.

NATIONAL INSURANCE
So, too, was the National Insurance Act of 1911. Workers earning less than £3 a week could now be treated free by a doctor. They could also draw 35 pence a week for up to 15 weeks (and no more) if they were unemployed. This was paid for by small payments each week from the worker, his employer and the government. Later reforms have made Lloyd George's National Insurance Act seem inadequate, but it started the move towards providing help for people in times of trouble.

TROUBLE WITH THE HOUSE OF LORDS
All these reforms had to be paid for and this led to trouble between the House of Commons and the House of Lords. There had long been a contradiction between the idea of democracy and the existence of the House of Lords. For the peers in the House were not elected. They were there simply because they were the sons of dukes, earls or barons. When Lloyd George, in his 'People's Budget' of 1909, proposed to increase taxes on those who could most easily afford them – the rich – the Lords refused to pass the budget.

By what right, asked the Liberals, have the Lords rejected our budget? For centuries – ever since the Civil Wars – the Commons has decided the taxes which the country pays. Why, in a democracy, should an unelected House of Lords be allowed to have any power at all?

In the end the Liberal government proposed a compromise. The Parliament Act of 1911 said that in future the Lords would have nothing to do with taxation. Any act that was passed by the Commons three times during two years would become law, even if the Lords rejected it. The Lords gave in and passed the act.

THE SUFFRAGETTES
If the existence of the House of Lords seemed to contradict the very idea of democracy, the fact that women could not vote in Parliamentary elections seemed even more unfair. Step by step during the 19th century more and more men had been given the vote. Now a campaign began to give votes to women.

△ *These Suffragettes are celebrating the release of two fellow campaigners, Edith New and Mary Leigh, from Holloway in 1908.*

In 1903 Mrs Emmeline Pankhurst formed the Women's Social and Political Union. She and her three daughters began to try to bring about votes for women by writing articles and holding public meetings and marches. They persuaded numbers of men that their cause was just. But when it became clear that the government would not help them, they turned to other methods.

From 1908 they called attention to their cause – the cause of the 'Suffragettes' ('suffrage' means vote) – by every method which did not include personal violence. They interrupted Liberal or Conservative Party public meetings with cries of "Votes for Women!" They chained themselves to the railings of 10 Downing Street. They ran down Oxford Street smashing shop windows. They endured cruel treatment by the police. They got themselves imprisoned and went on hunger strike in prison. One of their leaders, Emily Davison, threw herself under the hooves of the king's horse as it rode in the Derby – and killed herself. Six thousand women marched in her funeral procession.

The Suffragettes grew desperate. Mrs Pankhurst was arrested repeatedly. When she was released she made sure she was soon back in prison. The women who went on hunger strike were forcibly fed in prison. Christabel Pankhurst organized a campaign of burning houses and planting bombs in letter boxes. By sheer luck no one was hurt. By the outbreak of the First World War the Suffragettes had still not achieved their aim.

THE FIRST WORLD WAR
(1914–1918)

The First World War was one of the greatest disasters which Britain has experienced in its history. In four years nearly one million young British men were killed and over two million were wounded, many of them for life.

Yet the British entered the war in a cheerful mood. The recruiting offices were filled with volunteers. People thought it would be over by Christmas.

THE CAUSES OF WAR

Since the 1880s, Germany and Britain had been competing for colonies in Africa. From the battle of Trafalgar (1805) onwards, the British had dominated the world's seas. They resented the growing power of the German navy, which openly challenged that domination. Both countries competed frantically to build bigger and better battle ships.

After the Germans had defeated the French in the Franco–Prussian War of 1870, they had become the strongest military power in Europe. To the east, Russia feared the power of Germany and its ally, Austria–Hungary. In the west, France was itching for revenge.

Britain had become friendly with France, but it was by no means certain that it would join in if another war broke out between France and Germany.

On 28th June 1914, the Austrian heir to the throne, Franz Ferdinand, was assassinated at Sarajevo in Bosnia. By August the shooting had brought Europe close to war. Britain was still undecided.

It was the German attack on Belgium in August 1914 which made up the minds of the British Liberal government to enter the war on the French–Russian side (the Allied side). Britain had signed a treaty promising to help if Belgium was attacked. The Germans hoped to knock out the French army by surprise tactics before the French attacked them. On 3rd August the Germans attacked Belgium. They planned to march through Belgium, cross into France, and capture Paris in 40 days.

The British government and people had become convinced that the Germans had to be stopped. As in the Hundred Years' War and the French wars of 1793–1815, Britain feared that the greatest power in Europe – which had been France and was

now Germany – would control the whole coastline of northern Europe. Such control was certain to threaten British interests, and particularly British trade. War was declared on Germany on 4th August 1914.

The great majority of British people supported Britain's entry into the war. A few leaders opposed it, including two members of the Cabinet, and Ramsay MacDonald, later to become prime minister. There were also young men who refused to take part in any war on principle. These conscientious objectors were jeered at and scorned. They showed courage in facing such unpopularity.

HOW THE WAR DEVELOPED

The German generals had assumed that their men would be in Paris before the British armies had time to go into action. But the British Expeditionary Force arrived in France much sooner than the Germans expected. A hundred thousand British soldiers fought at Mons in Belgium on 23rd August 1914. They showed tremendous courage, though they were outnumbered and without machine-guns.

The German army was stopped outside Paris in the first battle of the Marne in September 1914. From then on millions of soldiers faced each other in northern France across a few hundred metres of churned-up mud. French, Britons (as well as thousands of Canadians, South Africans, Australians and New Zealanders) and Germans dug deep trenches on either side of this 'No Man's Land' and fought each other to a standstill. Millions of young men were killed. The Western Front – the line along which the troops fought – did not change by more than 15 kilometres in either direction in three and a half years.

FIGHTING FROM THE TRENCHES

The trenches were dug deep into the ground and connected with each other so that men could pass along kilometres of trenches, taking messages or bringing help to comrades. Here they ate, slept and hoped that a shell from an enemy gun would not explode on top of them.

Most men were killed taking part in an offensive or when they were on patrol. Patrols were sent to test out the defences of the other side. Most took place at night. The patrols had to cross No Man's Land and locate the nearest enemy trench. They would keep as close to the ground as possible. Wire-cutting squads went in front of them. If they reached their destination, they would silently cut the line of enemy barbed wire. Flares lit up the night. When they found the enemy trenches, the men lobbed bombs or grenades into them, then went in with their bayonets to kill the Germans and capture the trench.

Massive casualties also occurred when the generals decided that the time had come for a breakthrough. Then, for hour upon hour, shells whined over the heads of the tense, stooping troops waiting to go 'over the top'.

At last, the guns stopped firing and the infantrymen were ordered to advance. As the men attacked, they were fired on by enemy machine-gunners, who had somehow survived the bombardment, and shelled by enemy artillery. Thousands of young men fell dead before they even reached the enemy trenches.

▷ *This dramatic photograph was taken from inside one of the British trenches in the First World War. It shows troops going 'over the top' of the trench and into battle.*

The British lost 60,000 men in this way on the first day of the battle of the Somme in 1916. At the battle of Passchendaele in 1917, the fierce preliminary bombardment destroyed the drainage system of the German trenches. The British troops fought their way into great lakes of water and mud in which thousands drowned. They lost 324,000 men, killed and wounded, in this battle.

Other ways of achieving a breakthrough were tried. In 1915 the Germans used poison gas; the British soon used it back on them. But gas provided neither side with a clear advantage.

The invention of tanks by the British and the development of military aircraft by both sides promised to bring about a breakthrough on the western front. But the promise was not fulfilled.

The Allies hoped for victories in other parts of the world. Then the Germans would have to retreat on the western front. At the start of the war, Russian armies had taken the Germans by surprise. They advanced into eastern Germany and threatened the capital Berlin itself.

But the Germans sent back some of their best troops and commanders from France and Belgium in early September 1914. In this way, they saved Berlin, but probably ended their chance of occupying Paris. They defeated the Russians at the battle of Tannenberg in August 1914. The Russians retreated farther and farther into their own country. Finally, in 1917, hundreds of thousands of men deserted and Russia experienced two revolutions. The second was the Communist revolution. The Communist government took the Russians out of the war at the end of 1917.

In 1915 Britain decided to use her navy to land half a million men – including large numbers of Australian and New Zealand troops – on the Gallipoli Peninsula in Turkey. The Turks had entered the war on the German side. The British dreamed of capturing the Turkish capital, Constantinople (Istanbul), and of joining up with the Russian armies to the north. The plan proved a disaster. Half the troops were killed or wounded. The campaign was abandoned.

The Germans were the only country to see that U-boats (submarines) could win a war. They knew that the British relied on importing arms and food from the United States and Canada. In 1917 they began to sink American ships trading with Britain, although the United States was neutral. At one time Britain had only six weeks' supply of wheat left. But the German policy caused the United States to enter the war on the Allied side in April 1917.

THE FINAL STAGES OF THE WAR

The Germans' last chance of victory came in 1918. Now that their armies no longer had to fight the Russians, the Germans had more than three and a half million men on the western front. They advanced to within 60 kilometres of Paris. If they could occupy the capital before huge numbers of American soldiers joined the British and French, they would win.

But once again Paris was saved – at the second battle of the Marne in the spring of 1918. The Germans began to retreat. By early September 1918 the Americans were sending more than 250,000 troops a month into France. On 11th November 1918 the Germans surrendered before fighting reached German soil.

At least eight million young men were killed in the war and 20 million were seriously injured.

IRELAND ACHIEVES INDEPENDENCE

The outbreak of war in 1914 ended for the time being the Irish struggle to be free of British control. The Home Rule Bill, which was due to become law in August 1914, was postponed. Irish troops had a high reputation for courage. They fought alongside Scotsmen, Welshmen and Englishmen wherever Britain was waging war. Then everything changed in 1916 when the Irish Easter Rising occurred.

▽ *The future Prime Minister of Eire, Eamonn de Valera, is seen here campaigning for Sinn Fein. He told his supporters to fight in the trenches in Ireland, not in France.*

THE EASTER RISING (1916)

In 1916 Sir Roger Casement, an Irishman who worked in the British foreign service, went to Germany. There he tried to persuade Irish prisoners of war to join an Irish revolution, helped by the Germans. He planned to land in southern Ireland from a German submarine. Casement, who was in touch with Sinn Fein supporters in Ireland, planned the landing to coincide with a Sinn Fein rising in Dublin at Easter.

But Casement failed to recruit enough Irishmen in Germany, and on Good Friday he landed from a German submarine to tell the Sinn Feiners that the plan was cancelled. British intelligence officers were waiting for him on the beach.

On Easter Monday 1916 a group of Sinn Feiners, led by P.H. Pearse and James Connolly, seized the Dublin General Post Office and proclaimed an independent Irish republic. Fighting continued for four days before they finally surrendered.

The treatment of the Sinn Fein leaders turned Irish opinion against the British once and for all. Casement was hanged. Fifteen Sinn Feiners were shot. One other Irish leader, Eamonn de Valera, was given life imprisonment only because he had been born in the United States.

At the 1918 election the Irish showed their support for Sinn Fein by electing Sinn Fein MPs in every constituency in Ireland outside Ulster. The new MPs set up their own parliament, the Dail, in Dublin. The Dail established its own courts and taxes,

even its own postal services. De Valera escaped from jail and was declared president of the new republic.

Three years of war followed. The Irish Republican Army (the IRA), led by Michael Collins, received money from supporters in the United States. They were determined to shoot and bomb the British out of Ireland. Soldiers' barracks were bombed, railway lines blown up, lorries hijacked. The British recruited special regiments of soldiers – known from their uniforms as 'Black and Tans'. The IRA and the Black and Tans fought until December 1921. Each side committed terrible atrocities.

Finally, the British Prime Minister, Lloyd George, signed a treaty with Irish leaders by which 80 per cent of Ireland became an Irish Free State. British troops withdrew, though Ireland remained in the Commonwealth. Ulster, which became known as Northern Ireland, continued to be part of the United Kingdom.

△ *This is Earl Street, Dublin, after the Easter Rising of 1916 in which Sinn Fein announced the birth of the Irish Republic. The rising was suppressed after 4 days of street fighting.*

CIVIL WAR

Many leading Irishmen, including de Valera, opposed the treaty because the Irish Free State did not include Ulster. It was only passed in the Dail by 64 votes to 57. But those who supported it included Arthur Griffith, the founder of Sinn Fein, and Michael Collins, though Collins was soon to be shot by his own men.

Civil war now broke out between those Irish who supported the treaty and those who opposed it. The war lasted two years, before de Valera reluctantly accepted the temporary separation of Ulster. When he became Prime Minister of Ireland in 1937, the Irish Free State became the republic of Eire and broke all ties with Britain. Eire left the Commonwealth. During the Second World War Eire was neutral.

THE POSITION OF WOMEN

By the outbreak of the First World War in 1914 the Suffragettes' campaign had reached a dead-end. The chances of a male Parliament passing a bill that gave women the vote seemed as far away as ever. The war altered the situation.

WOMEN AT WORK DURING THE WAR
Women became deeply involved in war work. They staffed military hospitals in Britain and close to the front line in France. They drove army cars and did the bulk of the clerical work in offices.

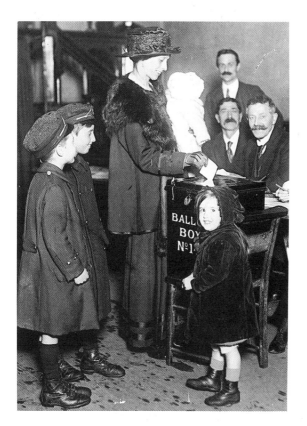

△ Women were finally given the vote in the election of 1918. Here, a first time voter, with her children, drops her vote into the ballot box.

When conscription was introduced in 1916 and more and more men of military age left for the trenches, opportunities for women became even greater. Now some were sent away from home to work on the land. Thousands more worked in the munitions factories.

THE VOTE AT LAST
Little of this survived the war. By 1921 the proportion of women in paid employment was smaller than it had been in 1913. But women's contribution to the war effort, both in Britain and on the battlefields, convinced the wartime Parliament that women should vote. In June 1918 a bill granting women the vote became law.

THE INTER-WAR YEARS
Despite the decline in their opportunities of work, the general position of women between the wars was improved. Thanks to better methods of birth control, families were now smaller, though they remained large among the working class. In working-class homes housework remained a drudgery. But in middle-class homes gas and electric cookers and vacuum cleaners multiplied. Middle-class wives had one or two domestic servants up to 1939 – far fewer than they had before the First World War. Nevertheless, few married women went out to work.

The education of girls was the same as that of boys. A small minority went on to university. Slowly more women began to follow full-time careers but only a very small proportion reached high positions in their companies.

BRITAIN BETWEEN THE WARS

After Lloyd George's wartime coalition government had broken up, Britain returned to party politics. Now there were three main parties, not two.

THE NEW POLITICAL SCENE
The Labour Party had won 53 seats in the election of 1906, at which the Liberals gained a large majority. The new party, which worked closely with the trade unions, aimed to improve the conditions of the poorest class in Britain – the working class. They were supported by many of those who returned from their wartime experiences determined to reduce the great differences that existed between the country's rich and poor.

Labour's opportunity came when the Liberal Party split into two separate groups, one following Lloyd George, the other Herbert Asquith.

In 1923, the first Labour government in Britain's history took office. Its prime minister was Ramsay MacDonald.

▽ *The 'No More War' demonstration in Hyde Park in 1923 summed up the between-wars feelings of millions, particularly the young.*

COUNCIL HOUSING

There was little the Labour government could do to carry out its policies, as it did not have a real majority (the Liberals held the balance of power). But MacDonald's Minister of Health, J. Wheatley, was determined to build large numbers of council houses.

Wheatley's policy was accepted, in fits and starts, by later governments. By the outbreak of the Second World War, one million council houses had been built all over Britain. Often for the first time in their lives, working people moved into well-built, three-bedroomed houses, with a separate kitchen, indoor toilet and bathroom, mains drainage and electricity. They rented them at cheap rents from their local council.

At the end of 1924 another general election was held. The Conservatives won with a large majority. From now on – except for a short period in which Labour held power from 1929 to 1931 – the Conservatives governed Britain until the start of the Second World War in September 1939. The most important event in Britain during these 15 years was the General Strike of 1926.

THE GENERAL STRIKE (1926)

In 1925 the pit owners announced a cut in miners' wages of 25 per cent. The two sides could reach no agreement. On 1st May 1926, the owners shut the mines.

They would not reopen them, they said, until the miners accepted lower wages and longer hours. The miners' leader, A.J. Cook, replied with the slogan: "Not a penny off the pay, not a minute on the day." The general council of the Trades Union Congress (the TUC), which represented the country's main unions,

△ *During the 1930s a growing number of more prosperous people, like this couple, moved out of the towns and into the suburbs.*

called on all its members to support the miners by going on strike. They responded on such a wide scale that their response was called the General Strike.

All the steelworks now shut. There were no trains, buses or trams. Building work stopped, and only emergency supplies of gas and electricity were provided. There were no national newspapers. A week later the shipyard workers and engineers joined the strike. The country faced the closest thing to a national shutdown it has ever experienced.

But the government stood firm. Volunteers drove buses and trams. Troops escorted food lorries from the docks through jeering crowds.

The TUC seems to have had little contact with the miners. Deep in their hearts the leaders of the other unions did not believe in the General Strike. On 12th May the TUC called the strike off. In December 1926 the miners went back to work. They accepted lower wages and longer hours – many pennies were taken off the pay and minutes added to the day.

UNEMPLOYMENT

There were between one and three million men and women who were unemployed between the wars, the worst time being during the worldwide Depression of 1929–1933. The worst unemployment was in the old industrial areas – South Wales, Lancashire, Yorkshire, Clydeside and the north-east of England – where industries had begun to do badly because of foreign competition.

△ *Unemployment between the two World Wars was very high, particularly in north-east England. In 1936 the unemployed marched from Jarrow in Tyne and Wear to London, to draw the nation's attention to their plight.*

In these areas life for hundreds of thousands of workers became a monotonous round. Once a week they would join the queue to draw unemployment benefit (or 'dole'). The money was barely enough to live on, and in 1931 it was cut further.

The unemployed would pass the day standing around on street corners, doing little jobs at home, reading the newspapers in the public library, and walking to the Labour Exchange to see if any vacancies had been posted up on the noticeboard. They struggled to bring up their families as best they could.

Only the coming of the Second World War brought jobs once more. The cotton workers spun shirts for the army, while the woollen workers wove uniforms. The shipyards of Jarrow and Glasgow built destroyers and frigates for the navy. As large supplies of coal were needed for the arms factories even miners had jobs.

Outside the areas of high unemployment life improved for most people. During the 1930s, councils carried out huge slum-clearance schemes. More and more families could now afford a week's holiday by the seaside every year. Almost every home had a radio – whose programmes were transmitted by the BBC – and most people read a daily newspaper. By 1939 there were two million cars on the road.

THE ABDICATION CRISIS

In January 1936 George V (1910–1936) died. His 41-year-old son, Edward VIII, became king. He was a bachelor, and as Prince of Wales he had been popular, particularly in areas that had high unemployment, for he sympathized with people's sufferings. When he announced that he wished to marry a twice-divorced American, Mrs Wallis Simpson, the prime minister insisted that he must choose between marriage and his throne. (Divorce was still frowned upon.) He chose marriage and on 11th December 1936 he abdicated. He was succeeded by his brother George VI.

THE DRIFT TO WAR

Right through the 1930s the outbreak of a Second World War seemed more and more likely. The Germans were eager for revenge after their defeat in 1918 and the humiliating peace treaty of Versailles which followed it. Germany was a democracy, but in 1933 Adolf Hitler, the leader of the German National Socialist Party – the Nazis – took over the government as a dictator. Hitler made no attempt to disguise his determination to conquer the whole of Europe.

The Conservative governments of the 1930s, under their prime ministers Baldwin and Neville Chamberlain, followed a policy of 'appeasing' Hitler and his Italian ally, the dictator Mussolini. They thought that if they let the dictators have their way, instead of opposing them, it would prevent a war. Neville Chamberlain, in particular, believed he could persuade Adolf Hitler to drop his war-like plans.

At the Munich Conference in September 1938, Chamberlain and Daladier (the French Prime Minister) agreed to let the Germans take over part of Czechoslovakia even though Czechoslovakia was Britain's and France's ally.

Chamberlain believed that the Munich Conference marked the end of Hitler's ambitions. He called it 'peace in our time'. Huge crowds cheered him from the airport when he returned from seeing Hitler. When he entered the House of Commons, MPs of all parties rose to their feet and cheered wildly. People remembered the terrible suffering in the trenches of the First World War and cried with relief when they were told that there would not be another war.

Such dreams were soon ended. In March 1939 Hitler took over the rest of Czechoslovakia by force. In September 1939 Germany attacked Poland, for whom Britain and France had promised to fight. But it was a poorly armed Britain which went to war again with Germany.

THE SECOND WORLD WAR
(1939–1945)

Six month passed before Britain felt the full effects of the Second World War. People had forecast that London would be flattened in the first 24 hours of war. Then nothing happened.

EVACUATION

The evacuation of three and a half million mothers and children from London and other big cities began the day war broke out. Evacuation had been carefully planned, and it worked amazingly smoothly. But when the bombing failed to come, millions of evacuees went home – only to return to the country later.

Many of the evacuees who arrived in the country from the big cities were poor and underfed, with ragged clothes and shoes which leaked. Most people had no idea such poverty existed in Britain.

Other precautions against bombing were also taken when war broke out. All the street lights went out. They stayed out until Germany was defeated.

No light could be shown in any house. Every person in Britain was given a gas mask, to carry at all times.

THE FALL OF EUROPE

In Europe the German armies soon overran Poland. French, British and German troops faced each other along the borders of France with Germany. Neither made a move. Then in April 1940 Hitler occupied Denmark and Norway. In May the Germans attacked France through Belgium. They quickly occupied Holland.

Winston Churchill took over from Neville Chamberlain as prime minister. The Labour and Liberal leaders joined him in a coalition government.

The Germans had learned the lessons of the First World War. They used regiments of tanks. Low-flying aircraft flew in front of their advancing armies. On 22 June 1940 France surrendered.

Hitler did not believe that Britain would want to continue fighting once France had surrendered. But the British were determined to do so. Their position was stronger than the Germans realized.

At the end of May the British Expeditionary Force had retreated to the French Channel port of Dunkirk. From here the troops were rescued by British ships and taken back to Britain. A total of 338,000 men were taken off the Dunkirk beaches, 200,000 of them British, the rest French. The evacuation took a week. The navy asked every boat available to help. Fishing boats, pleasure steamers, river ferries, yachts and dinghies responded. Though they lost almost all their guns and tanks, the troops reached Britain.

The German plan was to land an army on the coast between Hythe in Kent and Hastings in Sussex. Troops would be parachuted around Ashford in Kent before the men went ashore. But the German navy was not strong enough to convoy an invasion army across the Channel unless the German air force ruled the skies above. Hitler knew he could not invade England unless he controlled the Channel.

△ *Firemen battled bravely to put out the many fires caused by the 'Blitz'. German planes began by bombing London and then bombed other towns. London was attacked again just before the end of the war, this time by German flying bombs ('doodle bugs') and rockets.*

THE BATTLE OF BRITAIN

The German high command insisted that before any invasion could occur the German air force must control the skies over the Channel and the landing places. Their decision led to the Battle of Britain. On 13th August 1940 German bomber and fighter aircraft thundered over south-east England. For a month they bombed radar stations and airfields.

British fighter pilots shot down 1733 German planes in a month. They lost 915 planes themselves. On 17th September Hitler called the invasion off. It was certainly not worth such losses. He turned instead to plans of bombing London into surrender, while preparing to attack Russia the following summer.

People in London now settled down to night after night of bombing. From 7th September to 2nd November 1940 the Germans bombed London every night. Some Londoners took refuge in air-raid shelters in their gardens. In many areas, though, it was safer to take your bedding down to the London underground stations and sleep there. Nearly 200,000 people slept nightly in the stations, some for weeks on end. Londoners talked of this time as 'the Blitz' (from the German word 'Blitzkrieg' or 'lightning war').

From November 1940 the Germans concentrated on other targets, though London was still attacked. Britain's main industrial cities were badly bombed. The centre of Coventry, for instance, was destroyed. Bombardment from the air went on until May 1941, then it began to tail off. In all, over three and a half million British houses were damaged or destroyed. Thirty thousand people were killed, over half of them in London.

Since the surrender of France, Britain had been fighting Germany alone. But in June 1941 Hitler attacked Russia, and the Russians came into the war.

In December 1941 Germany's ally Japan launched a surprise attack on the United States' naval base in Hawaii, Pearl Harbor. War became worldwide – Britain, Russia and the United States fought Germany, Italy and Japan.

LIFE IN WARTIME BRITAIN
People worked together for the war effort. Many worked in factories to make weapons, tanks and aircraft. At night the men trained in the Home Guard, the civilian army which would fight with the army if invasion came. Women worked on the land in the 'land army'.

Conscientious objectors were sent to do work which helped the country. They were much less roughly treated than in the First World War.

Food was in short supply, so it was rationed. So were clothes, shoes, soap and sweets. No petrol was available for private motoring. Prices were controlled so that goods which were available were cheap.

Orange juice and milk were available cheaply for those who really needed them – for example, pregnant women and young children. The result was to make people in Britain healthier than ever before. Now everybody was eating much the same food. Now everybody had a job.

The country was united – more so even than in the First World War. People were all in it together. The wealthy were very heavily taxed.

The army authorities had learned from the mistakes of the First World War. The soldiers knew that their lives would not be thrown away so needlessly this time.

AIR ATTACKS ON GERMANY
The Royal Air Force began to bomb more and more German cities, chiefly at night. One night in 1942 the RAF used a thousand bombers to bomb Cologne.

Later the Americans joined in the bombing, flying chiefly by day. Many of Germany's great industrial towns, as well as the port of Hamburg and the capital, Berlin, were left in ruins. In February 1945 the RAF destroyed the ancient German city of Dresden. Nobody knows how many died that night. Some say 60,000; others a quarter of a million.

The British navy convoyed ships from the United States and Canada bringing food, soldiers and tanks to Britain. They also convoyed ships to Russia. Many ships were sunk by German U-boats.

THE WAR IN NORTH AFRICA
The first important battles which the British army fought were in Egypt. Here General Montgomery's Eighth Army defeated the German General Rommel's troops at the battle of El Alamein in October 1942. The Eighth Army went on

to join up with the Americans, who were landing in north Africa. The two armies went on to invade Italy in the summer of 1943. Slowly, they fought their way up Italy, entering Rome in 1944. The Italian dictator Mussolini was overthrown by his own people and killed by them in 1945.

During these years most of the German armies were fighting in Russia. At the battle of Stalingrad towards the end of 1942, the Germans were utterly defeated. Their long retreat from Russia now began.

▽ *During the Second World War people were encouraged to 'dig for victory'. The idea was that they should grow more of their own food, so that less food would have to be brought across the Atlantic. Here, a family is starting to turn a bomb-site into an allotment.*

THE D-DAY LANDINGS

In June 1944 the British and American armies, led by the American General Eisenhower, who had become Supreme Allied Commander, were carried across the Channel. They landed on the beaches of Normandy in northern France. The invasion had been planned in the greatest detail for two years. The British navy controlled the seas in the area of the Normandy landings. In the skies above the beaches the British and American planes kept out German aircraft. The men fought their way ashore and dug in.

For the next year British and American armies from the west and Russian armies from the east advanced first towards and then into Germany. The Germans fought bitterly all the way. But finally, in May

△ *The atomic bomb dropped by the Americans on Nagasaki in Japan, and the earlier bomb dropped on Hiroshima, brought the Second World War to an end. The bombs caused terrible destruction, both at the time and for years afterwards through radiation.*

1945, they surrendered. Hitler shot himself in his underground bunker under the ruins of Berlin.

THE WAR IN THE EAST

Since the end of 1941, the British and Americans had been fighting not only the Germans and Italians but the Japanese. The Japanese started with a number of remarkably quick victories. They occupied Malaysia and captured the great British naval base at Singapore. They advanced to within a few kilometres of Australia.

During 1942 huge American armies and navies began to drive back the Japanese. British troops stopped Japanese armies from invading India, and forced them to retreat through the jungles in Burma. It was here that British troops suffered some of the grimmest war experiences.

The American forces advanced during 1943 and 1944 further and further North from their starting point in Australia. By 1945 their bombers, from aircraft carriers, were in flying range of Japan itself.

THE ENDING OF THE WAR

Finally, in August 1945, American aircraft dropped atomic bombs on Hiroshima and Nagasaki. More than 110,000 people died immediately. Thousands more died later from the after-effects of radiation. Five days after the bombing of Nagasaki the Japanese surrendered.

From 1943 onwards, people began to look forward to the years after the war was over. William Beveridge announced a plan for post-war Britain. The main political parties supported it. He wanted a Britain in which all men and women had jobs, where people were insured against injuries at work and where mothers did not have to work immediately before and after they had babies. His plan promised medical care for all, whether poor or rich.

But the fear of a third world war hung over Britain as it hung over the rest of the world. The wartime friendship between Russia, the United States, and Britain had ended. In 1945 Europe was split between Russian-controlled Eastern Europe and the British-American West. Each side was armed with weapons of terrifying power. People were faced with a new and simple question: "With weapons like the atomic bomb is war ever worth fighting again?"

THE POST-WAR YEARS

After the Second World War it seemed that the British people were about to enter a new period in their history. For the first time everybody could expect a job, a house, good medical care and a decent school for their children. No longer, people hoped, would hundreds of thousands of people emigrate because there was no chance of a decent life for them in their own country. No longer would millions be without work.

The Labour Party, led by Clement Attlee, won the General Election in July 1945 with a huge majority. Their plans were similar to the Beveridge Plan.

LABOUR PARTY REFORMS
The government's first and most important aim was to give everybody the opportunity of a job. By careful planning this was achieved.

The National Insurance Act of 1946 was built on Beveridge lines. Every man and woman in the country who was at work had to pay national insurance money each

▽ At the end of the Second World War, planners had the opportunity to plan better housing, such as here in Stepney in the East End of London. The bomb-damaged houses were pulled down and new ones were built.

week. So did their employers. Out of the fund which was created, everyone who contributed could claim benefits if they became unable to earn a regular wage – the unemployed, mothers after the birth of their babies, and those off work through sickness. Old-age pensions were available for everybody.

THE WELFARE STATE

The government's boldest scheme was the National Health Service. The Labour Minister for Health, Aneurin Bevan, established a free service for everybody. It was paid for out of taxes. Now everyone was entitled to receive free treatment from a doctor or hospital. Nor did you have to pay anything if you went to the dentist or needed spectacles.

Aneurin Bevan was also responsible for the organization of house-building after the war. The shortage of houses and flats, particularly in the big cities, was a huge problem. Bevan believed that local councils could solve the problem by constructing well-built homes at cheap rents for those who needed them. Out of 850,000 houses built in the five years after the war, 650,000 were built by councils.

Many new schools were built during these years. In 1947 the school leaving age was raised to 15.

These improvements came to be known as the Welfare State. They were brought about at a particularly difficult time.

POST-WAR PROBLEMS AND AUSTERITY

During the war everyone had concentrated on the war effort. Now that the war was over the old social divisions returned. Britain was no longer the leading industrial power. Her industry's equipment was worn-out and out-of-date.

The Labour government believed that the main industries of the country should be owned by the government, and run in the interests of the British people, not for private profit. Therefore coal, steel, railways, airlines, gas and electricity were all nationalized.

Everyone in the country felt the effects of Britain's economic troubles. Food rationing continued for years after 1945. The rations themselves were sometimes even smaller than in wartime. During the very hard winter of 1946–1947 stocks of fuel ran low. Factories were forced to close. Families huddled round gas or electric fires that gave out little heat.

These shortages, to which people gave the general name 'austerity', made the government unpopular. In the 1950 election, a Labour government was re-elected, but with a small majority. In 1951 Winston Churchill, whose leadership during the war had inspired Britain, led the Conservatives to victory.

Britain now turned to neighbouring countries in western Europe for support. After the Second World War, NATO (the North Atlantic Treaty Organization) had been formed as an alliance of western European countries. They feared an attack by the Russians, who had taken over eastern Europe at the end of the war. The United States and Canada also joined NATO. From now on the British army was based mainly in Europe. British troops were combined with those of its allies more closely than ever before. But British governments insisted on developing their own atomic and hydrogen bombs and keeping control of them.

In 1952 George VI died and was succeeded by his daughter Elizabeth. Her Coronation created joy and optimism.

NEW OPTIMISM

The Conservative Government (1951–1955) led first by Winston Churchill and then by Sir Anthony Eden (1955–1957) caught the general mood of relief after war and austerity. Rationing ended. They set out to encourage people to use their initiative and so make Britain more prosperous.

During the 1950s and 1960s people lived much more comfortably than ever before. Millions of people bought their own homes by taking out a new type of long-term loan called a mortage. More and more people had cars. These crowded the roads and created new problems of traffic jams and petrol-polluted air.

The BBC television service had started broadcasting before the war, but in 1949 two-thirds of the population had never watched a television programme. In 1954 the Independent Television Authority (ITV) was established. It was financed by revenue from advertising. Both channels were transmitting in colour by 1969.

△ *During the 1950s more and more families owned cars. A picnic in the country was a popular way of spending Sunday afternoon.*

THE RETREAT FROM EMPIRE

In 1947 Attlee and Lord Louis Mountbatten – the British Viceroy of India – brought about the independence of India and Pakistan. Later governments negotiated the independence of Britain's African colonies. Within 15 years, starting from 1947, Britain withdrew from a quarter of the world and lost very few lives in the process. By the 1970s, all that Britain owned overseas were her bases, such as Hong Kong, Gibraltar and the Falkland Islands.

In October 1956 Egypt and Israel went to war. Britain and France attacked Egypt and began to occupy the Suez Canal to protect their interests. But an international outcry, led by the United States, forced them to withdraw their troops from Suez. Britain's international weakness was obvious for all to see.

A SOCIAL REVOLUTION

In the 1950s and 1960s about a million men and women came to Britain from the West Indies, India, Pakistan, Britain's ex-colonies in Africa and other overseas countries of the old empire. They came seeking work at higher wages than were available to them in their own countries. The possibility of well-paid jobs was advertised by the British public services such as the Post Office, hospitals, railways and buses. Without the immigrants who came to Britain these services would have been unable to run.

HOMES FOR THE IMMIGRANTS

The immigrants settled in the poorest and most deprived areas of the cities. They lived particularly in London, Birmingham, Bradford and the West Midlands. They would often join other members of their family who had come to Britain before them. They lived in overcrowded conditions and their children attended overcrowded schools. Many immigrants encountered racial prejudice. They were turned down for jobs or houses because of the colour of their skin.

The Race Relations Acts of 1965 and 1968 tried to prevent such prejudice (or discrimination) by making it illegal. Often prejudice was difficult to prove, but the acts helped to turn people's attitudes more in the immigrants' favour. After 1962 the numbers of immigrants allowed into the country were restricted. If you wished to emigrate to Britain you had to show that you had a job waiting there. Nevertheless large areas of Britain had become multi-racial by the early 1970s.

YOUTH CULTURE

During the 1950s a new type of Briton began to appear – the young person who became known as a 'teenager'. They danced to new sorts of music, wore new sorts of fashions, and played new sorts of records on new sorts of record players. Teenagers became big business. In 1961 young people spent £850 million on themselves. Thousands of people were employed in servicing their needs.

In the 1960s Britain became the leader of the 'pop' music world. British groups were admired everywhere. The most famous of them was the Beatles. Their records were to be heard the world over.

SECONDARY EDUCATION

The Education Act of 1944 established free secondary education for all boys and girls. Secondary schools were of three sorts – grammar, technical and secondary modern. Pupils were selected at 11. The 20 per cent who were best at school work went to grammar schools. The great majority of the rest went to secondary moderns and left school at 15.

In the 1960s increasing numbers of education authorities stopped selecting at age 11. The Labour governments (1964–1970) under Harold Wilson encouraged comprehensive schools (schools which admitted children of all abilities).

By 1970 there were 200,000 university students, four times the numbers in 1939. Thousands more joined the 'Open University'. They studied by correspondence and by listening to lectures on TV or radio.

△ In the 1950s thousands of people came to Britain from her ex-colonies, such as these new arrivals from the West Indies. They were wooed with promises of riches and a good life – but they were badly paid and faced discrimination.

At the end of the 1960s universities were disrupted by marches or 'sit-ins'. Students demanded changes to courses or protested about issues such as the war in Vietnam.

THE 1960s AND 1970s
The 13 years of Conservative government (1951–1964) came to an end at the general election of 1964. Harold Wilson's Labour governments (1964–1970) were determined to reduce the differences between rich and poor, and to bring Britain up to date. They continued the policies of the Welfare State, which the Conservatives had largely accepted. They encouraged councils to build many more council houses and to put more energy into clearing the slums of the big cities. They tried to move industry away from the constant conflict between workers and employers. Hanging was abolished. Men and women could vote at the age of 18.

During the 1960s homes, particularly kitchens, went on becoming more and more convenient places. Hire purchase schemes meant that you did not have to possess the money there and then to buy a refrigerator or a washing machine. You could pay for it by instalments – on the 'never-never', as it was called. An increasing number of families bought a car on the never-never. They used their cars to travel to work and for leisure activities. Most houses had no garages, so the cars stood in front of their owner's houses and blocked the streets.

The method of buying a house or flat by taking out a mortgage loan was now making it possible for hundreds of thousands of young couples to begin buying their own homes. In the years before and after the war, the dream of home-ownership would have seemed an impossible one to the majority of families. But couples now launched into buying their homes, knowing very well that they would probably be paying for them for the rest of their lives.

ANTI-SMOKING CAMPAIGNS

One national habit – almost universal amongst those under 40 who developed it during the war – now began to come under attack. Although it was not yet finally proved that smoking increased your risk of developing lung cancer, doctors were increasingly trying to persuade their patients to give up smoking, particularly cigarettes. They were keenest of all that young people should not start.

With higher wages and shorter working hours – it was a rare job which demanded Saturday morning work by the end of the sixties – people had money to spend on the leisure activities for which now at last they had time. Package tours and cheap holidays were now within the reach of millions, who would never previously have ventured abroad for their holidays.

PROBLEMS WITH THE ECONOMY

But the prosperity of the sixties began to look increasingly shaky, as the decade neared its end. In 1967 the government had been forced to devalue the pound. The cost of living was rising. The trade unions insisted that their members' wages must at least rise to keep pace with that cost. An attempt to persuade the unions to limit their demands failed.

In 1970 Edward Heath's Conservative government (1970–1974) took office. It soon became clear that people's wages were rising faster than the prices of goods in the shops. Soon the price of goods also rose. This meant that money was losing its value – inflation.

WAGE POLICIES FAIL

Both the Labour governments under Harold Wilson and the Conservative government under Edward Heath tried to persuade people to accept small but steady rises in wages – no more than the rise in the cost of the goods in the shops. These efforts, known as wages policies, were very unpopular with working people and the trade unions who represented them.

The government's main opponents were the miners. In 1972 and again in 1974 they refused the wage rises offered them. The miners' strikes which followed affected everybody. Stocks of coal went rapidly down. The power stations were forced to stop the supply of electricity for hours on end. Factories closed. During the strikes the only light people had indoors for much of each evening was candlelight.

Finally Labour governments with small majorities were elected at the two general elections of 1974. At first Harold Wilson continued as Prime Minister. In 1976 he was succeeded by James Callaghan.

JOINING THE EEC

Edward Heath's Conservative government decided that the only way out of Britain's economic difficulties was to form closer economic links with Europe. Several of the countries of western Europe had joined together in the 1950s to form the European Economic Community (EEC). These countries traded freely with each other. Heath's government brought Britain into the EEC in 1973. In 1975 there was a special vote – a referendum – to see whether or not the British people wanted the country to stay in the Community. Two out of every three British voters voted to remain in the EEC. From that time onwards, British life has been increasingly linked with Europe.

△ Power cuts caused by the strikes of the early 1970s meant that homes and stores had to be lit by gas lamps or candles.

The Labour governments of 1974–1979 continued their policies of improving the conditions of the nation's poorest people. They maintained the National Health Service. Like the Conservative government before them they formed large numbers of comprehensive schools. For the first time since 1945 a British government spent more on education than defence. But it became increasingly difficult to stick to the policies of the Welfare State when inflation was soaring.

MORE INDUSTRIAL ACTION

For a while the trade unions agreed that their members would not ask for more wages than government policy allowed. Inflation steadily dropped. Then, at the end of the seventies, another round of strikes broke out, in hospitals and local council services, such as refuse collection. The strikes on the railways meant that hundreds of thousands of people were held up for long hours travelling to and from work. They grew bitter and angry. The strikes helped the return of a Conservative government in the spring of 1979, now under the leadership of Margaret Thatcher, who was Britain's first woman prime minister.

THE POSITION OF WOMEN

By the end of the 1970s more and more women – married as well as single – were going out to work. One wage was usually not enough to make up the mortgage payment, which was rising steadily with inflation. The Equal Opportunities Act now made it illegal for an employer to offer a job to a man rather than a woman just because of his sex. The Equal Pay Act said that men and women must be paid the same money for the same work.

NORTHERN IRELAND AND 'THE TROUBLES'

After the Second World War Eire became a republic – the Republic of Ireland. Northern Ireland – Ulster – remained part of the United Kingdom with its own Parliament for local affairs. But many in the Republic would not accept that Ireland should be split. In Ulster the great majority of people were Protestants and had no wish to unite with the south.

The Roman Catholic minority in Ulster had long complained that Protestants took the best jobs (such as in the Belfast shipping industry) and that they jumped to the head of the queue for houses.

PROTESTS AND VIOLENCE

In 1968 a series of huge marches were held in Belfast and Londonderry. The marchers demanded civil rights for Roman Catholics. But soon 'the troubles' in the North became much more serious. The IRA began a violent campaign to force the British government to grant the union of north and south. They were supported by young men in the Catholic areas of Ulster, and were supplied with arms and money from the south, and the United States.

The Ulster Protestants hit back. There was street-fighting in Londonderry and Belfast. In 1969 the British army was sent in to prevent the street fights turning into civil war. In 1971, on 'Bloody Sunday', 13 people were killed in Londonderry when troops opened fire on rioters.

TERRORISM REACHES THE MAINLAND

The IRA's campaign of terror soon spread to the mainland. In 1974 they planted a bomb in a Birmingham pub, killing several people. They went on to explode bombs in Hyde Park and outside Harrods' store in West London. In 1984 they exploded a bomb in a Brighton hotel where Margaret Thatcher, the Prime Minister, and some of her ministers were staying. Five people were killed. Despite many attempts to bring about peace, 'the troubles' continue.

◁ *The 'troubles' in Ulster have now lasted 25 years, with no solution in sight. During that time many British soldiers have been sent out to patrol the streets of Belfast.*

THE EVER-CHANGING PRESENT

During the 1970s the government had given millions of pounds to industries such as the motor industry to prevent them from going bankrupt. For Britain was no longer one of the main exporting nations. Throughout the developed world, German, Japanese and American firms were selling cheaper, more popular goods and putting British companies out of business. In industry after industry – and above all on the land – machines were rapidly taking over the work of men and women. People began to fear a return to the mass unemployment of the 1920s and 1930s. With the return of a Conservative government under Margaret Thatcher in 1979, and again in 1983, the fears became reality.

UNEMPLOYMENT IN THE 1980s

During the 1980s unemployment rose to three million people, and never dropped below one million. During some years 85 out of every 100 workers had jobs, while 15 did not. The situation differed from the unemployment of the 1930s. When there were two earners in a home, as in the 1980s, one was generally at work.

Once again, unemployment was worst in the areas of the 19th-century Industrial Revolution – south Wales, Liverpool, Clydeside and the northeast of England. But now it was also found in the Midlands, in towns such as Birmingham and Coventry, for instance, which had been so prosperous in the 1950s and 1960s. Yet the southeast was still prosperous and wages there were high until the end of the 1980s.

△ In the 1970s and 1980s many factories were demolished. Old industries, such as coal, steel, textiles and ship-building, were no longer in world demand and their decline led to high unemployment. New, lighter industries such as electronics have created some new jobs but there are still high levels of unemployment.

The Conservatives believed in helping enterprising business people. They cut the income tax. They returned nationalized industries to private ownership by selling shares in them. At the same time the Conservatives cut government help to many industries, and cut the money spent on schools and hospitals. They succeeded in lowering the rate of inflation.

Governments during the 1980s were determined to make people stand on their own feet. They said that the welfare state policies of governments since 1945 had made people look to the state for help instead of helping themselves. They quickly cut the amount of strikes, and reduced the power of the trade unions.

THE MINERS' STRIKE (1984–1985)

In 1984 they faced their greatest test. As coal supplies dwindled underground, and industry used more oil and gas, coal pits were closing. To fight the closures the miners called an all-out strike. It lasted a year. The government had built up large stocks of coal, so industry did not suffer. The miners faced riot police. It was the bitterest strike since the General Strike. In the end, the miners were defeated.

INNER-CITY RIOTS

The poorest areas of the big cities suffered the worst unemployment. Thousands of young people left school and could find no job. They lived on unemployment benefit. They were bored and turned easily to crime and in many areas relations between the police and the community broke down. During the early 1980s there were serious riots in the Brixton and Tottenham areas of London, as there were in similar areas outside London, such as Toxteth in Liverpool.

▽ *During the miners' strike of 1984–1985 pickets massed outside the coal mines threatened with closure, such as this one at Kellingley in Yorkshire. The pickets were determined to blockade the pit so there would be no movement of people or coal to or from it.*

FALKLANDS WAR (1982)

After many years of peace Britain was involved, for a short time, in war in 1982. Though Britain had possessed the Falklands Islands ever since the 19th century, governments had made it clear that they did not wish them to remain a British colony if a better alternative could be found. Less than 2000 people lived there, almost all of British descent. The islanders were determined to remain under the British government. They did not want to be ruled by their neighbours, the Argentines, who claimed the islands belonged to them.

Suddenly, in late March 1982, the Argentines invaded the islands. If the Argentine government expected that the British would not take any action against them, they had made a terrible mistake. Within days Mrs Thatcher's government had arranged a force whose task it was to win the islands back.

As the 10,000 troops sailed south many people thought it would never come to war. They thought that the United Nations, the international body, would persuade the Argentines to withdraw their troops. But the Argentines did not withdraw. Though some ships and their crews were lost, British troops soon recaptured the islands. It was all over in three months.

NORTH SEA OIL

Coal and iron ore supplies might be dwindling. British industry might be losing markets to the Americans, Germans and Japanese. But the British had two great strokes of good fortune – they found huge fields of oil and gas underneath the North Sea. In 1975 the first North Sea oil was brought ashore, soon followed by gas. By the 1980s oil and gas from the North Sea were flowing not only into British cars, industries and homes. They were also in great demand abroad.

NUCLEAR WEAPONS

After the war Britain developed her own atomic and hydrogen bombs. The development came from decisions made by the Prime Ministers of the 1940s and 1950s. Bomb tests were carried out in the 1950s in Australia and some Pacific islands. Britain led the way over using nuclear power for peaceful energy during the years 1956–1976, before fears grew that it might be unsafe to dispose of nuclear waste.

But there was a growing horror about the country's possession of nuclear weapons. These were now far more destructive than the bomb used at Hiroshima in 1945. They could instantly destroy great modern cities like Moscow, New York or London.

In 1959 the Campaign for Nuclear Disarmament (CND) began a series of marches and 'sit-downs' at aerodromes and nuclear research stations. These reached a climax in the early 1980s when thousands marched to the American air base at Greenham Common.

Relations between the United States and the Soviet Union had grown worse. The Americans installed Cruise missiles, armed with nuclear warheads and targeted on the Soviet Union, at Greenham Common. Thousands of protesters linked hands around the fence which surrounded the base. At the end of the 1980s the missiles were withdrawn when relations between East and West improved. But the British retain their nuclear weapons, now to be sited on Trident submarines.

△ *Multi-racial classrooms are a common feature of today's Britain. In some areas of London and other big cities there are more children from the ethnic minorities in the schools than there are white children.*

THE 1990s

In 1992 the Conservatives won their fourth successive general election. It would be at least 17 years before there was any likely change of party control in Britain. But there had been one change. Margaret Thatcher, after 11 years as Prime Minister (the first woman to hold that office), was dismissed in 1990 by her own Cabinet and MPs. She was succeeded as Prime Minister by John Major. He waited 18 months before he called the election, where the Conservative majority was reduced.

In January 1991 British troops were involved in war again, this time as part of a United Nations force. (In practice most of the troops were American.) The UN army had been raised to help Kuwait, who had been invaded by Iraq. In a short desert war in the Persian Gulf Iraq was expelled from Kuwait with heavy casualties. Britain and the United States lost few soldiers.

CHANGING FAMILY PATTERNS

By the 1990s divorce had become much easier. One in three marriages were ending in divorce – a fact which worries many people who fear for the effect upon children. The divorces of Princess Margaret and the Princess Royal illustrated the fact that divorce had become common in every class. At the start of the 1990s one in three children were being raised by single parents. The traditional family was under threat.

The birth control 'pill' had been available on prescription since the 1960s. Couples could now time their children's arrival to suit their convenience. Some couples chose not to have children, so they could both follow their careers. Others saw no point in getting married. They lived together and brought up their children without a wedding.

Many fathers became more helpful in the home, particularly those who had lost their jobs while their partners were still in work. No longer was the kitchen thought of as a 'no-go' area for men. Men and women at best shared the housework.

MULTI-CULTURAL BRITAIN

Despite a high amount of unemployment, the early 1990s did show some signs of improvement for minorities. More black doctors, lawyers, policemen, teachers and nurses were being employed. There were four black MPs. Britain was starting to accept the fact that it was home for people of many races and many religions.

Throughout the 20th century regular church attendance has declined steadily. But Christianity and Judaism are not the only religions in modern Britain. British Muslims, Sikhs, Buddhists and Hindus have their own mosques and temples.

TOWARDS THE FUTURE

Events change so fast that it is impossible to foresee the future, but there are likely to be developments of tendencies we already can see.

Ever since 1945 Britain has been allied with the Western block of countries. Fearing the power of the Soviet Union, we have spent huge sums on defence. In the 'Cold War' between East and West both sides felt they must be strong to be safe. From 1989 the Soviet Union began to collapse and has now ceased to exist. It may be that in the future more money for peaceful purposes will be available.

SOCIAL PROBLEMS

The needs of the homeless in Britain are becoming increasingly glaring. In the cities hundreds of men and women – many of them young – have taken to begging openly. A prosperous country will want to find a solution to the problem. Nor should Britain be prepared for ever to tolerate two or three million unemployed.

Though women have grown more and more equal to men they are still not employed in nearly as many top jobs. This is likely to change in the future.

BRITAIN IN EUROPE

In the 1980s Britain has grown closer to her partners in the European Community, which the old EEC has now become. In 1993, the year of the single European Act, goods and workers will be able to go easily from one EC country to another. In that year too the Channel rail tunnel between France and Britain is due to open. Britain will need to decide if it is prepared slowly to lose its independence and to become part of a European state?

ENVIRONMENTAL CONCERNS

Finally there are the ecological or 'Green' problems. There are fears that emissions from British factories and cars may be contributing dangerously to global warming. Many experts believe that the ozone layer, which protects us from the harmful effects of the sun's rays, is being thinned by similar emissions. They fear the effect of modern farming methods on the soil and on wild life.

But history is made up of problems and is the story of continual change. Before we grow too depressed by our present-day problems, we should remember that the difficulties which faced our ancestors were very great too.

▽ *British and French workers began digging the Channel Tunnel from opposite sides of the Channel at the end of 1987. In December 1990 the two sides met amid much celebration. After 8000 years as an island, Britain was now physically joined to the Continent again.*

NOTES AND FURTHER READING

The quotations used in the text of this book are taken from the following sources:

1. Strabo. *Geography*. Translated by Horace Jones. Loeb Classical Library. Heinemann.
2. Caesar. *The Conquest of Gaul*. Translated by S.A. Handford. Penguin Classics, 1951 Copyright © S.A. Handford, 1951. Reprinted by permission of Penguin Books Ltd.
3. Grant, M. *Tacitus: The Annals of Imperial Rome*. London University Press, 1977.
4. Bede. *Ecclesiastical History*. Edited by Colgrage, Bertram and Mynors. Oxford University Press, 1977.
5. *Anglo-Saxon Poetry*. Translated and edited by Robert Kay Gordon. Dent/Everyman, 1927.
6. quoted by Snellgrove in *The Early Modern Age*. Longman.
7. quoted by C.V. Wedgwood in *The Trial of Charles I*. Collins, 1964.
8. quoted by A.J. Patrick in *History of Britain*. Reprinted by permission of Penguin Books Ltd.

A good way to find out how people lived in different periods is to read stories about them. Listed below are some you might try. You may also enjoy visiting some of the historic places described in this book, many of which are open to the public.

EARLY PEOPLE (2,000,000–75 BC)
King, Clive. *Stig of the Dump*. Kestrel, 1980.
Kipling, Rudyard. *Just So Stories*. Macmillan, 1965.
Robertson, Jenny. *Fear in the Glen*. Lion, 1990.
Sutcliff, Rosemary. *Warrior Scarlet*. Penguin, 1976.
Treece, Henry. *The Dream Time*. Heinemann, 1974.

THE ROMANS IN BRITAIN (55 BC–AD 407)
Sutcliff, Rosemary. *Eagle of the Ninth*. Puffin Books, 1977.
Trease, Geoffrey. *Word to Caesar*.
Treece, Henry. *Legions of the Eagle*. Penguin, 1970.

INVADERS AND SETTLERS (400–1042)
Atterton, Julian. *Fire of the Kings*. Julia MacRae, 1984.
Beowulf. Translated by M. Alexander. Penguin, 1973.
Hodges, C. Walter. *The Marsh King*. Penguin, 1970.
Hunter, Mollie. *The Stronghold*. Hamish Hamilton, 1974.
Manning-Sanders, Ruth. *Scottish Folk Tales*. Methuen, 1976.
Morris, Jan (Editor). *My Favourite Stories of Wales*. Lutterworth, 1980.
Simms, George Otto. *The Real Story of Patrick*. O'Brien Press, 1991.
St Patrick. *His Writings and Muirchu's Life*. Edited by A.B.E. Hood. Phillimore, 1978.
Sutcliff, Rosemary. *Blood Feud*. Puffin Books, 1988.
Sutcliff, Rosemary. *The High Deeds of Finn MacCool*. Puffin Books, 1968.
Sutcliff, Rosemary. *The Lantern Bearers*. Puffin Books, 1981.
The Burning of Njal. *Icelandic Saga*.
Trease, Geoffrey. *Mist Over Athelney*. Macmillan.
Treece, Henry. *Viking's Dawn*. Heinemann, 1971.
White, T.H. *The Sword In the Stone*. Collins, 1989.
Willard, Barbara. *Augustine Came to Kent*.

THE NORMANS (1042–1189)
Kingsley, Charles. *Hereward the Wake*. Macmillan, 1980.
Sutcliff, Rosemary. *Knight's Fee*. Oxford University Press, 1974.
Treece, Henry. *Man With A Sword*. Oxford University Press, 1974.

THE MIDDLE AGES (1189–1485)
Lively, Penelope. *Astercote*. Puffin Books, 1987.
Stephens, Peter J. *Shot From A Sling*. Andre Deutsch, 1975.
Tey, Josephine. *Daughter of Time*. Penguin Books, 1969.
Trease, Geoffrey. *Baron's Hostage*. Heinemann, 1975.
Walsh, Jill Paton. *Parcel of Patterns*. Penguin, 1988.
Welch, Ronald. *Bowman of Crecy*. Oxford University Press, 1966.

THE TUDORS (1486–1603)
Burton, Hester. *When The Beacons Blazed*. Hamish Hamilton, 1978.
Harnett, Cynthia. *Ring Out Bow Bells!* Methuen, 1953.
Harnett, Cynthia. *The Wool-pack*. Methuen, 1951.
Hodges, C. Walter. *Playhouse Tales*. G. Bell, 1974.
Sutcliff, Rosemary. *Brother Dusty-feet*. Oxford University Press, 1979.
Uttley, Alison. *A Traveller in Time*. Puffin Books, 1977.

Willard, Barbara. *The Mantlemass Novels.*
A series of novels set in the fifteenth, sixteenth and seventeenth centuries. They follow the lives of one family. All are now out of print but they may be available from a library. They are, in reading order:

The Lark and the Laurel.
The Sprig of Broom.
A Cold Wind Blowing.
The Eldest Son.
The Iron Lily.
A Flight of Swans.
Harrow and Harvest.
The Keys of Mantlemass.

THE STUARTS (1603–1714)
Burton, Hester. *Kate Rider.* Oxford University Press, 1974.
Burton, Hester. *Thomas.*
Doherty, Jim and Joe O'Donnell. *Journey to the Bay.* Brandon, 1991.
Harnett, Cynthia. *The Great House.* Penguin, 1968.
Hunter, Mollie. *Ghosts of Glencoe.* Hamish Hamilton.
Lively, Penelope. *The Ghost of Thomas Kempe.* Puffin Books, 1984.
Sutcliff, Rosemary. *Bonnie Dundee.* Puffin Books, 1985.
Trease, Geoffrey. *Popinjay Stairs.*
Trease, Geoffrey. *Saraband For Shadows.* Macmillan, 1982.
Trease, Geoffrey. *The Field of the Forty Footsteps.*
Welch, Ronald. *For The King.* Oxford University Press, 1969.

THE EIGHTEENTH CENTURY (1700–1801)
Aiken, Joan. *Midnight Is A Place.* Red Fox, 1991.
Aiken, Joan. *The Wolves of Willoughby Chase.* Penguin, 1971.
Aiken, Joan. *Three Cuckoo Tree.* Puffin Books, 1988.
Carter, Peter. *The Sentinels.* Oxford University Press, 1980.
Cross, Gillian. *The Iron Way.* Oxford University Press, 1979.
Darke, Marjorie. *Ride the Iron Horse.* Kestrel, 1975.
Darke, Marjorie. *The First of Midnight.* Murray, 1977.
Garfield, Leon. *Smith.* Kestrel, 1977.
Leeson, Robert. *Bess.*
Orczy, Baroness. *The Scarlet Pimpernel.* Hodder and Stoughton, 1968.
Peyton, K.M. *Right-hand Man.* Oxford University Press, 1977.
Scobie, Pamela. *A Twist of Fate.* Oxford University Press.
Stevenson, R.L. *Kidnapped.* Arrow Books, 1979.
Stevenson, R.L. *Treasure Island.* Collins, 1976.
Welch, Ronald. *Captain of Dragoons.* Oxford University Press, 1974.

THE NINETEENTH CENTURY (1801–1901)
Aiken, Joan. *Black Hearts in Battersea.* Puffin Books.
Avery, Gillian. *Call of the Valley.*
Burnett, Frances Hodgson. *The Little Princess.* Penguin, 1970.
Burton, Hester. *Time of Trial.* Oxford University Press, 1979.
Carter, Peter. *The Black Lamp.* Oxford University Press, 1973.
Conlon-McKenna, Marita. *Wildflower Girl.* O'Brien Press, 1991.
Darke, Marjorie. *Question of Courage.* Armada, 1978.
Garfield, Leon. *Blewcoat Boy.* Gollancz, 1988.
Lightwood, Donald. *The Baillie's Daughter.* Canongate, 1990.
Lutzier, Elizabeth. *The Coldest Winter.* Oxford University Press, 1991.
Mooney, Bel. *The Stove Haunting.* Puffin Books, 1988.
Pearce, Phillipa. *Tom's Midnight Garden.* Oxford University Press, 1958.
Tanton, Bruce. *Time's Lost Hero.* Hodder and Stoughton, 1990.
Trease, Geoffrey. *Comrades For the Charter.*

A number of non-fiction books on Victorian England are very worth reading such as:

Chaney, Lisa. *Breakfast.* A. & C. Black, 1989.
Evans, David. *How We Used to Live: Victorians Early and Late.* A. and C. Black, 1990.
MacDonald, Fiona and John James. *A 19th Century Railway Station.* Simon and Schuster, 1990.
Steel, Anne. *Victorian Children.* Wayland, 1990.
Stoppleman, Monica. *School Day.* A. & C. Black, 1989.
Thomson, Ruth. *In the Post.* A. & C. Black, 1989.
Thomson, Ruth. *Washday.* A. & C. Black, 1989.

THE TWENTIETH CENTURY (1901–1992)
Bawden, Nina. *Carrie's War.* Gollancz, 1973.
Frank, Anne. *The Diary of Anne Frank.* Pan, 1989.
Graves, Robert. *Goodbye to All That.* Penguin, 1969.
Kilner, Geoffrey. *Joe Burkinshaw's Progress.* Methuen, 1979.
Owen, Wilfred. *Collected Poems.* Chatto and Windus.
Peyton, K.M. *Flambards.* Penguin, 1980.
Remarque, E.M. *All Quiet On the Western Front.* Mayflower, 1968.
Richter, Hans Peter. *The Time of the Young Soldiers.* Armada, 1989.
Rowe, Alick. *Voices of Danger.* Methuen, 1990.
Shemin, Margaretha. *The Little Riders.* Julia MacRae, 1988.
Welch, Ronald. *Tank Commander.* Penguin, 1980.
Williams, Eric. *The Wooden Horse.* Armada, 1989.

INDEX